C000002410

NEW HORIZONS IN CRIMINOLOGY

A CRIMINOLOGY OF WAR?

Ross McGarry and Sandra Walklate

BRISTOL
UNIVERSITY
PRESS

First published in Great Britain in 2019 by

Bristol University Press
University of Bristol
1-9 Old Park Hill
Bristol
BS2 8BB
UK
t: +44 (0)117 954 5940
bup-info@bristol.ac.uk
www.bristoluniversitypress.co.uk

North America office:
Bristol University Press
c/o The University of Chicago Press
1427 East 60th Street
Chicago, IL 60637, USA
t: +1 773 702 7700
f: +1 773-702-9756
sales@press.uchicago.edu
www.press.uchicago.edu

© Bristol University Press 2019

British Library Cataloguing in Publication Data
A catalogue record for this book is available from the British Library

Library of Congress Cataloging-in-Publication Data
A catalog record for this book has been requested

ISBN 978-1-5292-0259-5 hardcover
ISBN 978-1-5292-0262-5 ePub
ISBN 978-1-5292-0260-1 Mobi
ISBN 978-1-5292-0261-8 ePdf

The right of Ross McGarry and Sandra Walklate to be identified as authors of this work has been asserted by them in accordance with the Copyright, Designs and Patents Act 1988.

All rights reserved: no part of this publication may be reproduced, stored in a retrieval system, or transmitted in any form or by any means, electronic, mechanical, photocopying, recording, or otherwise without the prior permission of Bristol University Press.

The statements and opinions contained within this publication are solely those of the authors and not of the University of Bristol or Bristol University Press. The University of Bristol and Bristol University Press disclaim responsibility for any injury to persons or property resulting from any material published in this publication.

Bristol University Press works to counter discrimination on grounds of gender, race, disability, age and sexuality.

Cover design by blu inc
Front cover image: © Ross McGarry 2019
Printed and bound in Great Britain by CPI Group (UK) Ltd, Croydon, CR0 4YY
Bristol University Press uses environmentally responsible print partners

Contents

Acknowledgements

No book is written without wider input from colleagues, friends and family. Ross would like to thank Sandra for her collegiality, friendship and good humour over the years working on a number of projects. This book is a testament to her substantial efforts guiding my intellectual development for the past decade. Thanks are also due to my wife Amanda for putting up with me during the writing process and for being an interested listener when I had surpassed the point of being interesting. The requirement to complete this manuscript hit Sandra at a particularly demanding time personally. Ross proved to be a stalwart and supportive colleague as he took the driving seat in ensuring the completion of this project while my husband Ron Wardale and my children ensured I stayed sane enough to deal with everything else. It would also be remiss of me not to acknowledge the support of my newer colleagues at Monash University, in particular Kate Fitz-Gibbon, JaneMaree Maher and Jude McCulloch. It is a delight working with you all. Both Sandra and Ross would like to jointly thank the following international base of colleagues for their kindness, generosity and input in reviewing sections of this book. Ruth Jamieson to whom we owe a great debt of gratitude for providing the impetus for the interdisciplinary study of 'war' within criminology, and whose feedback in this regard is reflected in Chapter Two and throughout the manuscript more generally. Gabe Mythen, our good colleague and friend in Liverpool who offered some characteristically detailed and considered comments on Chapter Three in ways we are lucky enough to have become accustomed to. Andrew Woolford for sharing his impressive and wide-ranging expertise on the study of genocide for Chapter Four, input which also had implications for some of the positioning within this book's conclusion. Ronald Kramer for graciously engaging our review and appraisal of his back-catalogue of scholarship addressing nuclear armament and war-related state crime, and whose feedback helped tweak our argument in Chapter Five with more accuracy and clarity. Vincenzo Ruggiero for his thoughtful and encouraging input for Chapter Six, capturing some sharp final insights which helped nuance the war technologies we were referring to. Finally, Chris Mullins for his thorough and considered feedback, and whose expertise of the field better allowed us to navigate the rather tricky issues we were attempting to connect in Chapter Seven. We also extend our thanks to colleagues at the Crime, Justice and Social Democracy Research Centre at Queensland University of Technology for awarding us both Scholarships in Southern Criminology, making possible our attendance at the 2017 Crime, Justice and Social Democracy conference in Cairns, Australia, where a version of this book's conclusion (Chapter Eight) was first presented. In particular, our thanks go to Kerry Carrington and Reece Walters for making this possible. Thanks also to the anonymous peer reviewer of the completed manuscript for their detailed and thoughtful feedback. Of course, our thanks also go to our wider network of colleagues in the Department of Sociology, Social Policy and Criminology at University of Liverpool for providing a spirited intellectual environment within which to produce such work. This book would not have been possible without all this collective support, influence and input.

Preface

Ross McGarry and Sandra Walklate are leading experts on the intersection between criminology and critical war studies and I am very pleased that they agreed to write this book. The aim of the New Horizons in Criminology series is to provide high quality and authoritative texts which reflect cutting-edge thought and theoretical development in criminology, have an international scope and are also accessible and concise. With *A Criminology of War?* Ross and Sandra have clearly fulfilled this brief. They rightly point out that criminologists have been interested in war for some time; for instance, citing the work of Hermann Mannheim (1941) and Ruth Jamieson (1998). The authors have also edited two volumes on the topic (Walklate and McGarry, 2015; McGarry and Walklate, 2016). Yet war is a subject that is often overlooked, or not regarded, as a central criminological concern. This is surprising. The anomie of conflict means crime and social harm are prevalent in times of war and often post-conflict as well. There are minor and more serious crimes, harms and human rights violations that can go hand-in-hand with military action, there are serious state crimes, questions regarding the legality of war and specific methods and technologies of warfare, the use of torture, genocide and terror. The authors highlight that the study of war is an inter- and intra-disciplinary endeavour, but there is clearly much that criminologists can contribute.

In this book, McGarry and Walklate build on their previous work. They draw on criminological, sociological and other literatures to explore key concerns pertinent to a criminological study of war. They consider definitions of war and different conceptions of 'old' and 'new' wars. The authors also focus on 'the decimation of civilians via "degenerate" war violence' as exemplified by nuclear war. There is specific attention on the historical and conceptual challenges of studying genocide as criminologists or sociologists – not least an acknowledgment of 'the discipline's "dark" input into the biological determinism of the Holocaust'. And the authors' claim that post-war, criminology ought to have been more concerned with genocide as a topic of interest.

McGarry and Walklate consider interconnected dialectics of war within criminology, the context being a transfer of risk over the course of the 20th and 21st centuries that seems to 'prioritise the lives of soldiers over the deaths of civilians'. The authors also look at the war on terrorism, which they regard as criminology's 'third war', and they consider gender, war and violence as criminology's 'fourth war'. The authors conclude by critiquing the 'new war paradigm'. And they are critical of criminology's focus on specific wars and conflicts at the expense of others. Conflicts in the Global South are noticeably absent, and – influenced by work on Southern criminology – the authors suggest a reorientation from 'the metropolitan hegemonic knowledge-base of criminology'.

The title of the book ends with a question mark and this is deliberate. McGarry and Walklate do not propose this to be the definitive criminology of war, and they are also uncertain of the merits of using the label 'a criminology of war' – suggesting it risks 'becoming yet another intellectual enclave of criminology'. Furthermore, they are not sure whether it is necessarily a 'new horizon' for criminological study (as suggested by the series title). But I think the authors are being modest. While war has been studied by criminologists before, this book offers something quite new in how it brings together disparate criminological and sociological literatures relevant to the study of war. The book is accessible but challenging in highlighting war and conflict as legitimate interests for criminology. It is also a challenge for criminologists who see their subject as merely a 'peacetime endeavour'. The book is highly recommended.

References

Jamieson, R. (1998) 'Towards a criminology of war in Europe', in V. Ruggiero, N. South and I. Taylor (eds) *The New European Criminology: Crime and Social Order in Europe*, London: Routledge.

Mannheim, H. (1941) *War and Crime*, London: Watts & Co.

McGarry, R. and Walklate, S. (eds) (2016) *The Palgrave Handbook of Criminology and War*, Basingstoke: Palgrave.

Walklate, S. and McGarry, R. (eds) (2015) *Criminology and War: Transgressing the Borders*, Abingdon: Routledge.

Preface

The study of war has a long tradition within the social sciences including the discipline of criminology. Yet despite historical evidence of war being influential within the lives, activities and the respective work of sociologists and criminologists, and the consistent emergence and cessation of wars, conflicts and genocides being the social and political tapestry against which these disciplines have developed (as variously addressed throughout this book), the study of war and its attendant subject matter have often been perceived as marginal, neglected or irrelevant to criminology (and sociology for that matter). While there may be some truth to observations of this kind, within this book we look to unsettle such ideas by making clear the connection of war with the study of criminology. At the outset of this book readers should be minded to consider (at least) two questions: is the study of war within criminology new? What is the relevance of writing this book? Let us offer some brief answers.

First, *is the study of war new to criminology?* As will become evident, the answer to the first question is quite simply no: the study of war within criminology is not at all a novel undertaking. Recent examples of the prestigious Radzinowicz Prize, annually awarded to the best academic article in the *British Journal of Criminology*, have addressed the illegal activities associated with the 2003 war in Iraq (Whyte, 2007), reconciliation processes in Afghanistan (Braithwaite and Wardak, 2013; Wardak and Braithwaite, 2013), and the Israeli occupation of Palestine (Shalhoub-Kevorkian, 2017). Each of the scholars receiving these awards had, of course, been thinking and writing about war for some time prior to this recognition. Interestingly, none of these scholars made reference to the seminal work of Ruth Jamieson (1998) who had long before outlined an agenda for war to be studied as an interdisciplinary endeavour within criminology. One scholar who had previously made acknowledgement of this work was Jock Young, cross-referencing it within *The Exclusive Society* (1999), *The Vertigo of Late Modernity* (2007) and *The Criminological Imagination* (2011). In this latter (final) contribution, Young (2011: 217) concluded by squarely situating Jamieson's (1998) 'pioneering work on the criminology of war' as part of the broader intellectual tradition of critical criminology. However, despite this awareness Young never offered any detailed reading of Jamieson's (1998) agenda, nor the work that it gave access to. Within this book we substantively pick up where Jock's comments concluded. Second, *is this book relevant?* Of course, we suggest readers make their own minds up when answering this sort of question. However, we are concerned to point out that war, conflict and genocide are (unfortunately) persistent social phenomenon demanding sociological and criminological attention. For example, during the time writing this book: Afghanistan was declared no longer a post-conflict environment by the United Nations as fighting there ensued once again; the Panmunjom Declaration between North and South Korea was signed proposing to denuclearise the peninsula (how meaningful and successful this will be remains to be seen); in the first case of its kind, representatives from Bangladeshi organisations and the UN have begun calling for the International Criminal Court to prosecute Myanmar authorities for their genocidal persecution of the Rohingya in Rakhine; and in the months following this book's submission, November 2018 is poised to commemorate a century since the armistice of the First World War. However, although such contemporary examples may offer this book some relevance, they still do not necessarily afford it uniqueness. As we will learn, this book could perhaps have been written during any point in history.

Ross McGarry and Sandra Walklate
Department of Sociology, Social Policy and Criminology,
University of Liverpool
September 2018

ONE

Introduction: Can there be a 'Criminology of War'?

Introduction

Some time ago Anthony Giddens noted an 'oddity' within sociology. When conceptualising ways of thinking about the nation-state he suggested that, 'it is very unlikely that he or she will discover any discussions of military institutions, or of the impact of military violence and war upon modern society' (Giddens, 1985: 22). The peculiarity insinuated by this remark is that the absence of war, as a common sociological interest, both past and present, is counterintuitive since war and war violence have had impacts on the social world in significant and undeniable ways throughout history (Giddens, 1985). As we will go on to discuss in Chapter Two, other scholars have pointed out more recently that the study of society, politics and culture have often been marginal interests to those studying war and military institutions; likewise, war and war violence are suggested to have been scarcely paid any significant attention by sociologists (see, for example, Barkawi, 2006; Ware, 2009). Although prominent works within historical sociology have been influential in addressing war in relation to state practices (for example, see Tilly, 1975, and of course, Giddens, 1985, noted above), such contributions 'have remained sporadic' (Eulriet, 2010: 61). Put simply, although 'war' and war violence has raged consistently in one form or another on every continent following the 'century of peace' (1815–1914), and certainly during the subsequent 100 years since the cessation of the First World War in 1918 to the present day (we are indeed writing parts of this book during 2018), sociological interest and attention to the incitement, perpetration and consequences of 'war' has failed to match the historical prevalence, global reach or influential scale of this violent social phenomenon.

Instead, attention to war and military issues within sociology has been largely relegated to the 'estranged' interests of military sociology (Eulriet, 2010: 62). Indeed, as Martin Shaw (1984: 4) noted some time ago within *War, State and Society*, 'Military sociology has been primarily concerned with institutional analysis, with the social organisation of armed forces and the way this influences their goals.' Heinecken (2015) suggests that the redirection of these interests to study the military institution, and the neglect of a detailed study of war and its relationship to social and political change within sociology, is the Achilles heel of the discipline. For Heinecken (2015: 5, emphasis added) this demonstrates 'a disciplinary weakness which has meant that the study of war has been left largely to those working in the field of political, international and security studies, *criminology* and law'.

These deficit views of a sociology in relation to the subject of war are not necessarily universal, however. In a detailed overview of political, cultural and historical sociological work relating to war, Wimmer (2014: 175) observed that 'the *lamento* over the lack of a sociological tradition of studying war is increasingly unjustified'. Although disproportionately concerned with the consequences, rather than causes, of war, particularly since the 1980s, Wimmer (2014) suggests that sociology has addressed broad thematic issues such as legitimacy and ideology, power relations and the arrangement of power, organisational development, and the long-term social trends and implications of war (some of which are addressed in subsequent chapters).

In relation to the primary focus for this book, there is also some disagreement on the relevance of Heinecken's (2015) assertion for criminology. This discipline has also been accused – albeit differently from sociology (discussed in Chapter Two) – of a limited engagement with understanding the causes and consequences of war and war violence. As Hagan et al (2012: 482) have pointed out, the discipline of criminology is 'only beginning to consider the mass violence associated with war, armed conflict, and political repression'. For example, in the wake of genocides occurring throughout the 20th and 21st centuries (discussed in Chapter Four), not only was health research said to have principally ignored violations of international laws in lieu of matters related to welfare, so too the discipline of criminology was alleged to have 'largely ignored war and human rights issues and still bears a disciplinary responsibility for this neglect' (Hagan and Rymond-Richmond, 2009: 63). More recently, in the decades following the 2003 Iraq war (discussed in Chapter Three) a similar accusation has been levelled against the discipline of criminology for being caught 'sleeping' (yet again) as a result of its alleged inability to sufficiently critique this war in socio-legal terms as a 'war of aggression', and its inability to bring its perpetrators to 'justice' (Hagan, 2015). What these accusations provisionally make clear is that, for Hagan, the criminological study of war has a moral and intellectual obligation to study not only war but those who perpetrate war, the ways in which war is committed and waged, the consequences that it brings, and how justice in the aftermath of war is pursued. As we will come to learn throughout this book, this positioning has been shared, and aired, by many of his contemporaries past and present. However, as Wimmer (2014: 180) identified, a notable emergence of sociological studies of war since the end of the Cold War era makes 'the refrain that sociology has little to offer to our understanding of war sound like an echo from the past'. In relation to the study of war within criminology, such 'refrains' also require further exploration.

To examine these observations further, we are compelled to expose the claims levelled against criminology to critical scrutiny. To do so, in this book we intend to interrogate the answer to a question similar to the one previously posed by Shaw (1984) in relation to the sociological study of war. However, rather than asking 'can there be a sociology of war?' (Shaw, 1984: 4), we pose an alternative question which looms over the broader conceptual framework of each chapter and is reflected in the given title of this book. We ask instead: can there be 'a criminology of war?' We address this question through an exploration of various objectives, established from work we have previously completed in this area (see for example Walklate and McGarry, 2015; McGarry and Walklate, 2016).

Objectives of this book

In the following pages we have attempted to build on our own previous work to continue a dialogue (largely between ourselves) that remains searching, broadminded, and questioning of the ways in which 'war' is studied within criminology. Our previous work in relation to the topic of war has enabled us to identify several key issues that have been useful in informing the conceptual approach taken in this book. These include:

- acknowledging that the study of war within criminology is not a new undertaking;
- recognising that the topic of war has, curiously, been paid less attention at key historical moments when war, conflict and genocides have emerged;
- illustrating that extant criminological literature addressing war has struggled to gain consistent traction within either mainstream facets of the discipline or those related to critical criminology; and
- appreciating that considerably more is required to be achieved to ensure that criminological scholarship has a continued relevance and contribution to make vis-à-vis the academic study of war.

The purpose of this book is to examine these reflections in further detail. We achieve this throughout the forthcoming chapters by foregrounding disparate bodies of work within criminology related to the study of war and connecting them to a wide range of extant sociological literature. The shorthand to our objectives, then, is to demonstrate that the study of war is a long-standing and interdisciplinary undertaking.

Defining 'war' for the purposes of this book

With our central question raised and objectives now outlined, next we wish to define at length our terms of reference for how 'war' is conceptualised for our purposes here. There are, of course, many ways in which this can be achieved. For example, in terms perhaps more sympathetic to mainstream criminological positions, Detter (2013: 9) describes in some detail a legal approach to explaining the concept of war as armed conflict between nation-states (that is, a 'state of war') whereupon 'certain rules are brought into operation' to arbitrate violence (that is, international law in the capacity of the laws of war) and protect civilians (that is, international humanitarian law). In this normative sense 'war' is the opposite of 'peace' (Detter, 2013). Or, in the post-9/11 era, war can be understood to have become more ambiguously defined and reluctantly declared when fought between or against non-state actors, such as the 'war on terror' (Detter, 2013). For Detter (2013), the notion of a 'state of war' therefore needs to be distinguished from 'other hostilities' such as armed attacks or raids, state-organised or intra-state terrorism, and distinctions made between what she terms 'traditional' (pre-9/11) and 'genocidal' (post-9/11) terrorism. So too must war be understood as being fought as either civil wars within fixed geographical localities, or 'internal' wars often turned into 'internationalised wars' if attracting 'international repercussions' from the likes of the United Nations (UN) or North Atlantic Treaty Organisation (NATO) (Detter, 2013: 54). Wars can also be 'programmatic' such as those historically fought for liberation (that is, from colonisation), or as acts of resistance, revolution or separatism and independence (Detter, 2013). Contemporarily wars are also said to be waged pre-emptively and with a stark asymmetry via the technologies of violence used (that is, 1991 Gulf war and subsequent 2003 Iraq war); or in what Detter (2013: 64) describes as 'methodological war' whereby fighting takes shape in innovative forms often to compensate for disparities of power (such as guerrilla warfare). The notion of war can therefore take many forms and be defined in multiple ways. However, in order to reconceptualise war

war is here... is 'Amote leg'Amote

— why should criminology be concerned?

outwith the trappings of the legal, and retaining the complexity of the outline offered above, our initial interests here are twofold. First, to establish a baseline from which the notion of war can be defined and, second, to create a platform to conceptually appreciate this definition's changing characteristics. It is for these reasons that we initially defer to the work of Carl von Clausewitz and Mary Kaldor to distinguish war in 'old' and 'new' forms.

Establishing a baseline definition of (Clausewitzean) war

Within his renowned work in *On War*, military strategist Carl von Clausewitz ([1832] 1997) defined war as an activity that brought together such elements as emotions, chance, passion and strategy that were linked to what he termed a 'trinity', including the apparatus of the state or political leaders, military leaders and the public (Kaldor, 2014). For Clausewitz ([1832] 1997: 333–6), the conceptualisation of 'absolute war' (as differentiated from the unwieldly and oppressive enactment of force during 'real war') was that which derived from three key actions. First, the capacity of the state to achieve its objectives in the face of opposition; second, its ability to immobilise its enemies; and third, an awareness that if war was to be waged, and citizens (almost exclusively men) were to be convinced to kill and be killed, entire populations had to be mobilised in support of war (Kaldor, 2014). Crucially, what was being fought for had to be perceived as legitimate and given a clear purpose (Kaldor, 2014). War is also said to include 'tensions' (Clausewitz, [1832] 1997: 195–7) between opposing drives (that is, emotion/reason; action/inaction; defence/offence) and 'frictions' (Clausewitz, [1832] 1997: 66–9), in that what is planned for in 'absolute war' preparations seldom materialised in the reality of 'real war' fighting (Kaldor, 2014). Clausewitz ([1832] 1997) therefore considered war an activity derived from social relations and society, rather than more abstract notions of the arts and culture, the experience of which was substantiated by realism. However, despite its relationship to emotionality and social interaction, key to this model was the establishment of war as a rational instrument of political state authority, or the state's 'monopolization of legitimate violence' (Kaldor, 2014: 19; see also Weber, 1919).

Conceptualised in rationalist terms, in Clausewitz's ([1832] 1997) model perhaps the most well-known aspect of war is its function as an apparatus of politics and government 'for definable political ends' (Kaldor, 2014: 17). This is otherwise understood as 'war' serving as a form of 'politics by other means'. He states,

> We see, therefore, that war is not a political act, but also a real political instrument, a continuation of political commerce, a carrying out of the same by other means ... for the political view is the object, war is the means, and the mean must always include the object in our conception. (Clausewitz, [1832] 1997: 22)

Fundamental to the establishment of war for Clausewitz was the constitution of standing armies, the demarcation of civilians from soldiers (as *external* forces who participated in war) and the distinction of soldiers from police officers (who dealt with *internal* matters of crime) (Kaldor, 2014). A lesser cited feature of Clausewitz's model however is the central purpose of war to enact the maximum use of violence necessary to defeat another, and the readiness to use force when needed (Kaldor, 2014). As Kaldor (2014) notes, for Clausewitz violence was literally the currency of war:

> *War therefore is an act of violence intended to compel our opponent to fulfil our will* ... Violence arms itself with the inventions of art and science in order to contend against violence ... Violence, that is to say, physical force (for there is no moral force without the conception of states and law), is therefore the means; the compulsory submission of the enemy to our will is the ultimate *object*. (Clausewitz, [1832] 1997: 5–6, emphasis in original)

In Clausewitzean terms, war is therefore an extreme violent activity, reserved for states with standing armies to conduct against one another – via the consent of the public – for political purposes and with extreme prejudice; the 'absolute' and destructive nature of which is ultimately constrained by inherent 'frictions' when experienced as 'real war' (Shaw, 1988a).

However, this book is not concerned with teaching the strategy of war making; quite the opposite. Instead, for our purposes Clausewitz's ([1832] 1997) model of war serves as both a working definition of how war has frequently been imagined intellectually, politically and within the public domain, and as a baseline of how war making is to be critically understood and developed within our own discussions. It has relevance to all forthcoming chapters in one way or another as a consistent reference point or counterpoint for how war is being defined, discussed, interpreted and reinterpreted within sociology and criminology. With this traditional definition of Clausewitzean war now foregrounded, we next turn to reimagine its contemporary forms. This will help inform our discussions of different types of war throughout the forthcoming chapters of this book.

The changing nature of war, from 'old' to 'new'

The rational model of war outlined above from Clausewitz ([1832] 1997) was developed following his experiences in the Napoleonic Wars (1803–15), and is said to have typified how war had generally emerged and developed from the beginning of the 18th century (Kaldor, 2014). It is the basis for what Kaldor (2014) terms 'old' wars. However, as Giddens (1985) notes, while traditional Clausewitzean views of war may have some historical consistency and application, the same assessment cannot simply be made of the meaning of wars in modernity. Clausewitz's ([1832] 1997) model of war is suggested by Kaldor (2014) not to have been realised again until the First World War. As we discuss in Chapter Two, this period of 'old' war first saw criminological commentary regarding war and militarism emerge from the work of Willem Bonger (1916).

During this period, the evolution of 'old' warfare was aided by several developments occurring throughout the 19th century, including advancements in communications technologies and the importance of establishing alliances to enact overwhelming force (that is, violence) (Kaldor, 2014). Other changes in what came to be known as 'absolute war' throughout the 20th century cause the 'tensions' noted by Clausewitz ([1832] 1997) to come under strain (Kaldor, 2014). Following the introduction of the 1928 Kellogg-Briand pact not to resort to war as a resolution to geopolitical issues and, in particular, the paradox occurring between the parallel emergence of the legal term 'genocide' (discussed in Chapter Four) and the 'terror bombing' of civilians by Allied forces during the Second World War (discussed in Chapter Six), an 'old' Clausewitzean 'legitimacy' of war soon became less politically convincing (Kaldor, 2014). Advances in weapons technologies also quickly began to outstrip their rational use, particularly during the Cold War era of nuclear armament following the catastrophic consequences caused by the nuclear bombings of Hiroshima and Nagasaki (discussed in Chapter Five; see also Kaldor, 2014). Finally, as Kaldor (2014) describes, state monopolies of violence became eroded with the post-war emergence of state military alliances such as NATO and geopolitical alliances such as the Association of Southeast Asian Nations (ASEAN). However, as demonstrated in the forthcoming chapters, violence committed by individual states as 'state crimes' well illustrate that 'monopolies of violence' (see Weber, 1919) still exist and are perpetrated via externalised acts of war or internal conflict and violence.

A further central component of the ways 'new' wars are conducted is their targeted use of counter-insurgency techniques to destabilise political and civic life, gain political control of populations and supress civic values and multiculturalism, rather than being driven by geopolitical or ideological goals and the capturing of geographical territory by military force (Kaldor, 2014). Kaldor suggests such techniques make use of identity politics – based on fear and hatred – to isolate targeted populations as 'other' and remove them from political debate through exclusionary techniques. These include repressive and arbitrary legislation, low intensity military operations, asymmetrical violence (that is, terrorism, discussed in Chapter Three), advanced technologies such as drones (see Wall and Monahan, 2011), and/or more widely available digital technologies such as Google Earth. At the extreme, this may involve killing and violence frequently undertaken by a range of actors who are no longer 'vertically organised' (that is, standing armies, as in 'old' wars), including, for example, paramilitary organisations, militia, traffickers and private military contractors (see, for example, White, 2010). It may also include organised crime gangs, or indeed war making as a form of organised criminality (Tilly, 1985).

Moreover, similar to Barkawi (2006) (whom we return to in the Conclusion), for Kaldor a central element to understanding the transition from 'old' to 'new' wars as they developed from the late 20th century onwards is globalisation. That is, 'the intensification of global interconnectedness – political, economic, military and cultural – and the changing character of political authority' (Kaldor, 2014: 5), distinguished by dynamic social relations, rather than being exclusively defined by technological advances. Kaldor (2014) suggests 'new' wars become visible in globalised terms through the different entities which openly participate in them, such as the UN or Médecins Sans Frontières, plus the 'members of a globally divided class' who are included and excluded through the ways these wars are fought. Including for example, those who on the one hand have access to modern communications technologies, participate in free movement and are fluent with the English language (included), and on the other hand, those whose movements are restricted, are in receipt of humanitarian aid and frequently exposed to famine, displacement, civil conflict and genocide (excluded) (Kaldor, 2014: 5). For Kaldor, this points us to the occurrence of 'new' wars mainly persisting in the Global South and Eastern Europe. However, given their globalised nature, they are also perpetrated by, or from within and against, sovereign territories of the metropolitan North (Kaldor, 2014). These are contentious issues and we return to them in our concluding Chapter Eight.

As such, when conceptualised in these terms, it is evident that war is not only a violent state-defined and enacted social phenomenon, it also needs to be considered in relation to its shifting characteristics across time, space, technologies, social relations and actors engaged with forms of war violence different from those defined by Clausewitz ([1832] 1997). There are, however, further characteristics of Kaldor's (2014) notions of 'old' and 'new' wars which connect more specifically to the direct concerns of this book. These relate to the ways in which war violence is 'legitimised', how laws regulating war are transgressed and suggestions on how war might be prevented.

Connecting 'old' and 'new' wars to the interests of this book

The formation of 'old' wars, as defined in Clausewitzean terms, is affirmed as a 'rational' state activity via the codification of the laws of war as we understand them today (see Detter, 2013, for an extended discussion). As Kaldor (2014: 26) observes:

> In a sense, they were an attempt to preserve the notion of war as a rational instrument of state policy in a context where the logic of war and the extremist tendencies of war, combined with growing technological capacities, were leading to ever-increasing levels of destructiveness.

Indeed, fully forming during the inter-war period (such as the Kellogg-Briand Pact 1928) and in the aftermath of the Second World War (with regards to the UN Charter 1945, and the Geneva Convention 1949 and its protocols), the laws of war demarcate extreme violent behaviour into 'legal' (that is, non-criminal) and 'illegal' (that is, criminal) forms. These developments, and the violence that they emerged from, made the social phenomenon of war intellectually relevant to early criminological scholars such as Willem Bonger, Hermann Mannheim, Sheldon Glueck and Edwin Sutherland (discussed in Chapter Two). However, in the transition from 'old' to 'new' wars, the enactment of war violence also brought the laws of war into view differently for other more contemporary sociological and critical criminological scholars. Fundamentally, this transition illuminated that the violence of war is now disproportionately targeted towards civilians (discussed in Chapters Four to Six), and those who perpetrate such violence (such as states, militia or private entities) engage in a range of atrocities contrary to (and in full knowledge of) the laws of war and international humanitarian law (Kaldor, 2014). War is therefore an inherently deviant activity with clear relevance to (critical) criminological interests, particularly when viewed as a 'rational' state activity within codified international laws. Moreover, while our analysis of war is often defined, and interpreted, throughout the forthcoming chapters of this book via the machinations of the laws of war, the 'legality' of war in such rationalist terms is regarded critically and with scepticism throughout our discussions; so too is our use of the term 'legitimacy'. For purposes of clarity, '*Legality* denotes compliance with the binding rules (substantive and procedural) of the political entity, while *legitimacy* denotes the normative belief by other members of the community that a rule or institution ought to be obeyed' (Chinkin, 2012: 220, emphasis added).

While it is beyond the confines of this book to unpack these terms more fully with regards to wars and 'humanitarian interventions', our references to notions of 'legality' and 'legitimacy' can be understood respectively as a resort to determinants of the law, and by perceptions of state action which are 'subjective and culturally, socially, and historically contingent' (Chinkin, 2012: 221). We recognise these terms are not mutually exclusive, however. When one is substituted for the other critical points of disjuncture can be found in their application; indeed 'an activity may be deemed legal and legitimate; legal and illegitimate; illegal and legitimate; or illegal and illegitimate' (Chinkin, 2012: 220; see also Falk et al, 2012, for a comprehensive insight of these terms across both 'old' and 'new' wars).

There are, of course, additional limitations to Kaldor's (2014) 'new wars' thesis which we return to fully in our Conclusion (Chapter Eight). The glaring absence of acknowledging the gendered nature of war in Kaldor's analysis notwithstanding (discussed in Chapter Seven), these also include: problems of viewing the corrective to war making as having 'cosmopolitan' solutions (that is, law, policing and justice), and the lack of a critical appraisal of colonialism and imperialism as modes of warfare. However, for our purposes, initially defining war in the terms outlined in this Introduction offers a broad conceptual backdrop against which criminological studies of war can be set in context from a sociological vantage point.

Outline and structure of this book

Taken as our baseline definition in the forthcoming chapters, the Clausewitzean notion of war will be subjected to various reinterpretations, from its appreciation within conflict theory of classical sociology (see Malešević, 2010a) to its more critical reinterpretation within contemporary sociological literature (see, for example, chapter 1 in Shaw, 2003). Following this Introduction, this book is structured across six interrelated chapters, in addition to the Conclusion. These chapters may be read in insolation from one another; however, the full clarity of our argument is better grasped by reading them consecutively.

In Chapter Two, 'Theorising "War" within Sociology and Criminology', we make use of both sociological and criminological scholarship to outline thematically some of the ways in which the subject of war has been studied as an interdisciplinary endeavour. This chapter serves two key purposes: first to illustrate that studying war has an identity politics of its own within criminology and sociology. Both historical and contemporary work help to reason the study of war as a critical and pacifistic endeavour, particularly via scholarship produced throughout the First and Second World Wars. Second, to make clear that although not sustained throughout its history, studying war is not necessarily a new endeavour for criminology (or sociology). With these conceptual observations made, in Chapter Three, 'The War on Terrorism: Criminology's "Third War"', we pose a central problematique. We suggest that the seemingly 'new' criminological study of war is a product of renewed interest to studying matters related to the 'war on terrorism' in the aftermath of the terrorist attacks on the World Trade Center on 11 September 2001 (9/11). Although by no means a criticism of the work produced during this period, we provide examples which indicate that the aftermath of 9/11 brought with it fresh impetus to study attendant matters of war and security within criminology which (inadvertently) diverted attention from previous relevant sociological and criminological scholarship. The remaining chapters of this book set about attempting to redress some of this oversight within the discipline.

In Chapters Four and Five, some of the most prolific work within criminology related to genocide and war are presented, to bring into view two long-standing agendas which have provided considerable coverage of war violence for two decades. In Chapter Four, 'The "Forgotten Criminology of Genocide"', some of the historical influences within criminology established in Chapter Two are revisited to highlight the connections the discipline has to the topic of genocide. In particular, these connections pertain to the Holocaust, defining genocide as an international crime in the aftermath of the Second World War, and thinking about how the contemporary notion of genocide can be informed sociologically to recognise its ongoing violence and pervasiveness throughout the 20th and 21st centuries. Next, in Chapter Five, 'From Nuclear to "Degenerate" War', we turn attention to criminological work produced in the aftermath of the Cold War, specifically related to nuclear warfare. In doing so, seminal work within criminology is used to provide an account of the ways in which the detonation, production and proliferation of nuclear weapons can be considered as forms of extortion, deviance and international state criminality. An intervention is then made in this work to suggest that, if alternatively understood as a form of 'degenerate war', then analytic attention would draw not only state criminality into view but, importantly, state victimisation. What both Chapters Four and Five endeavour to make clear is that the consequences of war violence fall disproportionately on civilians.

This issue is then taken up differently in Chapter Six, 'The "Dialectics of War" in Criminology'. In this chapter, the issue of 'terror bombing' is foregrounded as an extensive weapon of 'new' wars used against civilians throughout the 20th and 21st centuries. However, with the intention of transgressing this as merely a matter of 'state crime' this is redefined as a form of 'risk transfer' war wherein military lives are strategically prioritised over those of civilians. In making this observation, juxtapositions are proposed between civilian victims of war, the 'deviant' soldier, and what we term the politics of remembering and 'forgetting' war violence. These two 'dialectics of war' are outlined to illustrate how war is relational with society, and how certain matters relating to deviant military bodies have been prioritised ahead of the murder of civilians within the discipline of criminology past and present.

In Chapter Seven, 'Criminology's "Fourth War"? Gendering War and Its Violence(s)', a reanalysis of genocide is provided (as previously discussed in Chapter Four) via an analytic prism including: the sub discipline victimology, feminism (as broadly defined) and the study of gender (vis-à-vis masculinity). The main intention of this chapter is to make clear that the study of war (and crime) within criminology (and sociology) has frequently overlooked its inherently gendered masculine nature. In so doing, this chapter provides a corrective to much of the literature presented throughout previous chapters of this book, and gives affordance to critical ways of reflecting on other conceptual frameworks and concepts used, and assumptions made, in our discussion to this point.

Finally, in the Conclusion, 'Beyond a "New" Wars Paradigm: Bringing the Periphery into View' (Chapter Eight), the conceptual framework of 'old' and 'new' wars presented in this Introduction, and as generally applied throughout subsequent chapters, is revisited to offer a critique of the broader arrangement of material in this book. This brings into view ways of thinking critically about facets of the 'new wars paradigm' more generally, and helps us to illustrate omissions from the larger body of work that we have presented in Chapters Two to Seven. Key to the critique of 'new' wars, and a notable problematique of criminological literature related to war, is an intellectual fixity that largely omits an awareness and critical understanding of colonialism and imperialism as brutal acts of war violence.

In structuring the book in this way, against the conceptual backdrop of 'old' and 'new' wars, our purpose is to expose the study of war within criminology to an awareness of its past, its emergent trajectory over time, and to offer some mindfulness of the broader types of interdisciplinary literatures from which it derives and to which it relates. In so doing, we wish to disrupt the solidity and assuredness of knowledge which has fast accumulated under the rubric of a 'criminology of war' in the post-9/11 era (discussed in Chapter Three). Most of all, our intentions are to keep criminological scholars mindful that war is conceptually, historically, temporally and spatially dynamic; in brief, what we are discussing is a complex and changing social phenomenon with a considerable history and ongoing interdisciplinary relevance.

The intentions of this book

To be clear from the outset however, this book is not intended to be an attempt at solidifying disciplinary boundaries, nor authoritatively defining what has come to be known as a 'criminology of war' and the way it *should* be studied as an intellectual subject matter; hence the intentional use of a question mark in this book's title. As Jamieson (2012) has previously observed, 'the war/crime nexus is, or ought to be, an object of enquiry that belongs to no one, not even criminology.' Furthermore, rather than becoming yet another intellectual enclave of criminology, as DiPietro (2016) suggests, any attempt at studying war is de facto an inter- and intra-disciplinary endeavour. Indeed, as Jamieson (2014: xxx) has further made clear, the study of the interconnections between war, crime and victimisation 'cannot be unravelled without interdisciplinarity and an awareness of the theoretical and empirical advances made by scholars outside criminology who are thinking about war'.

As will become apparent throughout the forthcoming chapters, our underlying message is similarly rather straightforward: the study of war within criminology requires an engagement with scholarship from both within the discipline, and from the far-reaches outside of its own interests and spheres of influence. To this end, and for our own purposes in this book, we have chosen to make the most use of sociology.

TWO

Theorising 'War' within Sociology and Criminology

Introduction

It has been suggested that 'war' has been of lesser interest to the discipline of sociology than other normative social phenomenon. West and Matthewman (2016) have recently pointed out, rather than commanding the central attention of sociological analysis, the study of war and the military have either been broadly ignored within the discipline, discussed as an attendant matter related to social and political issues, or subsumed as a facet of peace studies. Indeed, they and other scholars (Barkawi, 2006; Ware, 2009; Eulriet, 2010) have noted that the academic study of war has conventionally been taken to be the preserve of the macro interests of international relations, 'tended to be understood in rationalist ways, as a mechanism in which sovereign states and elites engage as a means to pursue their interests, paying little attention to the dynamics and power of civil society' (West and Matthewman, 2016: 486).

Furthermore, the study of the military as a social entity has been seen as the territory of the niche, but longstanding, interest of military sociology (West and Matthewman, 2016); a subdiscipline of sociology emerging from US scholarship in the aftermath of the Second World War (see for example Coates and Pelligrin, 1965; Siebold, 2001; Caforio, 2006; Soeters, 2018). For West and Matthewman (2016), making a case for theorising and studying war as a 'strong program', requires surpassing such rationalist agendas set by international relations and military sociology, in order to better explore the interconnections between state conduct of/at war, and the impacts militarisation has on social relations. However, overlooked within the 'strong' agenda put forth by West and Matthewman (2016) has been the more marginal commentary from criminology.

Although such disciplinary boundaries are often artificial and entirely co-constructed by the knowledges, methods and practices that are – or are not – recognised within and by them, when studying the subject of war from a 'criminologically' oriented starting point (as we have in this book) such boundaries can and do become noticeable. They are therefore worth acknowledging in the interests of breaking them down in order to appreciate the subject of war as a social phenomenon with interdisciplinary relevance across the social sciences. To illustrate this point and help set the context in which this book is intended to be read, in this chapter we outline some of the ways in which the study of war has been theoretically conceptualised within sociology and criminology. To do so, this chapter is split into three interconnected parts. First, drawing on existing scholarship from contemporary sociology, the thematic interests of three classical sociologists who have variously addressed war in their work (Marx, Weber and Durkheim) are outlined. In section two, criminological literature is exposed to a similar approach identifying some of the key authors within the discipline, both past and present, who engaged with the study of war. In the third section, we take stock of the themes derived from both sets of literatures to provide a broadly constituted analytic framework for how this book conceptualises 'war' utilising a sociologically informed criminology. Finally, the concluding section postulates whether or not a 'criminology of war' is possible and indicates how a critical study of war will be pursued in the remainder of this book.

'War' as sociological subject matter

Eulriet (2010: 62) suggests, in noting the limited attention to war within the social sciences (such as sociology and criminology) we should be encouraged to ask ourselves *why* particular disciplinary interests have 'not contributed more to the understanding of this aspect of social life'? We consider this question a crucial starting point for framing the wider possibilities of what the study of war within criminology might entail. We first address this question with regards to sociology and then with reference to criminology. Parcelled in between these explorations, we highlight some key and emergent themes within the extant sociological and criminological literature relating to war. We begin with a view from sociology.

Whither a 'sociology of war': modernity, bellicosity and pacifism

For Giddens (1985) and Mann (1988), the disengagement from war within classical sociology is conceptualised as a problem related to modernity. The onset of industrialisation is assumed by both liberal and Marxist traditions within classical sociology to be a peaceful endeavour in which the advances in the technologies of industrialism make war redundant. As Mann (1988: 147) observes,

Comte

From the Enlightenment to Durkheim most major sociologists omitted war from the central problematic. This was not neglect; it was quite deliberate. They believed the future society would be pacific and transnational. Industrial, or capitalist, or 'modern' society would be unlike the preceding feudal, or theocratic, or militant societies. Power could now operate pacifically, without the use of force.

For example, Durkheim paid little attention to military power and violence in his accounts of modernity and considered the social phenomenon of war to be obsolete under the conditions of organic solidarity (Giddens, 1985). Taking a different view, despite perceiving the social world to be replete with conflict, Marx is said to have written 'nothing on the nature of war' and instead broadly considered the arrangement of the nation–state in economic terms, rather than in relation to military power (Giddens, 1985: 24). Different again is the view of Weber who 'tended to see violence as an inescapable part of the human condition' and for there to be only force lurking behind 'universal values' of social life defended by states that have coercive bureaucratic power and an apparatus of violence at its disposal (Giddens, 1985: 27). For Mann (1988: 146–9), the history of this disengagement runs deeper than this and is juxtaposed between what he categorises as a 'Marxist/Liberal' and 'Militarist' tradition within facets of European sociology. He suggests that a 'militant' tradition relates to historical scholarship which deemed war and war preparation (that is, militarism) 'as a normal and desirable social activity' derived from nation–states whose armies were defeated during the First and Second World Wars (Mann, 1988: 125).

As an extension of Mann's (1988) conceptualisation of 'war' within sociology, Hans Joas (2003) and Sinisa Malešević (2010a, 2010b) further unpack the historical tensions between the ways war was permitted or rejected as either a pacific or bellicose tradition within classical sociology. Like Mann (1988), Joas (2003) assumes modernity to be inherently peaceful and non–violent. He argues that a focus on war in classical (that is, European) sociological literature has been systematically forgotten due to its associations with fascism and violence during the First and Second World Wars, with the enduring passivity of modernity being prioritised instead. However, although Joas (2003) and Malešević (2010a, 2010b) concur with Mann (1988) in this regard, they both disagree on the historical consistency of a 'militarist' tradition within the discipline. Joas (2003) suggests there was little internal coherence between late 19th century sociologists and their commentaries on war that could constitute a lucid 'tradition' of militarism within classical sociology. In contrast, for Malešević (2010a, 2010b) there was a clear intellectual tradition within European and US sociology, although differing in political affiliation, which had provided a long-standing commentary on war with relevance for contemporary sociology. Following Mann (1988) and Joas (2003) Malešević (2010a, 2010b) explains this as deriving from the ways in which the classical sociological theory of Marx, Weber and Durkheim (plus others) had been reinterpreted in the aftermath of the Second World War in the spirit of an anti-militarist tradition. Subsequent sociological scholarship 'cleansed' sociology of the study of war and instead pursued a pacific interpretation of classical theory ignoring its 'bellicose' tradition, largely due to the fact that '[t]he distaste for war and violence on the part of the general public was shared by many post-WWII sociologists', alongside distaste for Nazi war crimes among non-bellicose intellectuals (Malešević, 2010b: 195). Instead, sociologists reformulated the discipline's interests in critical issues to address social structure, welfare and 'normative systems' (Malešević, 2010b).

How classical materials are read, therefore, is a matter of interpretation. For instance, for the historical sociologist Norbert Elias (1994) modernity encouraged a shift from the shame, repugnance, and 'informalisation' (that is, self-restraint) of the Middle Ages to 'figurations' (that is, obligations, pacification, increased empathy and so on) characteristic of the 'civilising' processes within society at large (as indicated above in relation to war by Giddens, 1985, and Mann, 1988). Coupled with a centralisation of power, including the capability of the state to be violent as one of its monopolies of force (including war), the formalisation of law, and the transitioning of punishment from a public spectacle to privately enacted 'rational' act (such as prison), the modernising project of industrialisation was conceived sociologically to have made societies less violent and more pacific (Elias, 1994). However, in the modernist process of 'civilising' Elias (1994) did not necessarily consider war to be obsolete nor the antithesis of peace. Instead, violence became an instrument of the civilising process, and – as Kaldor (2014) later noted vis-à-vis the transition between 'old' and 'new' wars – rivalries between states became reconfigured in order to wage war with less risk, but a continued capacity to pacify large geographical areas. For Elias (1994: 523):

> To begin with, there is the constant danger of war. War, to repeat the point in different words, is not the opposite of peace ... wars between smaller units have been, in the course of history up to now, inevitable stages and

instruments in the pacification of larger ones [that is, colonisation] ... [b]ut the fact that, in our day, just as earlier, the dynamics of increasing interdependence are impelling the figuration of state societies towards such conflicts, to the formation of monopolies of physical force over large areas of the earth [that is, geopolitical alliances such as NATO] and thus, through all the terrors and struggles, towards their pacification, is clear enough.

Therefore, Elias (1994) did have something to say about war, which was not merely reducible to it occurring less in an increasingly 'civilising' world. Instead, war, both historically and contemporarily, is the cosh of pacification wielded as a state monopoly of violence. The work of Marx, Weber and Durkheim has also been subjected to similar (re) interpretations.

Although we do not intend to resurrect or rejoinder the observations of Mann (1988), Joas (2003) or Malešević (2010a, 2010b) in the terms outlined above, in the central tenet of their arguments there are some useful thematic elements to begin a (re)conceptualisation of the historical contexts of a 'sociology of war'. By provisionally compartmentalising the 'anti-militarist' positions proposed by Giddens (1985) and Mann (1988) within classical sociology between their 'Marxist' and 'Liberal' perspectives, we can sketch how the dominant positions of Marx, Weber and Durkheim had indeed made contributions to sociological commentary on war.

To be clear however, by selectively focusing on these three popular scholars we do not consider them to constitute all commentary regarding war in classical or modern sociology. Indeed, we have intentionally left out the work of other important scholars such as George Simmel and Jane Addams, for example, who are both noted as making early contributions to studies of war and the military in relation to networks/groups and peace activism (see Soeters, 2018, chapters 4 and 5 respectively). However, in focusing our interests on the ideas of Marx, Weber and Durkheim we can distil some common historical influences from classical sociology to help begin conceptualising a sociologically informed study of war.

Conflict, power and 'legitimate' violence

Malešević (2010a) broadly conceptualises Marx's relevance to war in relation to traditional themes of class conflict, social change and revolutionary formation, informed by collective violence. As Malešević

(2010a) explains, Marx's general interests were not in relation to 'real war', killing or the extermination of the bourgeoisie by proletariat classes but in the appropriation and redistribution of their property. In these early ideas (as discussed in Chapter Three) war was considered in metaphorical terms (that is, class war) with violence reserved for the final stages of revolutionary epochal change to overthrow the brutality of economic classes. However, according to Malešević (2010a), violence in Marx's later work became more central following the Paris Commune of 1871 (the short-lived revolutionary takeover of the French government), taking two particular forms. For Marx violence was considered an integral part of capitalist modernity, both in relation to modes of production and revolution (Malešević, 2010a). Violence was not merely considered a normative function of social life but integral to capitalism itself. War violence and its perpetration has its own political economy benefiting from the expansion of militarisation due in part to the technological advancement and perpetuation of warfare requiring significant financial investment (Malešević, 2010a). The coercive foundations of capitalist states arranged in these ways were therefore recognised as having interlocking commercial, economic, (geo)political and ideological interests. Any changes in power to overthrow the established order would therefore require the complete dismantling and destruction of the existing nation-state itself formed and sustained by violence and thus legitimating a violent response (Malešević, 2010a).

This conceptual approach prevailed during a later upsurge in interest with war and sociology (see Creighton and Shaw, 1987). Writing in *The British Journal of Sociology* during the 1980s a debate emerged between the conservative philosopher Roger Scruton (1987, 1988) and sociologist Martin Shaw (1988b) exemplifying this. Both had differing opinions regarding the contemporary intellectual positionality and theoretical worth of what they debated as a 'sociology of war', the centre of which was its perceived Marxist ideology. For Scruton (1987: 296) the prevailing 'sociology of war' of the time had naively taken a broadly Marxist view of war (akin to that proposed by Malešević, 2010a) that was devoid of any understanding of it 'flowing from the political realm' or systems of government. Scruton (1987: 296) rejected what he considered a 'Marxian vision of politics as 'super structural" which he considered to have no appreciation of the complexities of war from a Clausewitzian (that is, military strategy) perspective (as noted in our Introduction). Understood in these terms, for Scruton (1987: 301) war was to be interpreted as the 'contrast between contract and fighting', insofar as the rationale, negotiation, control and avoidance of war is derived from the sovereign democratic power of government, in agreement with the body politic under its leadership.

For Shaw (1988b) however, this position was highly objectionable on two fronts. First, he opposed the view that the position being taken by sociologists interested in war was 'a simple Marxist view' (Shaw, 1988b: 616). For him, leading sociological theorists subsumed into this 'simple' viewpoint had been overlooked by Scruton (1987). For example, C. Wright Mills (1959), who in *The Causes of World War Three* (discussed in Chapter Five) alleged that the potential causes of nuclear war were not in the material conditions of nation–states, but in the mutual preparation of warfare and the autonomy afforded to the military in the bosom of political and economic systems (Shaw, 1988b). Similarly, Shaw also pointed to *The Nation State and Violence* by Anthony Giddens (1985) (referenced earlier) wherein it is argued that converging relations between domestic surveillance, state military force and the industrialisation of war had jointly contributed to an increase in internal (namely surveillance) and external (namely war) state violence, rather than capitalism being the causes of war per se (Shaw, 1988b; see also Jessop, 1986; Skocpol, 1987). Second, Shaw (1988b: 616) was exercised by the suggestion of a 'juridical concept of the state' offered by Scruton (1987). This conception requires the body politic entrusting governments with more clearly defined 'democratic' structures to adhere to the 'laws of war' they produce, and restrict (or enact) war violence for the purposes of peacekeeping and 'peacemaking' (Clausewitz, [1832] 1997). For Shaw (1988b), Scruton's (1987) view of the state in this guise was particularly selective in relation to how the international juridical power it wielded was understood. He notes that Scruton's (1987) argument did not,

> seek to explain away the fact that certain states based on the rule of law, such as the USA and the UK, have been involved in immense numbers of wars … he remains comfortably aloof from the messy facts of warfare, not bothering to explain to us whether or why the US invasion of Grenada was more legal than the Soviet invasion of Afghanistan, or US support for the Contras more so than Soviet support for left-wing guerrillas elsewhere. (Shaw, 1988b: 616)

He continues that despite Scruton's (1987) reference to Clausewitz's strategic view of war (as part of political decision making other than as a political act), the fundamental characteristics of war, namely violence and domination perpetrated under coercive state authority, had been overlooked. This is perhaps a lesser cited feature of Clausewitz's ([1832] 1997) work compared to war being considered 'politics by other means' (noted in our Introduction). However, as Kaldor (2014) has well observed (also noted in the Introduction), war defined in these terms needs to be considered as being a changing social phenomenon, from 'old' to 'new'. In modernity, war violence is no longer merely isolated to the overthrowing of feudal powers or military forces. The 'total wars' of the First and Second World Wars witnessed the mobilisation of civilian populations against a 'mass enemy of the people', signifying a shift in warfare facilitated by a more ubiquitous militarism with war violence concentrated on both military and civilian targets to weaken the fighting systems of nation-states (Giddens, 1985: 330). While this is not all there is to be said about these developments within the literature, this exchange between Scruton (1987) and Shaw (1988b) usefully captures the ways in which the tradition of Marxism had found purchase – usefully or not – in the later intellectual nomenclature of a 'sociology of war'.

According to both Mann (1988) and Joas (2003), Weber's intellectual contribution to understanding war and war violence sociologically has been noticeably rewritten within classical scholarship. They suggest that not only has this work been reinterpreted, it has also been repositioned and prioritised (along with Marxism) in contradistinction to bellicose intellectualism within social science (Mann, 1988; Joas, 2003). Malešević (2010a) illustrates how such work had been reinterpreted in these terms. For example, Weber considered the foundation of Western rationality to be structurally based on military organisation and customs; in contrast to Marxism, feudalism and the expansion of capitalism were not based on economic relations alone, but on a ruling class dedicated to military service, multiple sovereignties of power, and war (Malešević, 2010a). In addition, the 'growth of disciplinary techniques and practices' throughout social and political institutions during modernity were predicated on militarised discipline and war violence: in the arrangement of nation-states, the (later) industrialised context of factory labour, and/or in constituting mechanisms of social order such as the law or policing (Malešević, 2010a).

Perhaps most popularly recognised is Weber's (1919) conceptualisation of the modern nation-state assertively defined in terms of its own authority. In particular (as noted in our Introduction, citing Kaldor, 2014), state authority not only maintains a 'monopoly' and capacity to commit violence on its subjects or in the 'defence' of its borders, but it also does so by establishing rationally constituted laws providing its own 'legality' to do so (Weber, 1919). Understood in these terms,

Malešević (2010a) grounds his own argument within *The Sociology of War and Violence* in Weberian terms, engaging with the study of war between concepts of 'cumulative bureaucratisation of coercion' and 'centrifugal ideologisation'. These positions derive from the notion that states hold a 'legitimate' monopoly of violence (Weber, 1919) which is legitimatised and perpetrated via a ubiquitous state-orchestrated routinisation of bureaucratic rationality in everyday social life. However, as Mann (1988) further explains, caution is needed when relying on such a priori explanations of the 'state' across history, particularly with regards to notions of 'legitimacy' and a 'monopolisation' of violence applicable to centrally arranged bases of authority. He states,

> The problem of this definition (apart from the difficult word 'legitimate') is that it embodies both an *institutional* and *functional* element – the state being recognisable both because its institutions are centrally located and because it undertakes functions of legitimate violence. Difficulties arise when the two characteristics are empirically separable … those centralized institutions which we intuitively recognize as 'states' in feudalism – monarchies, duchies, etc. – sometimes did *not* possess a monopoly of the means of legitimate violence (either judicial or military force). Instead they shared these powers with church, local landlords and towns. (Mann, 1988: 74, emphasis in original)

These cautionary notes notwithstanding, as Malešević (2010a) continues, the state's capacity for violence in modernity, and the conditions of war this can frequently create, is not without other purposes. War creates opportunities for individual and collective sacrifices which can ascribe an enhanced meaning to the body politic in the face of death and destruction.

Perpetration and aftermath of 'war' violence: militarism and solidarity

In the aftermath of war, Weber observed that war violence can be afforded 'dignity' by repositioning state perpetrated violence as a noble endeavour. When interpreted as national/military 'victories' and 'losses', this is an attempt to add further legitimacy to the state's autonomy as both a coercive and protective force (Malešević, 2010a). Thus, in 'dignifying' war violence, the perpetration of warfare became important for social change since those who gain power through the violence of warfare may also promote its transformation as 'cultural prestige' (Malešević, 2010a). In doing so, Malešević (2010a) suggests that within modernity the 'prestige' formerly held by notions of 'heroism' come to be replaced with the bureaucratic rationality of military efficiency and effectiveness (Malešević, 2010a). Put simply, militarism is double-edged: it can both conjure the sentiment and ideology to perpetrate war violence, and in the aftermath of warfare it can create conditions which publicly encourage the 'remembrance' of specific prioritised activities, practices and populations, while privately 'forgetting' others (as discussed in Chapter Six). However, Weber was not the only classical scholar to comment on the interconnections between the state, war, its aftermath, and society. So too did Emile Durkheim.

For Joas (2003: 141) the work of Durkheim was a key liberal perspective that 'was guided by its belief in the pacific character of industrial society or of capitalism', and therefore more easily obscured from commentary relating to warfare than Marx and Weber. With a focus on matters of solidarity, Durkheim made two key contributions to the understanding of war. First, with the exception of altruistic suicide, war was considered to be 'inversely related' to suicide in that it strengthened moral and social order, and increased political and moral integration. This resulted in decreases in anomic and egoistic suicide (Malešević, 2010a). Second, war for Durkheim, particularly the First World War, was a large scale anomic and pathological situation which briefly returned society to a form of mechanic solidarity. However, as the state is understood as both the product and protector of moral autonomy, and the highest representative of shared morality, it represents the pacifism and solidarity of the body politic (Malešević, 2010a). As such, for Durkheim any attempts to impose militarism by autonomous state power (such as the Nazi German regime) was suggested to eventually fail due to the interdependency and shared beliefs evident in societies arranged by organic solidarity (Malešević, 2010a). Thus, Durkheim followed the most pacifistic tradition within classical sociology, considering war an aberration and something 'destined to disappear' as one form of solidarity (that is, mechanic) followed another (that is, organic), thereby creating little opportunity for collective violence to occur (Malešević, 2010a: 20). Unlike the views of Marx and Weber, who considered technological development a fundamental part of the economic conditions of capitalism and key to the militarisation and perpetration of state violence, for Durkheim such advances would instead foster and require peace thereby making war obsolete in the modern world (Malešević, 2010a). As history would show however, the assent of nuclear technology would demonstrate otherwise (discussed in Chapter Five).

However, despite war being considered an 'aberration' and of temporary influence on social solidarity, it is proposed that 'Durkheim deciphers war as useful' for social solidarity (Eulriet, 2010: 69). Eulriet (2010) suggests this 'usefulness' is derived from the tragedies and horrors of war, making 'vivid' the attachment of individuals to their wider social group. Moreover, war also facilitates the change and rearrangement of social systems, including the creation of new forms of solidarity and the recreation of the nation-state in the aftermath of warfare (as discussed in Chapter Six). Taken in the light of the criminological interests of this book, these observations are recognisably similar to Durkheim's (2013) commentary on crime as being in some ways functional for social order, particularly in maintaining a balanced appeal for punitiveness within the judicial system and popular sentiment. As Eulriet (2010: 69–70) states,

> the establishment of a parallel with Durkheim's views on crime is tempting. Hence he sees crime as useful for the development of morals and law: he was largely criticised, it is well known, for having stated that crime help maintaining and reinforcing solidarity within society. Yet if Durkheim identifies different forms and functions of solidarity in his reflection of war (as he did in his study of crime), caution seems to be required in the establishment of analogies.

Durkheim questioned if wars were inevitable, and given the geopolitical contexts within which warfare takes place, Eulriet (2010) proposes war should instead be considered quite different to the domestic context of crime (Jock Young had a different view and considered violence within these domains etiologically similar; see Young, 2003, 2007). Similar views regarding the precarious connection of Durkheim's alleged 'functional' view of crime (see Durkheim, 2013) and war has more recently been noted empirically by Caldwell and Mestrovic (2011) in relation to the anomic and 'deranged' conditions of the 2003 war in Iraq. Like Eulriet (2010), they caution simplistic interpretations of Durkheim's work in relation to war.

Thus, notions of solidarity are a key feature in Durkheim's comments regarding war as a means of appreciating the internal structural conditions of the outbreak of war and onset of militarism (Eulriet, 2010). This is not merely open to interpretation to civilian populations and civic space, but also to the solidarity and anomic conditions of war fighting for soldiers and combatants.

Taking stock of sociology and war

Having now arranged these first thematic insights, we can offer some initial thoughts to help conceptualise war critically within sociology. First, one of the key influences in the emergence of contemporary studies of war within sociology were approaches thought to be informed by Marxism. Here, war is considered from a macro view of conflict, whereby the act is synonymous with the pursuit of capital and state hegemony, and as a means to conceive of conflict as found within class struggle. Next, the work of Weber informs us that war may be conceptualised as a 'legitimate' act of violence, conducted by state entities via a 'monopoly' of force for the purposes of furthering political agendas, rather than as a political act per se. What we also learn is that war is conducted as a form a bureaucratic rationality during its preparation, perpetration and aftermath. As such the notion of 'war' becomes a political, cultural and social facilitator of militaristic values within civic life. Finally, from Durkheim we learn that war was a temporary aberration which influenced notions of social solidarity. Serving to offer a micro view of the impacts of war on society, it is understood as an act that can bring populations together, but also one that can create anomic conditions drawing them apart. With these basic themes now in view, next we turn to interrogate the study of war from the perspective of criminology.

'War' as a sociological problem for criminology

Some twenty years prior to the publication of this book, in his final essay *A Brief for Criminology* Leon Radzinowicz (1999: 460) stated that alongside many issues which 'crowd the agenda' for criminological attention, including substance abuse, violence against women and children, unemployment and poverty: 'Nor can criminology ignore the impact of international conflicts and tensions.' Radzinowicz is, of course, best known for establishing the Institute of Criminology at Cambridge University in the UK, and for his long running critical academic and social commentary on criminal justice policy. However, although not elaborating further on these comments, as a Polish émigré lawyer fleeing the Nazi German regime (see Hood, 2004), he was aware of the relevance of criminology to the issue of war. As Maier-Katkin et al (2009: 230) point out, like other criminological scholars of his time, Radzinowicz had 'worked during the war years with the Justice ministries of governments-in-exile of occupied European countries to document Nazi war crimes and plan for the possibility of post-war trials'.

As such, like sociologists, this indicates that criminologists have long-standing interests with the subject matter of war that may not be immediately apparent from their wider body of work. Although these interests are perhaps less pronounced than within sociology, it would be inaccurate to presuppose that criminologists have been inattentive to the study of war, or detached from its sociological relevance and historical occurrences. To unpack these observations further, we now turn to contextualise the historical backdrop of war as a sociological problem for criminology.

'Towards a criminology of war in Europe'

The comments above from Radzinowicz (1999) provide a useful historical anchor for the criminological literature related to war. They denote a significant reference point for the publication of a seminal chapter by Ruth Jamieson (1998) entitled 'Towards and Criminology of War in Europe'. In Jamieson's (1998: 480) extended essay/manifesto, she composed a sociological framework addressing why the study of war should be of central interest to criminologists. First, Jamieson suggested that the primary intention of war can be seen in its consequences: the perpetration of mass victimisation often taking the guise of 'state crimes' by frequently violating the human rights of innocent civilian populations. Next, as a social phenomenon war involves militias and militaries routinely engaging in gendered forms of (masculine) violent behaviour that is juxtaposed to non-militarised ways of civic life. Finally, the conditions of war both at home and abroad have a detrimental impact on civil liberties, bringing domestic citizens' lives under increasingly sophisticated technologies of policy and surveillance and exposed to more stringent social control and punitive judicial processes (Jamieson, 1998).

Yet, despite the clarity of this agenda – as is made clear in Chapter Three – its purchase within criminological literature during the twenty years hence has been sparsely recognised. This is particularly curious given its publication occurring at a time of numerous clusters of geopolitical violence, genocide and war within modernity which – as Radzinowicz (1999) suggested – warranted criminological attention. For example, Jamieson's (1998) essay emerged in the aftermath of the 1991 Gulf War in Iraq/Kuwait (see White, R., 2008), and followed the slaughter of approximately 800,000 Tutsi people and oppositional parties by Hutu army, police, civilians and militia (Interahamwe) throughout 100 days of violence during the Rwandan genocide (1994) (see Jamieson, 1999). It was also published during the same year as the Good Friday Agreement was signed ending political violence in Northern Ireland (1969–98) (see McEvoy and Mika, 2002); that same year the Rome Statute (1998) was adopted subsequently bringing into existence the International Criminal Court (see Rothe and Mullins, 2006). At the same time, war erupted in Kosovo following the collapse of the Dayton 'settlement' between Bosnia and Croatia resulting in the mass genocide of Albanian Muslims by Serbian forces (1998–99) (see Nikolic-Ristanovic 1998; and discussed in Chapter Six). In the years that followed, wars have emerged and raged across the Middle East in Afghanistan, Iraq and most recently Syria during the 'war on terrorism': violence which has continued since the terrorist attacks in the US on 11 September 2001 (discussed in Chapter Three), to the present day. In making these initial observations, we are not accusing an entire intellectual discipline of 'sleeping' in its ability to address war (Hagan, 2015). What this instead perhaps indicates, as Giddens (1985) noted of sociology, is that while wars and genocides have been consistent features of public and political life globally during the 20th and 21st centuries, the social phenomenon of war has perhaps been a central concern for very few scholars within criminology (some of whom are noted in the above). This is despite there being both a clear historical literature to tap into, and a prescient contemporary agenda awaiting its application. Most recently, Carrabine (2018: 1) has asserted that in the twenty years hence since Jamieson's (1998) call, 'three main approaches' have developed within criminology vis-à-vis the study of war, including: state crime, transnational militarised 'policing', and corporate crime. However, although accurate in some respects a closer reading of such literature, as developed from here and throughout this book, demonstrates there is much more to be contemplated.

Justice, 'unjust' wars and war crimes

Taking a historical view of war within criminology, Jamieson (1998: 481) noted that crimes occurring during times of war have been understood as 'a continuation of ordinary crime in an altered social (demographic), legal and political context'. Whereas 'war crimes', that is breaches of the 'laws of war', have often been treated as marginal concerns for the social sciences and criminology in particular. Previous insights from Bonger (1916, 1936) well illustrate a criminological preoccupation with crimes occurring during war as Jamieson (1998) observes. We return to this earlier work in due course. However, it was the scholarship emerging at the outset and throughout the Second World War that came to bring a distinct focus on 'war crimes' within criminology.

An early contribution to this literature is found in Hermann Mannheim's (1941), *War and Crime,* who in an extended set of published lectures provided a general overview of the causes of the yet to be known consequences of the Second World War. Writing at the outset of the War during August 1940, Mannheim (1941) provided an insight into the causes of war that – like crime – began to shift ideas of its perpetration from the individual to the collective actions of social groups and institutions. For Mannheim (1941) – himself a German lawyer and former member of the German artillery in exile from the Nazi regime (see Hood, 2004) – he proposed that during times of war economic crimes would rise, and crimes of violence would fall. Principally, he noted a distinction needed to be made between 'just' and 'unjust' wars. As Sutherland (1942: 639) proposed in a review of this work,

> The general analysis of the relation between war and crime is based on an ethical distinction between unjust wars, which are regarded analogous to crimes, and just wars, which are regarded as analogous to punishments ... He [Mannheim] realizes the difficulties involved in this distinction between just and unjust wars and expresses his desire for an international tribunal which may pronounce objectively as to the justice of wars.

From this perspective, war should therefore be regarded as 'unjust' when violating the sensibilities of international peace and enacted by nation-states without the agreement of the international community. The perpetration of 'unjust' war, in other words, should be understood as an activity not reducible to the individual but to social systems, institutions and groups who perpetrate, tolerate and support such injustice. In contrast, 'just' war should be reserved for the punishment of such acts, kept as a mode of 'justice' enacted by international judicial bodies (see Zolo, 2010 for critiques of 'victors' justice' in this regard, also discussed in our concluding Chapter Eight).

The pursuit of war crimes in such ways was realised shortly after in both the scholarly and socio-legal work of Harvard criminologist Sheldon Glueck. Although better known for work produced with

Eleanor Glueck regarding the biopsychological analysis of delinquent behaviour, the contributions that Sheldon Glueck made to the pursuit of justice for war crimes during and in the aftermath of the Second World War serve as considerable evidence of criminological engagement with both the material realities and punishment of acts of war. This work is captured in two influential texts: *War Criminals: Their Prosecution and Punishment* (Glueck, 1944) and *The Nuremberg Trial and Aggressive War* (Glueck, 1946). Hagan and Greer (2002) provide an authoritative account of his contribution to the institution of the Nuremberg trials which is largely unacknowledged within criminological literature. Despite his conceptual inclination towards reductionist accounts of criminality, Hagan and Greer (2002) depict how Glueck's pragmatic and legal realist approach to the ways Nazi war crimes should be pursued and prosecuted, fortified a position for the Nuremberg trials based on several key premises. First, that definitions of war crimes included and prioritised 'crimes against humanity' (discussed in Chapter Four) rather than 'wars of aggression' (as intimated by Mannheim, 1941). This included acts of knowing that permitted cruelty and atrocity to take place, and membership to criminal organisations that perpetrated acts of cruelty (such as the Gestapo) (Hagan and Greer, 2002). He advocated for the establishment of an international criminal court to be constructed, complete with standardised ways of practising international law, international humanitarian law and due process, to handle the trials and remain thereafter for subsequent use; he also rejected the proposition that war crimes could be defended on the basis of sovereignty, and introduced what came to be known as the 'Nuremberg principle', in that it was no defence to claim orders – deemed to be 'legally' given – were merely being followed unknowing that such activities were illegal (Hagan and Greer, 2002). Glueck's endeavours informed how the Nuremberg trials should be constituted and ensured that crimes against humanity and the atrocities of the Holocaust (discussed in Chapter Four) became the central features of the Nuremberg trials, rather than the (distracting and comparatively less serious) charge of crimes of aggressive war (Hagan and Greer, 2002).

Glueck also emphasised that crimes committed by 'powerful industrialists and bankers, manufacturers and businessmen' in the theft and receipt of stolen goods during the Second World War should be considered under the rubric of the Nuremberg trials (Hagan and Greer, 2002: 240). Similarly, Jamieson (1998) also acknowledged this latter premise, that war had been previously observed as 'a continuance of economic relations', profiteering from wartime regulation and the expansion of economic markets via opportunism created by war.

Different from Glueck however, Jamieson (1998) identified the later influential work of Sutherland's (1949: 190) *White Collar Crime*, wherein he commented at length as to what should constitute war crimes, 'when profits take priority to patriotism'. Sutherland (1949) added that war crimes constitute acts during times of war that look to profiteer from war making, trading with enemy forces (that is, treason) and tax evasion; all of which were most likely to be conducted by members of society in lofty positions of power, capitalising on a state of national emergency serving and protecting their own economic interests. Sutherland's (1949) analysis of these wartime issues, as he acknowledges, were previously addressed by Clinard (1946) in a detailed account of violations of US rationing regulation during the Second World War. Clinard's (1946) argument pointed out that 'business men' perpetrating violations of wartime ration pricing regulations not only caused more economic harm per capita but were also less likely to receive harsh sentences if turned over to the authorities because of their 'good' character, and because such crimes were perceived as less serious by the criminal justice system of the time. These arguments presented by Clinard (1946) and Sutherland (1949) sought to challenge the normativity of how conventional 'criminals' and 'crime' were perceived. They also offered an upward gaze of offending that stood in contrast to the more popular downward gaze on (frequently young male) criminality on the 'homefront' during war time (see Gault, 1918; Bonger, 1936; Bromberg, 1943).

Following these important historical contributions however, Hagan and Greer (2002: 256) note that, '[c]riminologists, including Sheldon Glueck, simply followed the great majority of the American public in focusing their attention in other directions after the war'. This perhaps gives some early indication as to why crimes of the powerful, as they related to war, were side-lined from future criminological interests in the post-war years.

Militarism, social disorganisation and pacifism

Looking to historical criminological literature related to war, Jamieson (1998) also drew attention to the early work of Marxist criminologist, Willem Bonger (1916, 1936). In his brief comments on war he presented two explanations of war and crime, initially during the First World War and then prior to the beginning of the Second World War. First, Bonger (1916) was preoccupied with the problem of 'militarism' (discussed in Chapter Six) taking two particular forms. Emulating the ideas of Marx that were later reflected in the work of Mann and

Giddens (discussed earlier), for Bonger (1916: 375) militarism was primarily a result of capitalism, with war – and more specifically the army – serving as a double-edged instrument: 'for its function is to furnish the bourgeoisie with the means of restraining the proletariat at home, and of repulsing or attacking the forces of foreign countries'. War was conducted by colonial Western nation-states for the specific economic purposes of expanding capitalist (that is, imperial) interests into exploitable territories (discussed in our concluding Chapter Eight) (Bonger, 1916). Thus the auspices of war affected workers and free labour on the homefront, with state agencies of social control (that is, police and military) employed to control disruption to the economic means of production from striking workforces before and during war, and thereafter (as Winston Churchill had done with striking Welsh miners at Tonypandy in 1910/11, and Llanelly in 1926; see O'Brien-Mòr, 1994, for a historical review of these contested issues, and Bonger, 1916). Furthermore, echoing Weberian sentiments in relation to the expansion of militarised bureaucratic rationality, Bonger (1916) pointed to the original source of military discipline itself as having degenerative consequences for those who join (either voluntarily or through conscription). He states, 'It is naturally only by a discipline of iron that order can be maintained and the recruits taught their trade. As soon as a man is debased by excessive discipline to the role of a machine, his moral qualities deteriorate' (Bonger, 1916: 517)

The 'debasement' of soldiers through the 'evil influence of military life' would consequently become evident in domestic crime statistics when returning home from war but, because of time and space, remain less visible for crimes perpetrated during war fighting itself (as discussed earlier; see also Caldwell and Mestrovic, 2011, for a contemporary view, and Bonger, 1916). As such, opposing Weber and Durkheim, for Bonger (1916) the cohesive impacts of war were 'rare', and only evident when wars were popularly and widely supported by the public for economic purposes (following Marx, see for example Malešević, 2010a). Even then however, the consequences of the violence of militarism at home and abroad would persist (Bonger, 1916).

This latter point became the narrative of Bonger's second explanation of war. In his later brief commentary (Bonger, 1936) war is understood as a cause of social disorganisation which perpetuated crime on many fronts, including family separation, child neglect, sexual demoralisation, poverty and destitution, and killing and destruction (Jamieson, 1998). As Ruggiero (2005, 2006) later noted, this view of Bonger's (1936) reflected an opposing narrative from sociological functionalist perspectives of war: instead of serving as cohesive and progressive periods in history (following Durkheim, see for example Malešević, 2010a), war is understood as criminogenic both during its occurrence and thereafter. Like Caldwell and Mestrovic (2011), war is perceived as creating anomic conditions that weaken – not strengthen – social bonds, undermine social solidarity and create social disorganisation both on the homefront and at war (Ruggiero, 2005). Jamieson (1998) also suggested this latter view of Bonger's (1936) was more associated with a Durkheimian perspective of war causing social disorganisation and fostering anomic social conditions; a view she considered akin to that of Pitirim Sorokin.

For Sorokin ([1937] 1962), the onset of war afforded pervasive state-military influence over/within civic life that would be dubious during times of 'peace'. The imposition of emergency domestic conditions during war is said to witness government control becoming 'unquestionably' expanded, laws transformed to cater for wartime activities (that is, conscription, rationing, security, etc.), and the rights and liberties of citizens constricted (Sorokin, [1937] 1962). The longer conditions of war persisted, the more of a 'habitual' foothold such state-military activity (or 'systematic militarism'; see Sorokin, 1944) gained between government and civic life. The extreme of these conditions was totalitarian rule from wartime governments, juxtaposed with the (utopian) notion of 'peace' which, as Sorokin ([1937] 1962: 198) points out, 'tends to work in the opposite way'. As we learn from Jaworski (1993: 69), Sorokin (1944) went on to believe that declines in what he termed 'sensate culture', evidenced by increasing social individualism brought on by modernity, corresponded with this emerging form of 'systemic militarism'. Such militarism permeated all aspects of civic, familial, and political life, creating and maintaining disparities of power throughout society, further polarising the rich and poor (via property ownership for example), causing criminality (Bonger, 1916, 1936) and allowing the state to operate as an ethically and morally bankrupt political entity (Sorokin, 1944; Jaworski, 1993). For Sorokin (1944), such conditions were untenable foundations on which peace could be built and maintained. His solutions to war were thereby driven by a *pacifistic*, rather than *pacific*, vision to deconstruct sovereign and geopolitical military authority, reallocate the economic capital of the industry of war for peaceful purposes, and for all nation-states to disarm and end experimentation with nuclear weapons (discussed in Chapter Five) (Jaworski, 1993). In brief, the conditions of war presented militarism as a form of social disorganisation affecting all aspects of public and private life. As long as this persisted, and the more entrenched it became, the less likely it was to establish peaceable ends to 'old' war (Kaldor, 2014) and its consequences.

For 'a pacifist criminology' of war: victimisation, state crime and prevention

Appreciating how war had been understood in sociological terms was therefore a core feature of the agenda Jamieson (1998) outlined. Several years later, Vincenzo Ruggiero (2005: 240) offered some further developments on how a 'sociological-criminological analysis of war' could be similarly envisaged. Ruggiero (2005) framed the attention of criminological concerns with war to concentrate on approaches that were distinctly non-bellicose, non-militarist and pacifistic. He reinforced the agenda Jamieson (1998) had outlined espousing that '[a] criminology of war, therefore, will focus on mass, devastating victimisation, violations of human rights and other forms of state crime', and pointed to the importance of recognising the difference between 'crime in war' (that is, interpersonal crimes; see Bonger, 1916, 1936) and 'war crimes' (that is, state crimes; see Mannheim, 1941; Glueck, 1944, 1946) (Ruggiero, 2005: 247). The former of these crimes were to be considered critically using concepts such as 'social disorganisation' (noted previously) to understand how crime can become a recurrent domestic feature during times of war, whereby 'legitimised' institutionalised violence or state violence decreed 'legal' by the law (that is, police and military) become difficult to 'see' (Ruggiero, 2005: 246). The latter problem of 'war crimes' (discussed earlier) were said to be perpetrated by nation-states using modes of 'denial' (Cohen, 2001) and 'techniques of neutralisation' (Sykes and Matza, 1957) to mask and evade responsibility for causing violence, abuse and violating human rights, international law and international humanitarian law (Ruggiero, 2005). However, borrowing from Weber, for Ruggiero (2005) such practices were only required when war is conducted outwith the 'legality' of state violence. When enacted (or framed) within the 'laws of war', not only is war violence able to be presented as a 'legitimate' function of the state (as intimated by Scruton, 1988, earlier), but it can also come to shape national identities (discussed in Chapter Six), inform notions of citizenship and belonging, and be imbued with righteousness and morality.

With attention firmly fixed on conceptualising war as a non-bellicose sociological criminological concern, for Ruggiero (2005: 248) a 'criminology of war' (understood in Jamieson's, 1998, terms) provided 'the background for a logical extension of its own arguments, namely for a definitive criminalization of war itself'. In presenting a 'thematic manifesto for a pacifist criminology', criminology should be considered as capable of pursuing a 'ceasefire' to warfare (Ruggiero, 2005: 249). Notwithstanding the earlier caution drawn to misinterpreting Durkheim's outlook on the 'functional' nature of war, Ruggiero (2005, 2006) suggests criminological studies of war should first and foremost be antithetical to any notions of shared memory and solidarity that collectivise national sentiment to war and its sacrifices (that is, militarism). Describing solidarity in relation to war memorialisation as 'cancer', this is to be tackled through the application of further theoretical and practical approaches (discussed in Chapter Six). For example, 'moral entrepreneurs', whose job it is to label 'deviant' behaviour, should instead be understood as those who commit deviant activities in the preparedness and perpetration of war (that is, militarism). The ousting and labelling of warmongering activities should be undertaken as a routine part of 'civilising' processes (Elias, 1994); and victimology is invoked as the corrective to conflict theory to more effectively identify the victimisation and harm experienced by civilians (and other less visible groups) (discussed in Chapter Seven) (Ruggiero, 2005). As a means of preventing warfare from occurring, criminological research is further encouraged to take note of its inherent peace-making interests by reinterpreting approaches to abolitionism, restorative justice and reparation (as more recently accomplished by Braithwaite and Wardak, 2013; Braithwaite and Rashed 2014; and Marsavelski et al, 2017, for example) (Ruggiero, 2005). The overall purpose of all of this is to approach geopolitical conflict resolution with peaceful alternatives to war, reject political and legal notions of 'just war' in the same ways as 'just deserts' is received as socially harmful, emphasise the need for strong social bonds to be fostered to decrease interpersonal violence domestically, and for the reallocation and redistribution of wealth and resources globally to aid crime prevention, help mitigate civil wars, and reduce the global inequalities which exacerbate war, conflict and genocide (Ruggiero, 2005).

Having now explicated some of the core early literature relating to the study of war from within sociology and criminology, it is now worth drawing together how each can serve to inform a broader conceptual and theoretical framework to facilitate a critical and interdisciplinary study of war.

Learning from the sociological and criminological literature on war

From our earlier discussion of sociological literature, we learn that 'war' can be understood in terms of its relationship to power and economic relations, both between nation-states and for its influences within sovereign borders. What we understand is that states can and do hold a 'monopoly of force' with which to enact geopolitical violence and coercive social control with 'legality', 'legitimacy' and impunity. This is made operational through the development of military institutions and the amassing of fortified military technologies, or is indeed facilitated using the imprint of militarised principles and routinised practices. Ways in which the coercive power of state violence becomes identifiable (beyond the enactment of war violence itself) is via activities and practices associated with 'militarism', that is 'an attitude and a set of institutions which regard war and the preparation for war as a normal and desirable social activity' (Mann, 1984: 25). However, as Shaw (1991) notes, war preparedness does not simply cultivate 'militarism'. This can become established and enduring throughout the experience of war violence and within its aftermath. In doing so, the ideological or symbolic imposition of military values onto, or within our social, cultural and political lives may become entrenched within economic and civic life, and the realities of the consequences of war become figuratively reinvented with different cultural capital within the public imaginary (Shaw, 1991). Thus acts of war are produced by, and have influence on, social structure, social and political change, and can hold cultural meaning for individuals, social, and political groups during war, and in the transitional periods of its aftermath. We can also appreciate what the notion of 'war' entails and how its circumstances and consequences, understood in sociological terms, are not fixed but need to be grasped within historical and contemporary contexts across time, place and space. Finally, and quite crucially, we learn from these initial discussions that few connections are made within the sociological literature between the issues of war and crime. Durkheim is perhaps the most explicit in doing this. However, as Eulriet (2010), and Caldwell and Mestrovic (2011) note, bald connections must not be assumed between the parallel natures of these two social phenomenon. As we will come to learn throughout the pages of this book, each operate within contextually different conditions and circumstances, and both are subject to quite different social, juridical and moral practices (Eulriet, 2010). As for the issue of victimisation, this appears to be even further abstracted from the literature than the issue of crime.

From the criminological contributions in the literature outlined above, we can identify some further thematic features of conceptualising war that bring issues of crime and victimisation into view. First, drawing from Shaw's (1988b: 616) disagreement with Scruton's (1988) 'juridical concept of the state', we are encouraged to conceptualise the perpetration of warfare within the socio-legal context in which it is considered deviant and criminal (that is, the laws of war). War as a 'criminal' act is indeed of relevant criminological concern, and for Hagan (2015) this is the context in which the discipline had been 'caught sleeping' in its analysis of war. Second, what is less explicit within the early sociological literature, but (as we will come to learn in subsequent chapters) a more prominent feature of later sociological work and criminological literature, is a focus on war as a violent cause of victimisation and social harm, particularly to civilians. This is another long-standing criminological interest from scholars such Schwendinger and Schwendinger (1970) and Cohen (1993, 2001), that has been afforded some attention in relation to human rights abuses and denials of state victimisation, although perhaps less prolific than one might expect. What we also learn as being of relevance to criminological studies of war are themes relating to the consequences – rather than facilitation – of warfare, namely militarism, social disorganisation and a tradition of pacifism. On this latter point, what is also evident, but again less abundant within the literature, is a focus on the resolution of war and conflict via peace-making.

Whither a 'criminology of war': mainstream interests and state rationality

Returning to where this chapter began, Eulriet (2010: 62) urged us to question *why* disciplinary interests (such as sociology) have 'not contributed more to the understanding' of war. This is a question also applicable to criminology. Moreover, it is from the seminal work of Jamieson (1998) we begin to glean an understanding why the subject matter of war has been less prolifically studied within criminology than one might expect. Jamieson (1998) suggests that 'disciplinary criminology' (that is, mainstream criminology) had obscured complex agendas relating to war through more than paradigmatic preference. Different from the identity politics said to have caused war to be deprioritised within sociology, criminological scholarship did so by seeking to account for the impacts of war on domestic crime rates, migration and displacement, and in seeking to highlight how the recruitment of young men into the military would either increase or decrease crime (Jamieson, 1998). Such a focus on domestic matters of crime and social disorder order, occurring as a result of war and thereafter, successfully obscured a wider assortment of critical issues from criminological scrutiny (discussed in Chapter Six), including: the creation of new offences and expansion of technologies of violence under the auspices of 'emergencies' and 'securitization' (see also Pollard, 1941); the cultural salience of militarised masculinities and hyper-sexuality; and increased levels of gendered, racialised and ethnicised violence directed towards vulnerable social groups during times of war and thereafter (Jamieson, 1998). For Jamieson (1998), the conservative nature of mainstream criminological literature was incapable of conceptualising such problems, of dealing with the emotional consequences of war violence, or occurrences of moral and immoral acts during times of war and peace.

In brief, war had been kept from most agendas due to mainstream criminology being fixated on matters of domestic crime, disorder and punishment during times of war and thereafter. Different from both Jamieson (1998) and later Hagan (2015), for Ruggiero (2005), war had become a marginal interest within the criminological canon due to warfare being an inherent feature of state rationality and interests. Moreover, it was synonymous with law and order, the very field that mainstream criminologists have a vested interest to protect for themselves (Ruggiero, 2005). Of course, underpinning each of these considerations – explicitly or implicitly – is that acts of war both 'old' and 'new' are fundamentally, first and foremost, acts of violent victimisation.

Conclusion: is a 'criminology of war' possible?

In this chapter, while we have been necessarily selective with the sources we have used and the sociological reasoning we have outlined, it is crucial to recognise that the study of war as a social phenomenon is a subject matter required to be understood as derived from the contested ways in which it has been embraced or displaced as part of the intellectual canon of sociology. Viewed in this way, the study of war is not a neglected facet of sociology or criminology; instead its visibility within each discipline is wedded to particular identity politics and disciplinary interests. Each of the first two sections of this chapter have illustrated a concern with addressing war in both its conceptual and material forms that differ in their approaches and scope but are nonetheless complementary in informing a study of war, war violence and its victimisation as a critical, non-bellicose, sociological endeavour.

Having documented the sociological and criminological study of war in relation to *some* of its historical and theoretical origins we are therefore able to better identify conceptual ideas to draw on for the purposes of unpacking what a 'criminology of war' might entail, as detailed in the third section of this chapter. Doing so also permits us to consider further gaps or omissions we may not have contemplated, and for which we can seek answers to within other scholarship. For example, in addition to not being a complete reading of historical or contemporary sociology, the sources that we have used in this chapter also have some significant omissions. Most notably, despite its comprehensiveness the work of Malešević (2010a) failed to address the phenomena of genocide or ethnic cleansing as part of a detailed analysis of war (discussed in Chapter Four); so too it misses out discussions of terrorism and security (discussed in Chapter Three) that would have carried some weighty contemporary salience, particularly for criminology (see Riga, 2011). However, unlike the contributions from classical (that is, Marx, Durkheim and Weber) or historical sociology (Giddens, 1985; Mann, 1988) Malešević (2010a: 307) did encourage war to be understood for its gendered dimensions, in particular for the recognition of masculinity as being prioritised (and separated from femininity) to make warfare 'possible and socially meaningful'. Despite making this argument however, and in overlooking genocide, the prevalence of sexual violence as a weapon of war is a notable further omission (discussed in Chapter Seven).

Other notable exceptions have of course used the nomenclature of a 'criminology of war' previously (see inter alia Young, J., 1999, 2003, 2007, 2011; Ruggiero, 2006). However, Jamieson's (1998) work, and other historical literature as presented throughout this chapter, has seldom been afforded a detailed unpacking and closer reading. For example, in addition to the insights offered above, similar to classical sociological commentary regarding war, Jamieson (1998) drew importance to recognising wars as occurring within specific historical periods, taking place during longer-standing periods of international political violence, and changing over time and with technology (evident in Chapters Five and Six). She also advocated for critical and philosophical recognition that a function of government, when perpetrating war, was the facilitation of immorality against other humans; and a legal and conceptual understanding of war as being a politicised activity within state institution when experienced by or against the public (discussed in Chapter Six; see also Jamieson, 1998). Unlike classical sociological literature related to war, however, Jamieson (1998) further encouraged war to be considered seriously for its gendered dimensions through prioritising militarised forms of masculinity, and causing emotional and traumatic consequences serving to reproduce normative assumptions and constructions of gender (that is, femininity/vulnerability and masculinity/heroism; discussed in Chapter Seven). Absent from all of these accounts however appears to be matters of globalism, colonialism and imperialism (discussed in our concluding Chapter Eight).

As such, we come to understand that although studied marginally, both sociological and criminological scholarship has not been disengaged from the topic of war. From the overview provided here we assert that if a 'criminology of war' is indeed possible, then (within the confines of this book at least) it is usefully informed by sociological ideas and traditions related to the consequences, rather causes, of war (Wimmer, 2014). As such, we can regard the study of war as an interdisciplinary pursuit that is inherently non-bellicose in its traditions, interests, nature and intentions. The remaining chapters of this book offer some directions in which the subject of war might now continue to be pursued from this critical vantage point. In the next chapter we begin by orienting the contemporary study of war within criminology during the 'war on terrorism'.

THREE

The War on Terrorism: Criminology's 'Third War'

Introduction

In a 2003 special issue of *Theoretical Criminology*, Ruth Jamieson assembled a collection of essays which variously addressed war and human rights. Their purpose was to highlight, as Kaldor (2014) also suggests, 'new' wars are often 'internal civil conflicts' that emphasise the 'local expression of global processes, politics and sentiments' (Jamieson, 2003: 259). Jamieson concluded these essays had 'necessarily produced omissions', which most obviously included

> the subject matter of The Hague and Arusha Tribunals (grave breaches of the Geneva Conventions, crimes against humanity, sexual violence and armed conflict, genocide, violations of the laws and customs of war) or with *the post-9/11 renewal of interest in (global) terrorism, just war theory, the arms trade or the need to rethink the issue of policing, 'securitization' and the convergence of internal and external security.* (Jamieson, 2003: 262, emphasis added)

While we go on to deal with many of these issues in later chapters, in this chapter we wish to draw attention to the 'omissions' noted above, which we instead interpret as key focal points for the contemporary criminological study of war. The chapter begins by suggesting that in the aftermath of 9/11 the 'war on terrorism' became the main interest of criminological studies related to war. Here this is understood as conceptualising war in metaphorical terms reflecting two emergent agendas. First, we outline a 'crime/security nexus' illustrated by studies taking counterterrorism and matters of 'security' as their main concern post-9/11 in order to address the (internal/domestic) consequences of the 'war on terror'. Second, we outline examples from the literature addressing the (external/global) consequences of the 'war on terrorism' as a 'war/crime nexus' (Jamieson, 1998); identified at macro, meso and micro levels of analysis. In presenting these two prongs of the literature, we argue that the post-9/11 era can be understood as a period of increased activity within criminology that overwhelmingly interwove a 'renewal of interest' (Jamieson, 2003: 262) between matters of war, crime and security, under the auspices of the 'war on terrorism'. We conclude, this agenda provides the foundation for the critique of, and departure from, criminological engagement with war found in the remainder of this book: that is, following 9/11 the contemporary meaning of a 'criminology of war' became tantamount to the 'war on terrorism'.

11 September 2001: criminology's 'third war'

When placed alongside mainstream criminological concerns (that of crime, disorder and social control), the discipline of criminology is said to have been historically engaged in three 'wars', namely: crime, drugs and terrorism (LaFree, 2009). Although establishing 'criminology's three wars' as distinct social problems, LaFree (2009) argues their main point of difference is that the 'war on terrorism' has been afforded less attention within (mainstream) criminology than the 'wars' declared on other dangerous nouns. While this may well have been true prior to 9/11, it is certainly no longer the case. As LaFree and Freilich (2016: 11, our emphasis) recently commented, the 'criminology of terrorism' is now a more established field within the discipline in which 'criminologists have made substantial strides towards developing a *science-based* approach to understanding terrorism and its consequences'. Such 'scientific' approaches in criminology's 'third war' (LaFree, 2009) has seemingly prioritised theories of social control and rational choice, among other mainstream perspectives, that have helped proliferate counterterrorism strategies as normative modalities of (criminal) 'justice' (in accordance with Freilich and LaFree, 2014, and LaFree and Dugan, 2015, for example). However, when presented as criminology's 'third war', the 'fight' against terrorism fosters (at least) two glaring problems for a 'criminology of war'. First, while the criminological study of terrorism has advanced apace post-9/11 to focus on the advancement (and critique) of domestic counterterrorism strategies and internal matters of security, blatant acts of warfare, conflict and genocide have consistently emerged and been perpetrated as a grim backdrop to its ascension. Second, at the same time, although having less coverage within criminological scholarship, interest in the topic of war experienced a resurgence in the wake of 9/11. Albeit in the peripheral vision of 'criminology's third war', this attention was directed to more external concerns of the 'war on terrorism', specifically the 2003 Iraq war. We suggest it is at this point the contemporary (read post-9/11) agenda for a 'criminology of war' emerged as a 'new horizon' for the discipline. To unpack this further however, it is useful to first grasp the notion of war in its figurative, rather than literal, form. As we will see, this allows us to connect both the internal and external concerns of 'criminology's third war'.

The 'metaphor of war'

Jamieson (1998) and Ruggiero (2005) noted the meaning of war within criminology had often been taken as synonymous with symbolic and coercive forms of social control. As Jamieson (1998) pointed out, war, law and social order have overlapping structural similarities: representations of war are assimilated into the practices of punishment, and notions of 'justice' and righteousness are frequently used to inform the conduct and perpetration of warfare. Expressed in these ways, the study of war has frequently been conceptualised within criminology in figurative terms. This ubiquitous use of the term 'war' within the discipline has similarly been described by Steinert (2003) as a metaphorical device.

For Steinert (2003), the 20th and 21st centuries witnessed a gradual conflation of three state monopolies of force (Weber, 1919): policing, punishment, war. Understood ideologically, policing as a form of peacekeeping, disarmament and 'pacification' – enacted via the proportional use of force – was assimilated with punishment; namely physical and structural violence aimed at containing crime and cultivating social order, achieved via practices of social exclusion (that is, of/against crime and 'criminals') (Steinert, 2003). So too 'policing' seems to have been reinterpreted from the consensual management of internal conflict (that is, crime and social disorder) aimed at protecting domestic citizens, to the management of social conflict as a form of confrontation. In so doing this requires an assumed universal set of shared morals and values (that is, for 'us', the non-criminals) to be defended against crime and 'criminals' as a common 'enemy' (that is, 'them') (Steinert, 2003). Thus, Steinert (2003) suggests the principles of peacekeeping became superseded by punishment and 'justice', pursued via (external) Clausewitzean models of war (discussed in the Introduction). Through this blurring of state monopolies of force, criminal justice (used to regulate police activity) was transformed as an obstacle to be overcome, in order to wage 'war' domestically in these punitive terms, and punishment – as a form of social exclusion (see Young, J., 1999) – became normalised as a key objective of 'justice', realised via discourses of war (Steinert, 2003). When placed alongside mainstream criminological concerns (that of crime, disorder and social control), Steinert's (2003) notion of a 'metaphor of war' can therefore been understood as a principal feature of 'criminology's three wars' (LaFree, 2009). In particular, the metaphorical use of the term 'war' became more pronounced within criminal justice discourse in the aftermath of 9/11.

Therefore, the 'metaphor of war' has an enduring articulation within criminology that typifies the 'renewal of interest' in war noted by Jamieson (2003: 262) during the post-9/11 era. In the following sections, we suggest this renewal of interest can be identified via two primary areas of concern: first in relation to a 'crime/security nexus' connected to counterterrorism and security, and second regarding a 'war/crime nexus' vis-à-vis the 2003 war in Iraq. To address the two prongs of our argument we first turn attention to (internal) matters of counterterrorism and (in)security, to offer a *critical* account of the issues associated with LaFree's (2009) version of 'criminology's third war'.

Crime/security nexus

As detailed by Aas (2013) in *Globalization & Crime*, during the post-9/11 era a number of frontiers converged for criminology, including the appending of securitisation as a new rationale to tackle the domestic problem of crime, alongside the local (internal) and global (external) risk from terrorism. While it is important to note the contested nature of the term 'terrorism' our concern here is its uncontested embrace and linkage with war within criminology. Moreover for the discipline, of additional importance was the emergent use of 'war' in metaphorical terms; deployed as part of the same lexicon for tackling crimes which seemingly transgressed the fluidity of geopolitical borders, including 'crime', drugs, trafficking and 'terrorism' (Aas, 2013). Aas goes on to assert

> The terminology of war can be a dangerous metaphor in several ways, justifying extreme means in order to defend the perceived enemies of the state and therefore endangering traditional civil rights and liberties. The discussion that ensued in the aftermath of 9/11, on whether these attacks were acts of war or whether they were criminal acts, mirrors this dilemma. (Aas, 2013: 25)

As noted above, the restructuring of state monopolies of violence (that is, policing and war), to entrench war as a metaphorical device for the purposes of punishment and 'justice' rather than peacemaking, can be mobilised by various social and political practices (Steinert, 2003). This included the invocation of a crisis against an 'enemy' (that is, crime or terrorism), and the establishment of populist positions/interventions, upheld by emotional appeals to/from the public (Steinert, 2003). In addition, this resort to 'universal' (masculine) values and appeal to patriarchal notions of solidarity and 'community', results in the requirement that all must participate in confronting a 'common enemy' (Steinert, 2003). Through the mobilisation of these practices, war metaphors are continually deployed at 'low-intensity' through the 'ingredients' of populist, political and social structures (Steinert, 2003). Importantly, as Steinert (2003: 282) observes, 'today terrorism is the most popular figure of thought that helps to extend principles of warfare to what should properly be the area of peacekeeping'. We find these 'ingredients' within criminological literature concerned with counterterrorism.

(In)security, risk and the 'new' suspect communities

It is important to acknowledge that while the 9/11 moment might have been extraordinary, it was not historically unique. Finnane (2013) usefully documents the international and long-reaching dimensions to terrorism from the taking of hostages at the 1972 Munich Olympics, to the activities of ETA in Spain, and the Baader-Meinhof group in Germany. The US has within its own history a similar catalogue of events. In each of these countries, both legal and extra-legal mechanisms for responding to threats of this kind were well established (Walklate and Mythen, 2014). Indeed, by 2001 the UK had become well accustomed to dealing with a wide range of 'security' incidents consequent to what was euphemistically referred to as the 'Irish Troubles' (1969–98): a civil conflict concerning British occupation of Northern Ireland and a fight for independence by the Republican south (see Dawson et al, 2016). The history of this securitisation is well documented in Hillyard's (1993) *Suspect Community: People's Experience of the Prevention of Terrorism Acts in Britain*. For Hillyard, security legislation (namely iterations of the Prevention of Terrorism Act 1974) produced by the UK government throughout the 1970–80s to tackle terrorism from Irish fundamentalism (that is, the Irish Republican Army) produced far-reaching consequences for the Irish diaspora. In what Hillyard (1993: 262) describes as the 'terror of prevention', the Prevention of

Terrorism Acts created a duplicity of powers directly targeted at Irish people (both Catholic and Protestant), making it easier to facilitate their arrest, detention and ability to be searched without evidence. In other words they were placed under constant surveillance and excluded from travelling at border crossing points into the UK. All of which came at the expense of significant restrictions to the human rights and civil liberties of Irish people, including their freedom of speech (Hillyard, 1993). The farther-reaching consequences of this legislation became their capacity to influence structural change within the criminal justice system in the UK. This included creating a 'dual system' of justice whereby those accused under counterterrorism legislation were treated in exception to the standards of due process resulting in the normalisation of arbitrary legislation and its assimilation into the wider assemblage of criminal justice. This, as Hillyard (1993) suggests, undermined democracy through using the law as a state monopoly of force, rather than to help arbitrate violent state (and non-state) activity. The result of these entrenched 'ingredients' (Steinert, 2003) of repressive counterterrorism legislation was the targeting of Irish people as a population singled out through legal and political mechanisms, not because of any known crimes committed by them but on the basis of their assumed membership (racial, linguistic, gender, religious and so on) of what Hillyard (1993) termed a 'suspect community'.

Why 9/11 took on the status that it did need not concern us in detail here. But suffice it to say, as Howie (2012) has argued, these events became emblematic of the global uncertainties of the 21st century and resulted in consequences and responses both exceptional and mundane. In the UK the contemporary post-9/11 processes of 'suspectification' reflected the historical legacy associated with the Irish Troubles (Hickman et al, 2011) documented above. Indeed, drawing on Hillyard's (1993) analysis, in a special issue of *The British Journal of Criminology* dedicated to the 'war on terrorism' (see Hudson and Walters, 2009) Pantazis and Pemberton (2009) have argued following the introduction of the Terrorism Act 2000 (which expanded the definition of terrorism to include international threats), subsequent UK counterterrorism legislation emerging post-9/11 served to construct Muslim 'communities' (rather than individuals), and those mistaken to be Muslim due to the racialisation of their identities, as a new 'suspect community' (for a critical review of the use of this term in this context, and the body of work from which it derives and pertains, see the exchanges between Greer, 2010, and Pantazis and Pemberton, 2011). Pantazis and Pemberton (2009: 654) make clear, central to multiple counterterrorism legislations developing from the foundations of the

Terrorism Act 2000 has been the further perpetuation of the 'terror of prevention' through arbitrary policing practices operating on 'a continuum with stop and search at one end and shoot to kill practices at the other' (see, for example, McCulloch and Sentas, 2006; Kennison and Loumansky, 2007). Therefore, identifying those individuals, groups and states considered risky and a threat to security is an issue necessarily framed by the political rhetoric of the times. However, the targeting of those considered 'suspect' post-9/11 developed apace elsewhere too (see Maira, 2009, on the US, and Camilleri, 2012, on France). In each of these contexts, the domestic targets 'othered' (mostly individuals) were not too dissimilar from the states 'othered' (to whom the individuals were *assumed* to belong). At the level of the individual, those suspected were primarily young, Asian (a label usually applied in an undifferentiated manner) males, in countries from the US to Denmark, Germany, France and the UK (see Walklate and Mythen, 2014). At the same time, as these kinds of targeted policy responses were being put in place, criminology was not slow to offer understandings and explanations for the kinds of terrorist behaviour with which many societies became increasingly familiar.

From the individual to subculture

Criminological interventions into these developments reflect, for the most part, the mainstream domain assumptions of the discipline alluded to in Chapter Two. It is possible to identify four main approaches here: (i) the 'lone wolf', (ii) strain theory, (iii) subcultural, and (iv) structural approaches. 'Lone wolf' terrorism has featured frequently in newspaper headlines throughout the 21st century, and as the label implies this approach tries to make sense of violent extremism by reference to the innate characteristics of the individuals concerned. Hamm and Spaaij (2017) endeavour to offer an explanatory framework within this vein. This work, thoughtful as it is, erases both individual connections with organised groups (many of those identified as lone terrorists have been found subsequently to have links with organised terrorist groups) and of course, erases any connections between their activities and 'war'. A second approach within criminology related to these developments is found in the work of Agnew (2010) under the rubric of strain theory. Agnew (2010: 136) argues that 'collective strains' have a high impact on individuals when they are seen to be unjust, and when they are seen to be the result of powerful others 'with whom the members of the strained collective have weak ties'. Hence those individuals with a psychological propensity for violent extremism will be particularly vulnerable to engaging in it under these conditions. Indeed, the vignettes of each of those involved in the January 2015 Paris attacks illustrate the presence of such 'strains' (Walklate and Mythen, 2016). However, why some people react with violence under these conditions and others do not is a question which remains unanswered (Dalgaard-Nielsen, 2010). This question has led some to consider the relevance of a variation of strain theory referred to as the 'culture of violence thesis' (Mullins and Young, 2012). In this vein, Cottee (2011) has considered the importance of both 'sub-cultural style' and structure in understanding the commitment to Jihadism with the emphasis on 'style' having been taken to the next level by Picart (2017). Yet it is important to remember that subcultural processes do not exist in a vacuum. They are always formed within a structural context. For those criminologists focusing attention on structure, social exclusion and disenfranchisement can lead to extreme and violent subcultures. Yet again, even here the explanatory equation is neither simple nor straightforward. For example, Kreuger and Maleckova (2003) reported that the vast majority of materially and geographically dispossessed Palestinians do not engage in political violence, and the impoverished and persecuted Rohingya Muslims of Myanmar (discussed in Chapter Four) fled en masse under persecution, rather than responding with force. Moreover, there are numerous examples of individuals from non-deprived backgrounds engaging in violent extremism (see Post, 2007) including Anders Behring Brehvik and the so-called 'Hamburg cell' who executed the 9/11 attacks.

From this brief overview, it is possible to see that the criminological explanations associated with terrorism/violent extremism unsurprisingly mirror the kinds of criminological explanations found on crime more generally. Yet, given the context in which this work emerged it is surprising that each perspective shares a common muting on the role of religious belief in provoking this particular kind of violent extremism/ terrorism (see Cottee, 2014). They also erase the biographical experiences of perpetrators of violent extremism and given the prominence of life-course approaches within criminology this absence is telling. Each of these perspectives, along with many perspectives claiming to make sense of 'security', also downplays the salience of gender (discussed in Chapter Seven) (see Walklate et al, 2019). Taken together these perspectives are also mute on the role of the state and state (in)action in having a contributory role in the development of terrorism. Expectedly then, these assessments situate thinking about and responding to 'security' squarely within the domain of 'crime'. They are all also silent on the question of 'war' and its inter-connections with the processes of suspectification (as outlined above), and the potential for violent extremism as a response to such processes. In addition, this work is silent on the question of victimisation and the impact of victimisation on those rendered 'suspect' along with the impact and extension of the 'terror of prevention' (Hillyard, 1993) by the state on all its citizens; all put in place in the interests of security. It is here that the third theme of crime/security nexus can be found.

Pre-emption and prevention

The 2015 attacks in Paris, Verviers, Copenhagen, Tunis and London, among others, have added fuel to Western concerns about terrorist attacks. These concerns have been heightened by the potential for such attacks by individuals who have had experience of using military equipment when fighting with Islamist militant groups in war zones in Syria, Iraq, Afghanistan and Yemen. Beck (2009) has referred to these conflicts as 'risk wars', especially given that under the conditions of global mobility and permeable borders, security is pivotal (Aas, 2013). However, one key development in the practices of security post-9/11 has been the ever-increasing presence of *pre-emptive* policies (see Ashworth and Zedner, 2014; McCulloch and Wilson, 2016), driven by the worst-case scenario of the 'unknown terrorist' (Amoore, 2014). Put simply, prevention focuses attention on known risk factors; pre-emption shifts attention towards the unknown and is driven by concerns about what might happen. However, in all of this a fundamental question is overlooked: under these post-9/11 conditions, whose security counts?

Security is a ~~promi~~scuous notion (Zedner, 2000, 2009) and as a concept has undoubtedly been stretched (Walklate and Mythen, 2016). Criminologists have tended to treat security as part of a zero-sum game, as something that somebody has at someone else's expense (Hudson and Ugelvik, 2012). This vision of security as a tug-of-war affords a number of potentially different possible relationships between liberty and security. For example, liberty and security could be inversely related (more of one produces less of the other); security can be a prerequisite for liberty (to be secure liberties have to be sacrificed); only through liberty is it possible to attain security; and finally, security could exist in a precarious relationship with liberty (Crawford, 2014; Walklate and Mythen, 2016). When taken together, these possibilities convey the view that security is both immeasurable and precarious. Apart from feminist work which has a long tradition of exploring this concern (from Brownmiller, 1975, to Cockburn, 2013, discussed in Chapter

Seven), and work concerning itself with the consequences of security practices for the lived realities of Asian minority ethnic groups in the UK (see, among others, Mythen et al, 2009, 2013), these visions rarely examine what security is like as a lived experience. At the same time the terrorist risk and its unknowability has moved governments increasingly towards refined security 'ingredients' (Steinert, 2003) designed to protect 'us' from the threat posed by 'them', using the logic of anticipatory risk and metaphorical discourses of war. This logic is driven by pre-emption (that is, what is unknown) and thus constitutes much more than conventional criminological notions of prevention (that is, what are known risk factors).

Understood as different from prevention, pre-emptive risk logic deems early action as justified to protect the majority on a *just in case* basis (Hudson and Ugelvik, 2012). It reflects an institutional and political preference for early intervention – even if this means a reduction in the civil liberties of a minority – since the larger threat posed to public safety is deemed unthinkable (Maras, 2013). This drive to 'think security' (de Lint and Virta, 2004) has underpinned a wide range of legislative and regulatory frameworks across the globe (such as those noted earlier). Nonetheless, they have the potential to affect everyone everywhere, from what it is possible to take on board an aeroplane, to how the business of banking is conducted, to the routine need for documentary identification evidence for relatively mundane tasks: all of which become more focused for an individual belonging to a 'suspect community' (Hillyard, 1993). Walklate and Mythen (2016) have pointed to the iatrogenic effects of these processes which continue to be facilitated by both the unfettered and ongoing powers of the state generated under conditions of 'exception' (Agamben, 2005), and the failure of academic (including criminological) agendas to think differently about the interconnections between these 'crimes' and 'war'. Both of these processes are hidden in plain sight.

From 'security' to war

During the same time at which the rise of securitisation served to obscure war as the context in which these practices were being justified, the conflation of crime, security and war facilitated by the 21st century preoccupation with terrorism has, for some commentators, enabled the furtherance of combativeness and punitiveness within public and political, domestic and international discourses regarding both criminal justice (for example, McCulloch and Wilson, 2016; Lea, 2015, 2016) and social justice (for example, Evans, 2017). We do not have the space to unpack these attendant matters of 'militarisation' in further detail. Suffice it to say however, as Degenhardt (2010) points out, during the wars in Afghanistan and Iraq, the blurring of distinctions within discourses of war between criminal justice and military activities was nothing new. It had been previously evident in US containment policies throughout the 'war on drugs' that witnessed US military forces engaging in policing roles internationally (particularly in South America), and conversely aided the militarised transformation of police forces domestically (McCulloch, 2004; Kraska, 2007).

What the discussion above makes clear however is that the post-9/11 era brought the local and global contexts of crime into view as interrelated concerns for criminologists, whereby 'the security landscape does not resemble a neatly organised world where the division between internal and external, military and police, and war and crime is clear; all these categories are blurred at best and non-existent at worst' (Loader and Percy, 2012: 216).

What also becomes clear is that the 'metaphor of war' usefully identifies a significant irony within the 'war on terrorism'. As Steinert (2003; 284) points out, not only do metaphorical appeals to 'old war' not match the realities of 'new wars', neither do 'new' forms of warfare – roused by the 'metaphor of war' – produce the desired outcome of 'security at home'. This is particularly the case for those who experience the violence of war directly. It is at this juncture we now point towards the second prong of 'criminology's third war' whereby the 'war on terrorism' comes into view through the 'war/crime nexus' (Jamieson, 1998) and the 2003 Iraq war.

War/crime nexus

As Jamieson (1998) points out, and as our above discussion indicates, significant moments of social transformation or crisis (such as the aftermath of a terrorist attack) have a direct relationship with punishment, and the regulation of social disorganisation whether this is real or imagined (for a historical view see Pollard, 1941). Shortly after the events of 9/11 occurred, different commentary soon emerged articulating the significance of the attacks in terms of 'crime' and the complexity of their interrelatedness to the occurrence of 'war' rather than 'security' (see for example Scraton, 2002). An early example from Hayward and Morrison (2002) considered the geographical space of 'ground zero' (the name given to the physical location where the Twin Towers of the World Trade Center were attacked and collapsed) which quickly transcended space and place, situating the events within and beyond both domestic and geopolitical domains. Indeed, for Hayward and Morrison (2002: 145), 'the effects of the attack were both local and global', and made possible by US authorities and popular media promoting official responses to the events – and those they considered culpable – in a fragmented discourse which used the terms 'crime' (local) and 'war' (global) interchangeably. In doing so, this discourse located and articulated 9/11 in a political and cultural dialogue which intertwined the terms 'war' and 'crime', and overlaid their meaning to become symbolic of the same issue: 'terrorism' (Hayward and Morrison, 2002). Interestingly this discourse also deployed criminological, historical, and religious articulations of these crimes and the response to them in terms of 'good' and 'evil'.

Hayward and Morrison (2002: 150) suggested this conflation of terms was a veiled exercise by the US security services to 'reassure' the North American public that the US administration understood the events of 9/11 (ontologically), and could be trusted to 'mobilise resources' to retaliate against the perpetrators and prevent such violence from occurring again. As Morrison (2006) later described in *Criminology, Civilisation and the New World Order*, these activities and what followed them were fundamental to revealing the existence – rather than *creation* – of global imbalances of power and domination by Western democratic nations. In the aftermath of 9/11, '[c]reating an image of a coherent 'we' was a staple of the communications media in the US and Britain, to name but a few arenas, around which images of victim-hood, potential threats, discourse of crime and war revolved, and invocations of powerful sovereign power resonated' (Morrison, 2006: 33).

Indeed, as Steinert (2003) observes, for 9/11 to be perceived as an act of war, it had to be conceptually and legally situated in exception of other domestic criminal acts (see McGarry, 2016). Instead, 9/11 was reconfigured as a conflict perpetrated by an external 'enemy', which presupposed 'war' – namely the 'war on terrorism' – in more literal Clausewitzean terms. The visualisation of these events in news media, and the narratives which formed around the responses to them, Hayward and Morrison (2002) suggest, divided those watching them in its aftermath into 'included' communities who felt threatened by the events they were witnessing, and 'excluded' communities who saw the attacks and collapse of the World Trade Center as symbolic of their own exclusion (see also Young, J., 2003, 2007). Such exclusion rendered them 'suspect' (Hillyard, 1993). Almost two decades since 9/11, the consequences of this schism have been bleakly practised and evidenced under the axiom of the 'war on terrorism'. Although now well rehearsed, these practices (as discussed above) broadly comprise the targeted expansion of both domestic and international counterterrorism policies and strategies towards local citizens with 'foreign' identities and/or (assumingly) belonging to Muslim communities, along with the instigation of retaliatory, 'liberating', and counter-insurgency wars towards Islamic majority nations by US, UK and coalition military forces.

As discussed above, the former of these two issues emphasise how matters of counterterrorism and security took centre stage within the post-9/11 context of the discipline vis-à-vis 'criminology's third war' – that is, the 'war on terrorism' (LaFree, 2009). The latter of these two issues illustrate the primary ways in which critical criminological interest in 'war' was 'renewed' in the aftermath of 9/11. Although not wanting to oversimplify these matters nor suggest that they do not overlap (they each can and do), we propose this interest can be discerned at several levels of analysis broadly resembling the layered approach of Kramer and Michalowski's (2006) model of 'state-corporate crime': war as a crime of the powerful (macro/structural level), war as 'justice' and punishment (meso/organisational level), and war as civilian victimisation (micro/interactional level). We briefly outline each of these in turn below.

War as a 'crime of the powerful'

Examining the enactment, perpetration and consequences of the wars waged in the aftermath of 9/11, Morrison (2006: 33) sought to question 'which territory, institutions or justice was invoked?' by such imperial violence. Following 9/11, the offending territories invoked as 'deviant' and 'criminal' were principally Afghanistan and Iraq, invaded by US, UK and coalition military forces during 2001 and 2002/03 respectively. For more than a decade, these two arenas became the sites of what Kaldor (2014: 180) termed 'technologically-intensive old war', wherein new technologies such as drones, 'precision weapons' and unpiloted aerial vehicles were used to focus on 'old war' objectives, such as defeating enemy entities militarily (that is, Al Qaeda). As Kaldor (2014: 180) describes:

> Where this new version of old war differs from, say, World War II, is that it does not require sacrifice from the American population. They do not have to pay additional war taxes ... nor are they conscripted to fight in the war, and, unlike the ground war in Iraq and Afghanistan, there are no American casualties in drone attacks.

These territories became the focus of much activity for criminologists interested in war, and although not all attention within the literature was directed to the 2003 war in Iraq (see for example, Braithwaite and Wardak's, 2013, and Wardak and Braithwaite's, 2013, excellent studies of local and state–community conflict resolution strategies in Afghanistan), in the immediate years after 9/11 criminologists became engaged with the study of this particular war as a matter of critical concern. In the beginning this was largely due to its perceived illegitimacy as an act of 'just war'. This war had neither been sanctioned within international law by the United Nations (UN) Security Council under Article 51 of the UN Charter (see also Braithwaite's, 2010, rationale for why the war in Afghanistan did not meet the threshold of 'just war' either), nor under the rubric of international humanitarian law (IHL) such as the Geneva Conventions. So, critical criminologists variously approached the war in Iraq as a war of aggression under the headings of it being 'state crime' and a form of organised criminality. For example, for Kramer and Michalowski (2005) the way in which war was declared on Iraq was a demonstrable act of imperialism by the US administration who knowingly neglected the UN Charter, disregarded the UN Security Council's authority, and flouted both international law in relation to its conduct of lethal violence as a warring party and IHL in its duty of care as an (illegal) occupying force in Iraq thereafter. Such illegality, they argue, capitalised on the historical legacy of the first Gulf War (1991) – whereby sanctions were placed on Saddam Hussein and the Baath party by the UN through disarmament and the oil-for-food programme – to invade an already impoverished Iraqi state (Kramer and Michalowski, 2005; see also Green and Ward, 2004). Against the backdrop of previous UN resolutions and a weakened Iraqi infrastructure, the 2003 war in Iraq was launched under the auspices of humanitarian intervention to 'liberate' a persecuted civilian population, and to demobilise weapons of mass destruction from the region (see also Kramer and Michalowski, 2006).

Following the illegal instigation and perpetration of this war, further dimensions of 'state-corporate criminality' (Michalowski and Kramer, 2006) were also unleashed on Iraq by the West. Rothe's (2006) account of how war profiteering was prolific throughout the Bush–Cheney administration during the 2003 Iraq war stands as a formidable contemporary example of Clinard's (1946) 'violations of wartime regulations', and what Whyte (2015: 39) later described as 'state-corporate war-making.' The vast military-industrial complex manufactured by the war in Iraq during 2003 onwards was served by an 'incestuous' relationship between former US vice president, Dick

Cheney, Halliburton Corporation (the company for whom he was previously the chief executive officer), and the neoconservative Bush administration (Rothe, 2006: 236). This relationship witnessed the unregulated 'systematic practice of over-costs, overcharges, failure to provide services charged for, and kickback profits' by Halliburton to the sum of billions of US tax dollars and privatised investment; all procured to sustain the violence of the Iraq war, the activities from which turned a considerable personal profit for Dick Cheney and other 'power elites' (Rothe, 2006: 236; see also Mills, [1956] 2000). Furthermore, as Whyte (2007) details, Iraq was not only dominated militarily and politically, but also economically via a 'neo-colonial' rule from its occupiers in pursuit of its prized natural resource: oil. The corporate occupation of Iraq, it is argued, was fostered via corrupt relations between the US and Iraqi authorities and multinational oil corporations to ensure privileged access to embezzled state funds, corporate wealth and resources while circumnavigating trade regulations and international law (Whyte, 2007).

As critical criminologists began to observe, in addition to causing a proliferation of state-corporate criminality, declaring 'war' in the geopolitical domain as a response to the domestically occurring crime of 'terrorism' also had corresponding 'securitised' and material consequences for local contexts at home (discussed earlier) and overseas. These issues made evident that localities had begun reflecting the growth of global instability, insecurity and exclusionism (Degenhardt, 2010).

Just war as punishment and 'justice'

Returning briefly to the work of Jamieson (1998), war can also be understood as a catalyst for creating the conditions on which state violence is legitimated as a normative solution to social problems once war has seceded. If the earlier examples are illustrative of the prevailing ways in which state-organised crime were understood in the aftermath of the Iraq war, the 'justice' invoked following 9/11 (Morrison, 2006) became the guise under which such criminality was perpetrated as a form of 'punishment' (Degenhardt, 2010).

In the immediate aftermath of 9/11 the crime of 'terrorism' was established and then entrenched within political discourse as a means of framing a response to ensure the pursuit of 'justice' was prioritised (Hayward and Morrison, 2002). However, this did not have the trappings of the kind of jurisprudence one might expect of justice pursued for criminal activity. During the 'war on terror', Degenhardt

(2010) suggests acts of war became represented as forms of punishment against the 'offending' states of Afghanistan and Iraq. Such punishment was constructed as a 'form of governance in the international sphere', one that assumed a set of universal values and social ordering processes as legitimate modalities of international social control, while at the same time flouting international legal mechanisms, such as international law and the UN Charter (Degenhardt, 2010: 296). For Degenhardt (2015), the redistribution of punishment in these organisational terms provides a less normative and more consequential assessment of state and military logics and practices used to 'resolve' geopolitical problems in the aftermath of 9/11. Beyond the normative problematiques of state-corporate crime, lies the deployment of military forces internationally for the purposes of protecting some (Western) populations, while designating 'other' (non-Western) populations as threats to international social order (Degenhardt, 2015a). This was enacted by 'legitimised' international state (that is, military) violence (Weber, 1919), both with and without reference to international (that is, metropolitan) criminal justice frameworks (Degenhardt, 2015a). In redistributing punishment in such ways, notions of criminality and deviance became (and continue to be) entrenched within the geopolitical imagination, ascribed by Western 'power elites' (Mills, [1956] 2000) against 'offending' (that is, non-Western) nation-states.

The metaphorical use of the term 'war' within these practices also became the means of overcoming necessary legal 'obstacles' of due process (Packer, 1964). These obstacles aim to prevent miscarriages of justice within criminal law (that is, fair and public trials, the preservation of privacy, freedom from cruel and inhumane treatment, and so on). Under the rubric of 'justice', the 'metaphor of war' was employed to rationalise geopolitical military violence as a 'legitimate' and 'logical' response to domestically occurring problems (Hayward and Morrison, 2002). For other criminological scholars, in the aftermath of 9/11 the notion of 'justice' had been further manipulated as a matter of 'security' (though this was not new; see Zedner, 2000, 2009). For Hudson (2009), the broader setting of the 'war on terrorism' witnessed the term 'justice' modified (in the ways described by Hayward and Morrison, 2002) to legitimise political authorities to undertake exceptional levels of state violence against particular 'suspect communities' (Hillyard, 1993) within and outwith its own citizenship (as detailed in our earlier discussion). In the aftermath of 9/11 the language of 'justice' had therefore become inverted and operationalised in paradoxical terms by prioritising and legitimising the identities and violence(s) of certain prescribed (Western) interests. As Hudson (2009: 715) put it, rather than be used for the purposes of eroding human dignity and perpetuating human suffering, instead 'Justice in a time of terror demands expanding institutions to lessen global inequalities and expanding mechanisms to maintain controls on violence, striving for perpetual peace rather than "just war".'

However, it is argued by Hudson (2009) that 'justice' pursued under the auspices of 'just war' within both Afghanistan and Iraq, gave way to crime control (Packer, 1964). As discussed above, such 'justice' was driven by an identity politics exposing 'new suspect communities' (Pantazis and Pemberton, 2009) to torture, extraordinary rendition and a suspension of individual human rights and civil liberties (Hudson, 2009).

War as criminal victimisation

The approaches to state–corporate crime addressed above are emblematic of the 'normative' ways in which criminology has conceptualised war throughout its history (Degenhardt, 2010). However, within the post-9/11 context the complex nexus of 'crime' and 'war' also had a far-reaching 'political spatiality', particularly in terms of policing, biopolitics, the management of risky identities, and identity politics (Holmqvist, 2012). In the decade and more following 9/11, the global ordering processes of 'justice' and punishment (noted above), operating along the lines of hegemonic Western military power, rendered nations (such as Iraq, Libya, Pakistan, Yemen and Somalia) 'other' as the targets of geopolitical modes of 'justice' under international law, and placed the consequences experienced by their populations in 'exception' of both domestic law and IHL (Degenhardt, 2015a). For Degenhardt (2016a: 3), in the aftermath of 9/11 the concerns of criminological scholars (such as ourselves; see Walklate and McGarry, 2015) largely overlooked 'the now prominent concerns for civilians in war'. However, although marginally addressed during this period, not all criminological work had disregarded the consequences of this war on civilian victims.

From 2003 to date, there have been more than 200,000 Iraqi civilians killed either as a direct or indirect result of the war (Iraq Body Count, 2018). Indeed, as a direct consequence of the US invasion of Iraq, deaths, murder and interpersonal violence to both civilians and combatants were exacerbated – and continue to date – in its aftermath; particularly gender-based violence against women, gay communities and transgender people (Green and Ward, 2009). The invasion also caused significant destabilising impacts on crime locally within the region. As Green and Ward (2009: 621) observed, organised crime and militia violence – said to be reminiscent of a 'tribal politics' – concurrently served political ends locally in the wake of the Iraq war, and facilitated individual pursuits of vengeance, profit and opportunism for those willing to participate in violent crime. In perhaps less extraordinary, but more routine cases, criminal victimisation also proliferated throughout Iraqi households. Illustrating the vast extent of the types of criminal victimisation observed by Green and Ward (2009), Hagan et al (2012) detailed the immense 'collateral economic losses' of this war for some civilian populations, with the greatest losses being experienced by Sunni Muslims. While US 'power elites' (Mills, [1956] 2000) financially profiteered war making in Iraq (Rothe, 2006), Iraq as a nation is reported to have suffered an estimated economic cost of US$309 billion from war-related crime; the upper limit of which is estimated to be as much as over US$1 trillion, with other monetary costs incurred in Baghdad alone amounting to over US$90 billion (Hagan et al, 2012). These economic costs were experienced across a variety of crimes exacerbated by the local occurrence of war, including blackmail, kidnapping/ransom payments, medical expenses incurred due to violence, moving costs to escape violence and insecurity, losses of businesses, homes, cars and other large costs (Hagan et al, 2012).

Other more difficult-to-quantify violence and torture was differently captured in the interpersonal violence of 'criminal soldiers' (Green and Ward, 2004) against civilians and combatant detainees during the war. For example, using now well-known and disturbing images of male Iraqi prisoners (such as the 'hooded man') within Abu Ghraib prison during the US military occupation of Iraq, Hamm (2007) added the less visible and more temporally detached violence of this war to the criminological canon. Within these images, US military personnel were depicted as willingly engaging in the torture, abuse and debasement of both Iraqi prisoners and the war dead (Hamm, 2007). Such abuse made clear that the violence(s) of war extended far beyond the confines of state–corporate crime as entrenched matters of intimate violence. They also significantly undermined any notion of 'justice' that had been originally mobilised to rationalise a 'just war' doctrine in Iraq (see also Scraton, 2007, chapter 10). Instead, such acts more readily resembled punitive forms of punishment in the guise of crimes against humanity (discussed in Chapter Four), and it has been argued that the totality of the physical and structural violence experienced by Iraqi civilians is symptomatic of genocide in all but name (see McGarry and Walklate, 2015b, chapter 3).

The zenith of such criminological work established in this context was later produced by Hagan et al (2015) in *Iraq and the Crimes of*

Aggressive War: The Legal Cynicism of Criminal Militarism. Drawing on a range of qualitative and quantitative secondary data sets, Hagan et al (2015) determine the social and political contexts under which the 2003 war in Iraq was 'legitimised', waged and fought as a 'war of aggression' by US and coalition military forces. Importantly, extending previous research in this area as noted above (see Hagan et al, 2012), this work also provides fundamental insights into the extent to which such 'criminal militarism' (Hagan et al, 2015) was experienced as lived everyday consequences by members of the civilian Iraqi public. As Mannheim (1965) had observed some time earlier, micro or interactional issues such as these and those outlined above, macabrely illustrate that war leaves both direct criminogenic consequences and lasting violent legacies long after war fighting abates. Indeed, they are illustrative of the 'deranged' anomic conditions within which war violence unfolded in Iraq between Western military forces and local populations (Caldwell and Mestrovic, 2011).

Conclusion

In this chapter we have presented a bifurcated approach to the contemporary study of a 'criminology of war', namely: the 'war on terrorism'. First taking war to be understood in metaphorical terms, we have suggested that criminological work emerging in the aftermath of 9/11 to have addressed the 'war on terrorism' in terms of an (internal) crime/security nexus, and an (external) war/crime nexus. The former nexus draws attention to domestic matters of counterterrorism targeted at 'suspect communities', individual and cultural motivations of 'terrorists', and pre-emptive security agendas. The latter nexus makes clear that the 'war on terrorism' was also waged as warfare against another sovereign nation, with attention drawn to crimes of the powerful, rationales used for 'just war' being enacted as forms of international punishment and 'justice', and the macabre criminal and victimising consequences of waging war largely against civilians.

We acknowledge the discussions presented throughout this chapter do not represent the full expanse of literature relating to the 'war on terrorism' within criminology. Our intentions for this chapter have been intentionally illustrative to help propose a fundamental critical point of departure for the remainder of this book. By drawing attention to the emergence of 'criminology's third war', we suggest that the popularity of studying war within the discipline over the past nearly two decades has often been fixed in time (including by ourselves) to refer to the post-9/11 context. As a result, we suggest contemporary attempts at imagining a 'criminology of war' have become synonymous with the 'war on terrorism'. Yet, despite an agenda having been firmly outlined by Jamieson (1998) and others prior to the events of 9/11 (discussed in Chapter Two), few scholars attracted to the study of war within criminology have made much reference to it and the debate has been largely forgotten in the immediate aftermath of 9/11 (one major exception was Jock Young, 1999, 2003, 2007, 2011, [1973] 2013). It is therefore our contention that it is through this lens that the study of 'war' within criminology has become considered a recent endeavour – indeed a 'new horizon' – when in truth, this is far from the case.

However, a further problem arises from this discussion. Despite civilians disproportionately experiencing criminal victimisation and harm as consequences of war violence in Iraq, civilian victimisation took a less prominent focus in critical criminological analyses of the war. Kauzlarich and Matthews (2006) point to this as a methodological 'gap' within critical criminological studies, which focus as they do on the structural and organisational practices of state-corporate criminality and deviance. As they suggest, this 'may be filled by designing studies that tap into the lived experience of the actors and victims associated with the crimes' (Kauzlarich and Matthews, 2006: 243). However, in the aftermath of 9/11 it was instead the identities, biopolitics and experiences of soldiers as 'criminals' and 'victims' of the wars in Afghanistan and Iraq (a long-standing attention within the criminological study of war) that reappeared on the discipline's horizon. We return to critically consider both the 'deviant' soldier and the 'soldier as victim' within Chapter Six, but in the next chapter we explore one issue in which the victimisation of civilians cannot be ignored: genocide.

FOUR

The 'Forgotten Criminology of Genocide'?

Introduction

In Chapter Three we posed a central problematique that the study of war within criminology has become synonymous with the 'war on terrorism'. In this chapter (and those that follow) we offer this position some reinterpretation and development. This is done first by evidencing past and present criminological connections to the worst crimes conceivable under the broad rubric of 'war'. Here we provide a general rejoinder to observations posed in William Laufer's (1999) 'Forgotten criminology of genocide'. Following Laufer (1999) we illustrate criminology's historical relationship to genocide and, more specifically, with the Holocaust. Next, we define and critically discuss the term 'genocide' as an international crime. Finally, we outline some of the ways in which criminologists have addressed genocide throughout the 20th and into the 21st century. Here we consider most recent scholarship in this area focusing attention on genocidal violence occurring in South and Southeast Asia at the time of writing. This is followed by some concluding thoughts on the continued challenges facing the criminological study of genocide.

In discussing the social phenomenon of genocide in these ways we do not intend to offer an exhaustive overview of the histories or interdisciplinarity of genocide studies, nor provide detailed case studies and profiles of genocides past and present. Others have already achieved these things successfully outwith criminology (see Totten and Bartrop, 2009; Bartrop, 2015), as well as within the discipline. Instead, the discussion here is dedicated to some of the historical and conceptual challenges of studying genocide as a criminological and sociological endeavour, thereby illustrating emergent agendas for criminological studies of war to address.

The Holocaust: connecting criminology to genocide

Returning briefly to Hagan and Greer's (2002) criminological account of the Nuremberg trials (Chapter Two), despite Glueck's substantial contribution to international legal practices relating to war crimes, this involvement was short lived. As Hagan and Greer (2002: 255) note, notwithstanding his influence in foregrounding crimes against humanity within the Nuremberg trials (discussed later), Glueck 'joined other criminologists in ignoring war crimes' for the remainder of his career and, 'like those who surrounded him in post-war policymaking circles, he displayed little inclination to take on the culture and social structure that allowed the Holocaust to happen'. It was not until later contributions from scholars such as Alex Alvarez (1997) that sociologically informed 'first generation' studies of genocide focusing on the Holocaust began to emerge within criminology (Woolford, 2013; discussed further in our Conclusion).

Alvarez's (1997) application of Sykes and Matza's (1957) 'techniques of neutralisation' theory to the Holocaust (1933–45; discussed later), proposed ways of conceptualising how 'ordinary' people 'repackaged' their internal values to rationalise individual participation in genocidal mass murder, and suppressed their internal opposition to such activities by having their collective 'vocabularies of motive' constructed within, and reinforced by, their social, political and cultural milieu. The purpose of this argument was to enhance (not supplant) traditional explanations for how these atrocities were perpetrated, to demonstrate the value of criminological knowledge to studying genocide, and to contribute to how understanding genocidal criminality could perhaps assist in its prevention (Alvarez, 1997). Taking this as our entry point, and before further exploring what Laufer (1999) termed the 'forgotten criminology of genocide', it is first important to situate the role of criminology within the production and perpetration of genocide. This particular 'forgotten' account therefore begins with the Holocaust.

Criminology's 'darkest hour'

Perpetrated by the Nazi German government under the fascist totalitarian leadership of Adolf Hitler, the Nazi regime committed the systematic mass murder of six million innocent Jewish (their primary target group) men, women and children, in addition to the mass murder of 10 million Slav civilians, three million Soviet war prisoners, 250,000 Roma and Sinti peoples, more than 200,000 homosexuals, and up to 100,000 people with mental and physical disabilities, in addition to Jehovah's Witnesses and communists (see Shaw, 2003; Savelsberg, 2010; Rafter, 2016). Added to the calculated mass slaughter of innocent civilians at the hands of the Nazi regime, millions more innocents were physically and mentally tortured; persecuted through displacement from their homes and homelands, communities and families; forced into ghettos, robbed of their belongings and livelihoods, had their cultural and religious heritages and practices decimated, and were exposed to despicable acts of cruelty, violence, inhumane treatment, experimentation, disease and social exclusion. During the process of this 'horrific orgy of destruction' (Shaw, 2003: 78), millions were murdered in gas chambers and within the torturous conditions of concentration camps at Buchenwald, Dachau, Neuengamme, Auschwitz-Birkenau, Treblinka, Majdanek and Sobibor. Throughout the Holocaust, the intention of the Nazi regime was not only to exterminate human lives, but also to completely eradicate the racial, religious, cultural, economic, political and social identities of all those they targeted as ideological 'enemies' (Shaw, 2003; Savelsberg, 2010; Rafter, 2016).

As we learn from Nicole Rafter (2008: 287), during what she termed criminology's 'darkest hour', the discipline was deeply implicated in these atrocities, stemming from its intellectual origins in biological determinism. Prior to Germany's one-party Nazi state, the Weimar Republic was influenced by the work of one of the 'founding fathers' of criminology, Cesare Lombroso:

> Conceived in the late 19th century by Cesare Lombroso … and his followers, criminology was still an immature field when the Nazis became interested in it. In countries such as England, France and the United States, criminology was turning in sociological directions; elsewhere it developed along biological lines. In Nazi Germany it fed into a political program of mass extermination. German criminal-biology was not directly responsible for that programme, but it did provide one justification for it. (Rafter, 2008: 288)

Lombroso's medicalised rationale that societies should exclude, remove and incarcerate 'born criminals' is said to have 'dovetailed' with an acceptance of 'scientific' (that is, biological) explanations for criminality and deviant behaviour, and a belief in individual sacrifice on behalf of the German nation (Rafter, 2008: 291). The establishment of a 'crime science' underpinned by criminal biologism – wherein scientific knowledge was intentionally used to categorise and exclude individuals and groups targeted specifically as habitual, hereditary, and psychopathic 'criminals' – grounded a biologically deterministic criminology within the Weimar Republic (Rafter, 2008). And, although the eugenic intentions of 'Weimar criminology' were said to have been 'relatively muted', its scientism had entrenched political and public notions of racial superiority/inferiority, making available the knowledge and technologies required for the Nazi regime to establish and pursue a murderous and prejudicial eugenic state apparatus (Rafter, 2008: 293). Consisting of eugenics and 'racial hygiene' programmes, this was initially used to target Jewish, Sinti and Roma peoples, and later targeted homeless people, homosexuals, communists and other social groups deemed as 'hereditary deviants' by the Nazi regime (Rafter, 2008: 294).

Although Woolford (2006: 90) calls for caution in merely assuming criminology to be 'simply a corrupt science perverted by the ideology of racial hatred' during this period, the murderous ideology of the Nazi state was clearly influenced and informed by a biologically deterministic criminology. Moreover, criminology's inherent conceptual tendency to exclude and criminalise as a fundamental part of its intellectual concerns, arguably assisted in making the murderous agenda of the Holocaust become 'thinkable' by the Nazi state (Woolford, 2006: 91). Indeed, as Zygmunt Bauman (1989: 12–13) observed within *Modernity and the Holocaust*,

> The Hobbesian world of the Holocaust did not surface from its too-shallow grave, resurrected by the tumult of irrational emotions. It arrived in a factory-produced vehicle, wielding weapons only the most advanced science could supply, and following an itinerary designed by scientifically managed organizations … It was the rational modern world of modern civilization that made the Holocaust thinkable.

Criminologists working in Germany during Nazi Party rule failed to prevent the Holocaust taking place; first by actively contributing to Nazi programmes to opportunistically pursue their own research agendas, and second through complicity by not deeming racist and exclusionary terms used in their daily work as problematic (Woolford, 2006). Conversely, the Nazi Party was also responsible for jettisoning more sociologically informed criminologists from positions of influence during the 1930s (Rafter, 2008). As noted by Hood (2004) and Rafter (2008), once in power the 'proto-genocidal' policy (Shaw, 2003) of the Nuremberg Laws was implemented by the Nazi state and used to neutralise resistance from positions of authority, ban Jewish people and communists from working in government positions and universities, and force those who remained to collaborate with Nazi activities. This witnessed several criminologists exiled from Germany and Poland to the UK and North America. As history came to show, those in exile, such as Mannheim, Radzinowicz (noted in Chapter Two) and Hans von Hentig, became influential in establishing the discipline of criminology, and subdiscipline victimology (discussed in Chapter Seven). Indeed, the third International Symposium on Victimology in 1979 was dedicated to the genocidal victimisation of these scholars (see Schneider, 1982a). As Rafter (2008: 295) observes, 'through its own racism, Germany sent into exile some of its best criminologists, some of whom might have tempered its criminological biologism with environmentalist perspectives'.

The 'forgotten criminology of genocide'?

As Rafter (2008: 288) continues, although 'this line of historical research is unfamiliar to most criminologists', when considered alongside the contribution of Glueck to the Nuremberg trials (Chapter Two), it is evident that the mass atrocities of the Holocaust were not isolated from the history of the discipline, nor the personal experiences of some of its eminent 'founding fathers'. Nor was the historical and contemporary significance of these atrocities 'forgotten'. For example, as William Laufer recalls from attending a dinner during 1997 with Marvin Wolfgang and Leon Radzinowicz, these distinguished criminologists were not only cognisant of the intellectual importance of studying genocide, they also had personal experiences of the Holocaust's genocidal consequences:

> At that small dining room table sat a criminologist who had fought with the allied troops in World War II [Wolfgang], one who was displaced from his homeland [Poland] as a result of the war [Radzinowicz], and a 'second generation' refugee from Nazi Germany who lost close relatives to starvation, disease, and execution in concentration camps in Poland and Germany [Laufer]. From the ethnic, religious and nationalistic campaigns of death in Burundi and Uganda, to the inexplicable killings in Paraguay and Indonesia, we were all too aware of the devastation that is genocide. (Laufer, 1999: 72)

In observing the Holocaust, and other genocides and mass killings occurring globally (considered to be the focus of 'second generation' genocide research; see Woolford, 2013), Laufer, Wolfgang and Radzinowicz were perplexed as to why the study of genocide had not become a more central feature of criminology's development and maturity following the cessation of the Second World War (Laufer, 1999). Soon after, by foregrounding the Holocaust as being of key criminological importance, David Friedrichs (2000) provided some initial thoughts as to why this may have been the case.

'Crime of the century'

Friedrichs (2000) advocated for the Holocaust to be considered the 'crime of the century', not only due to the mass scale of the murders and persecution that were perpetrated, but also as a result of the destructive totality of the atrocities which took place, and their enduring aftermath and legacy. As the most 'famous twentieth century case of genocide', rather than the only historical case of genocide (see Savelsberg, 2010), Friedrichs (2000: 24) notes there are no other criminal events in history so severe, that have captured the attention of so many, and produced such an expansive literature than the Holocaust. As Friedrichs (2000: 35) continues, foregrounding the Holocaust within criminological scholarship as the most serious of all crimes would not only situate it as the worst crime imaginable. It would offer credence to the study of 'state crime', and provide a rationale for the discipline to pay attention to the study of genocide more routinely (Friedrichs, 2000). It is worth noting, of course, that critical genocide studies scholars point to possible 'conceptual constraints' of studying genocides as 'prototypical' within the social sciences if considered in isolation of one another (see Moshman, 2011).

Nevertheless, Friedrichs (2000) and Yacoubian (2000) suggest that the marginality of genocide to criminology is entrenched, in one way or another, in the restrictive 'moorings' of the criminological imagination (Young, J., 2011). Friedrichs (2000: 24) suggests the Holocaust may have been 'neglected' due to being too 'overwhelming' for criminologists to address, and considered more appropriately dealt with by other cognate disciplines (history, for example); or perhaps causing 'a sense of impotence' in being unable to respond to the complexity of genocide as a crime (discussed later). For Yacoubian (2000: 13), although criminology had 'virtually ignored' genocide this was not 'merely because there is no subjective interest in the crime itself'. If war and genocides perpetuate extreme forms of crime and victimisation, and if crime and victimisation are the routine interests of criminologists, then the study of genocide should intuitively fall within the criminological canon (Jamieson, 1998; Yacoubian, 2000). That it has not relates to fundamental institutional, intellectual and geographical issues: funding has previously been scarce within mainstream (Western) criminology to research state crimes (although see research council-funded studies from Green et al, 2015, 2018, noted later), and (Western) criminologists are often either preoccupied with their own localised concerns with normative crimes and domestic criminal justice, or lack the historical, cultural and geographical knowledge to address the study of genocide, and successfully pass this on within academic curricula (Yacoubian, 2000). These are issues Tombs and Whyte (2003) noted in their later critique of the disregard of 'crimes of the powerful' in the conjoined interests of UK academia, funding bodies (again see how the work of Green et al, 2015, 2018, was recently funded) and government institutions. Thus it may be that the Holocaust, other genocides and crimes against humanity (discussed later), have often been part of a wider assemblage of neglect within the discipline.

Latterly, Savelsberg (2010) has attempted to stimulate the relevance of criminology to the study of genocide. Acknowledging the disparate conceptual approaches within (mainstream) criminology and genocide studies, which respectively (and generally) focus on individual causation and state/collective action, Savelsberg (2010) opens up an analysis of genocide from micro to macro perspectives. This is not an approach we intend to replicate within this chapter. However, we do wish to encourage conceptual ways of thinking to illustrate its farther-reaching complexities – and relevance – for criminological studies of war. However, before turning our attentions to such matters, we first conceptualise how this social phenomenon came to be defined internationally as crime.

International crime of genocide

Prior to the cessation of the Second World War, the term 'genocide' was coined by Raphael Lemkin (1944) within *Axis Rule in Occupied Europe*. Lemkin (1944) observed that the atrocities perpetrated by the Nazi regime were without a name. Terms such as 'denationalization' or 'Germanization', used up to this point, inadequately conveyed the scale and complexity of the atrocities being perpetrated throughout the Holocaust. As Lemkin (1944: 79) states,

> New conceptions require new terms. By 'genocide' we mean the destruction of a nation or of an ethnic group. This new word, coined ... to denote an old practice in its modern development, is made from the ancient Greek word *genos* (race, tribe) and the Latin *cide* (killing) ... Genocide is directed against the national group as an entity, and the actions involved are directed against individuals, not in their individual capacity, but as members of the national group.

Central to this definition were both physical and cultural destruction (Short, 2010, 2016). Lemkin (1944) explains that genocide first destroys the 'national pattern' of those targeted (that is, those who are oppressed), then imposes the 'national pattern' of those doing the targeting (that is, the oppressor) onto the oppressed. The result is either the enduring oppression of the remaining population or the total *colonisation* of the territory by the oppressor. The 'techniques' identified as being used to facilitate the Holocaust included the targeting of political, social, cultural, religious, moral and economic institutions (Lemkin, 1944). Most profound during the Holocaust was the targeting of Jewish people and other oppressed groups; abolishing births or malnourishing parents to reduce birth rates (Lemkin, 1944). The 'physical debilitation and even annihilation of national groups in occupied countries' (Lemkin, 1944: 87) during the Holocaust were therefore perpetrated via physical violence, including mass murder, incarceration in concentration camps and being put to death in gas chambers (Shaw, 2003). In addition to other forms of structural violence, such as food rationing unequally distributed under racist terms, with health intentionally endangered through withholding vital fuels and medicines, and housing Jewish people and other targeted groups in squalid conditions and ghettos (Lemkin, 1944). The atrocities of the Holocaust, perpetrated before and throughout the Second World War by the Nazi German state, therefore set the historical context for the definition of genocide as it is contemporarily understood within international law (Savelsberg, 2010).

Contemporary definition of genocide as an international crime

The outline offered by Lemkin (1944) was later simplified for a public audience (see Lemkin, 1945). The term 'genocide' was said thereafter to be 'occasionally' used in the drafting of, and submissions to, the Nuremberg trials when prosecuting 'crimes against humanity', but did not feature in the trials' final verdict during October 1946 (Schabas, n.d.). Most significantly however, Lemkin's (1944) definition was *partially* used by the newly formed United Nations (UN) to ratify 'genocide' as an international crime (Savelsberg, 2010). On 9 December 1948 the UN General Assembly resolution 260A (III) declared that 'genocide is a crime under international law, contrary to the spirit and aims of the United Nations and condemned by the civilized world' (UN, 1948: 174). Ratified on 12 January 1951 and outlined across 19 separate Articles within the *United Nations Convention on the Prevention and Punishment of the Crime of Genocide* (the 'Genocide Convention') (United Nations, 1948: 174, Article II), genocide constitutes:

> acts committed with the intent to destroy, in whole or in part, a national, ethnical, racial or religious group, as such:
>
> (a) Killing members of the group;
> (b) Causing serious bodily or mental harm to members of the group;
> (c) Deliberately inflicting on the group conditions of life calculated to bring about its physical destruction in whole or in part;
> (d) Imposing measures intended to prevent births within the group;
> (e) Forcibly transferring children of the group to another group.

Under the Genocide Convention, not only is genocide punishable as an international crime, so too is conspiracy and incitement to commit the offence, and complicity in perpetrating, facilitating or supporting genocide (UN, 1948, Article III).

As the definition above makes clear, for acts of genocide to be formally acknowledged, accuracy is required within its definition and application (Bartrop, 2015). Indeed, as with criminal law, for genocidal acts to be formally defined as 'crime' both actus reus (the act itself) and mens rea (intent) need to be demonstrated towards the partial or entire annihilation of the target group (Mullins and Rothe, 2008). Those charged with offences under the Genocide Convention should be tried by a military tribunal within the state where the atrocities took place, or by an international tribunal with jurisdiction (UN, 1948, Article VI; Savelsberg, 2010). The first historic example of this occurred over 40 years after the Nuremberg trials, at the UN International Criminal Tribunal for the Former Yugoslavia (1993–2017) (UNICTY, n.d.a). Here, Serbian leaders were put on trial for crimes against humanity, war crimes and genocide against Muslims during the war in Bosnia-

Herzegovina (1992–95) (discussed in Chapter Six). In November 2017, former Serbian commander Ratko Mladić was convicted of genocide for the massacre of almost 8,000 Muslim men and boys in Srebrenica during July 1995 (UNICTY, n.d.b). Becoming the last person to be convicted before the conclusion of the ICTY after 24 years, questions of whether 'justice' has been achieved by the tribunal, and if reconciliation is possible in its aftermath are now likely to ensue (Brennan, 2017).

The above discussion is just one reading of Lemkin's (1944) work, and the Genocide Convention definition we prioritise is not without further controversy and contestation (see, for example, McDonnell and Moses, 2005; Short, 2016). Indeed, for Short (2010: 839, emphasis in original), 'the foundational conceptual ingredient in genocide for Lemkin was *culture* not "civilian"'. By decoupling Lemkin's (1944) central conception of *colonisation* within 'genocide' from the codified definition (noted earlier), the Genocide Convention de facto *colonised* the term (issues we return to in Chapter Eight) (Short, 2010, 2016). However, for the purposes of this chapter we are concerned with other conceptual ways of thinking critically about the term as defined by the Genocide Convention.

Thinking conceptually about the term 'genocide'

As Helen Fein (1990) observes, the definition of genocide within the Genocide Convention is restrictive in terms of its 'intent and extent', or in other words what is included and excluded in this definition. Despite its fundamental importance (Bartrop, 2015), within the UN definition the matter of 'intent' is problematic given it is difficult to demonstrate with absolute certainty, and some acts which may *appear* genocidal fall short of being captured within the Genocide Convention (Fein, 1990). Furthermore, the extent of the official definition of genocide is not wholly inclusive of a variety of other groups or collectivities, including social classes, political institutions and minority sexual identities, for example (Fein, 1990; Shaw, 2003). Taken together, these matters raise critical questions for what is counted as an act of genocide, and who counts as genocide victims.

The definition aside, other conceptual problems also arise in the conflation of genocidal acts with acts of war. As witnessed during the Holocaust, formal state militaries can and do perpetrate genocide. War also 'contains within it the potential for a genocidal regime to realise its aims, and probably more easily than in peacetime' (Bartrop, 2015: 116). As Bartrop (2015) and Shaw (2003) point out, although war and genocide are events which *may* have their perpetration facilitated by the other, they are not synonymous. Formal armies and militias do not need to be invoked, and war does not have to be under way, for genocide to take place (Bartrop, 2015). Yet these issues are paradoxical. Genocidal acts *do* frequently occur during war (Savelsberg, 2010) and their perpetration often overlaps with war crimes and human rights violations, making it difficult to distinguish them legally from other war crimes (Alvarez, 2010). Furthermore, many genocides throughout history (such as the Cambodian genocide perpetrated by the Khmer Rouge, 1975–79), need to be understood as continuous with war and its cessation (such as the Vietnam War, 1955–75) (Shaw, 2003). Considered in these ways, as Alvarez (2010) points out, capturing genocide in one certified form (as outlined earlier) is problematic for how the UN definition of genocide is invoked and applied contemporarily, and for how genocidal acts are conceptualised, intervened with and prevented. As with normative definitions of crime, thinking critically with regards the definition and application of the legal term genocide allows us to challenge some of its conceptual (read 'first generation', see Woolford, 2013) problems.

Crimes against humanity: abstracting or expanding the parameters of understanding?

One way of addressing such issues is to propose alternative notions of how acts of atrocity could be meaningfully conceptualised to ensure they are not overlooked or erased from history. For example, Hagan and Rymond-Richmond (2009: 509) assert, 'more abstract terms, such as "crimes against public health" and "crimes against humanity" also have their place'. The 1998 Rome Statute of the International Criminal Court (ICC) Article 5 captured both genocide and 'crimes against humanity' as the gravest of crimes facing the international community (Mullins and Rothe, 2008). For Schabas (2005) and Savelsberg (2010), the 'place' of this term is as historically prescient as 'genocide', and broadens the scope of what may be considered an international crime.

Savelsberg (2010) documents that historical accounts of atrocities have been consistently recorded as far back as the 13th century rule of Genghis Khan. Over time, and with changes in the acceptability and perception of violence in an allegedly 'civilising' and globalised world, the notion of atrocity has shifted from being perceived as historical acts of 'heroic' conquering to barbaric acts of inhumanity (Savelsberg, 2010). Prior to the definition of genocide being coined by Lemkin (1944) and formalised in the Genocide Convention, the term 'crime against humanity' was first formally used during 1915 to address the massacre of the minority Armenian population in Turkey by the Ottoman government (Schneider, 1982b; Schabas, 2005; Rafter and Walklate, 2012). It then re-emerged during the 1940s as a response to the atrocities of the Nazis before and during the Second World War (Schabas, 2005). The term 'crimes against humanity' was first adopted into law on 8 August 1945 within the Charter of the Nuremberg Tribunal, Article VI, alongside 'war crimes' and 'crimes against peace' (Schabas, 2005). The term includes two elements: (i) acts that generally correspond to all punishable acts within domestic criminal law (i.e. murder, enslavement, etc.), and (ii) the perpetration of these acts as motivated by discrimination and prejudice, and targeted towards widespread attacks on civilian populations. (Schabas, 2005).

Unlike genocide however (which could occur in times of war *and* peace), under the Nuremberg Charter crimes against humanity were initially wedded to acts of 'aggressive war' (discussed in Chapter Two) (Schabas, 2005). This 'nexus' was later resolved by the constitution of the 1998 Rome Statute, which formally recognised their capacity to also be perpetrated in times of peace (Schabas, 2005).

Although Hagan and Rymond-Richmond (2009: 509) suggest this term 'can often have an abstract quality and a quieting or even silencing effect that the term 'genocide' intentionally seeks to overcome', Schabas (2005: 81) notes that the 'contextual elements' of the term broadened out the scope of who could be included within it when recognised as 'widespread or systematic attacks on civilian populations'. In doing so, the populations to which the term applies has been expanded to include not only political, racial and religious minorities (as per the UN definition of genocide), but also those identifiable on grounds of nationality, ethnicity, culture and gender (although the persecution of minority sexual groups and people with disabilities are still only captured under the notion of 'other inhumane acts') (Schabas, 2005). The term has also extended punishable acts to include crimes such as apartheid, rape, forced disappearance of persons, and modern forms of slavery such as trafficking women and children (Schabas, 2005). Schabas (2005), like Savelsberg (2010), also observes that crimes against humanity can perhaps be understood as akin to human rights violations. However, the consequences for committing either differ markedly. Violations of human rights often only require victim compensation and a change to current practices, whereas punishment for a crime against humanity will carry a long term of imprisonment (as demonstrated by the UNICTY, n.d.a) (Schabas, 2005).

Schabas (2005) therefore suggests that all acts of genocide may be collapsed within the term as the most extreme form of 'crimes against humanity'. However, some complexity arises when attempting to associate the term with contemporary acts of terrorism (discussed in Chapter Three). This arises because terrorist organisations, such as Al Qaeda and ISIS, have no formal attachment to state entities (that is, government), are not non-state actors, nor state-like actors with de facto control over national regions; nor are they formally engaged with the enactment of atrocities via formal social policy (Schabas, 2005). All of which are important facets of recognising crimes against humanity. As it stands, however, like Cohen (2001), Hagan and Greer (2002: 257) note crimes against humanity – akin to genocide and human rights issues (see Schwendinger and Schwendinger, 1970; Murphy and Whitty, 2013) – have similarly remained a 'criminological blind spot' within the discipline's broader interests.

'Genocidal impulse' as social, political and cultural processes

In one alternative sociological case reconceptualising genocide, Fein (1990) proposed a way to expose the opacity of genocidal violence, and better account for genocide victims as belonging to a range of collectivities. Fein (1990) suggested an adherence to the Genocide Convention definition, but encouraged:

- clarity over what specifically are / not included as genocidal acts;
- suggestions as to what demarcates genocide based on concepts better able to be applied to real-world occurrences;
- the opportunity for a broader inclusion of groups that are more representative of the societies to which the definition applies; and
- conformity to a universal notion of what constitutes 'justice', and a respect for the coexistence of all non-violent groups.

Such a reconceptualisation also urges us to consider the social, political and cultural processes involved in the perpetration of genocide. Although genocidal acts are driven by a 'genocidal impulse' to 'remove and destroy a population within a community', they are rarely spontaneous acts of random violence (Alvarez, 2016: 30). Genocidal ideologies are based on pseudo-scientific, irrational and fantastical beliefs of genocidists (Shaw, 2003), which require public acceptance of dogmatic and murderous ideology, and the cultivation of essentialism within public sentiment, social policy and the political lexicon, 'influenced by emotive elements', such as fear and hatred (Alvarez, 2016: 30; see also Alvarez, 2010). Pre- or proto-genocidal acts are found in discriminatory beliefs and practices which direct hostility towards specifically targeted social groups and collectivities (for example, via anti-Semitism, racism, chauvinism), and signify the beginnings of the threat of genocide (Shaw, 2003). Therefore, as Shaw makes clear, genocide needs to be understood not as simply equated with the 'completed destruction of a group', but also in terms of the practices leading towards and throughout its perpetration. It is therefore important to recognise the 'relational' nature of genocide, and to understand how it comes to be perpetrated by collectivities and – importantly – experienced collectively as victimisation (see Powell, 2007).

Drawing from Bauman (1989), Jamieson (1999) later noted that for those who are killed as a result of genocide, they are murdered not for what they have done, but for *who* they are and *what* they are *perceived* to become. Addressing gendered violence and victimisation during the Bosnia-Herzegovina (1992) and Rwandan (1994) (see UNICTR, n.d.) genocides, Jamieson (1999) suggests that one of the defining features of genocide transcends its physical violence and is characterised by the systematic demonisation, dehumanisation, essentialising and gendered exclusion of the 'other'. The systematic marginalisation of 'othered' collectivities by genocidists through such exclusionary processes juxtapose a fear of the 'other' with a warped and fabricated construction of their supposed unified identity (Alvarez, 2010). Such political and cultural constructions render entire groups biologically, socially and culturally inferior and become a fundamental feature of the structural conditions under which the 'genocidal impulse' is realised and made possible (Jamieson, 1999). Cultivated in these ways, as Fein (1990) noted, there is nothing that the victims of genocide could or could not do – be they submissive or militant – that would prevent their attempted eradication by genocidists (Jamieson, 1999). Once nurtured, genocidal acts then become facilitated through state policies, political propaganda and social consensus, with the backing of armies and government organisations to execute them (Alvarez, 2010).

Genocide in all its manifestations is therefore a planned, bureaucratic act employing a multiplicity of gendered violence(s) and social exclusion in extremis, made possible by being rationalised in the public interest (Alvarez, 2010). Bauman (1989: 18) referred to this as the 'social production of moral indifference'; rearticulated by Jamieson (1999) in criminological terms as the most extreme form of social exclusion. Therefore, understanding the dangers of targeting groups within social policy can identify potential escalation into genocidal behaviour and actions (Shaw, 2003). Furthermore, acknowledging that beyond the mass violence of large genocidal death tolls lie other social processes which *cultivate* genocidal behaviour, urges us to be cognisant that overt physical violence is often the latent result of long-standing prejudicial, discriminatory and proto-genocidal behaviour.

Genocide as an assemblage of violence

Mindful of the subjugation of 'culture' within the Genocide Convention definition (noted earlier), it is also important not to disregard some of the other key characteristics outlined within Lemkin's (1944) original explanation of genocide (see also Short, 2010, 2016). As Alvarez (2010) notes, there is more than militarised violence and the use of conventional weaponry deployed on genocide victims. They are also exposed to indirect methods of starvation, disease and displacement, in addition to forced sterilisation and the decimation of their cultural, religious and social identities (Alvarez, 2010). It must also not be overlooked that genocide exhibits deeply gendered acts of violence wherein rape and sexual violence are used against women (disproportionately) and men as weapons of mass degradation (issues we return to in Chapter Seven). Furthermore, genocide creates a challenging paradox of violence and victimisation to that found within mainstream criminological *and* victimological interests. During genocides, not only are women frequently victims of sexual violence and men of physical violence (with men as the main perpetrators), each of these roles can be the converse of conventional ideas of criminality and victimhood: men can become victims of physical and sexual violence, and women can also become the perpetrators (Jamieson, 1999; Alvarez, 2016; Rafter, 2016).

With these historical and conceptual outlines now in view, next we turn to illustrate contemporary examples of how criminological work has, and continues to address, genocide throughout the 20th and into the 21st centuries.

'Criminology of genocide' into the 21st century

Following Alvarez's (1997) contribution to the study of genocide, other notable 'second generation' additions followed, attentive to experiences in the Global South (Woolford, 2013). Mullins and Rothe's (2008) *Blood and Bedlam: Violations of International Law in Post-Colonial Africa* provides a multi-level case study analysis of genocide, crimes against humanity and violations of international law within and across the postcolonial nations of Rwanda, Uganda, Democratic Republic of the Congo and Darfur (see also Mullins and Rothe, 2007, on Darfur). This book was the first comprehensive criminological work dedicated to these issues as matters of state crime and international violations of the law, providing an awareness of how mass violence descends within these states, how militia and militaries become engaged in war crimes against one another and civilians, and the efficacy of international humanitarian law to protect against such violence (see also Barak, 2009; Okafo, 2009). Hagan and Rymond-Richmond (2009) later published *Darfur and the Crime of Genocide*. In this book, secondary victimisation data from 'The Atrocities Documentation Survey' conducted by the US State Department during 2004 was analysed to address the occurrences of genocidal violence within Darfur. Profound in this work is the finding that a triumvirate of violence was committed, including war crimes, genocide and crimes against humanity (Savelsberg, 2010). Hagan and Rymond-Richmond (2009) identified that the victims were racially constructed by the Sudanese president (al-Bashir), government and militia through derogatory 'racial epithets' to make them the targets of genocidal violence (see also Hagan and Kaiser, 2011, on Darfur). Although this strategy is a consistent aspect of the 'genocidal impulse', it is seldom isolated from other facets of its inhumane processes (Shaw, 2010; see also Rafter, 2009). For example, sexual victimisation was found to be most common where attacks were frequently accompanied by racial epithets, and – interestingly – victimisation was found to occur with the greatest frequency in areas with the most abundant land (Savelsberg, 2010).

Following Mullins and Rothe (2008), in *The Crime of all Crimes: Towards a Criminology of Genocide* Rafter (2016) presents a case study analysis of eight genocides spanning the 20th century, from the Herero genocide (1904–07) to the Rwandan genocide (1994). Like Mullins and Rothe (2008), Rafter (2016) offers a multi-level analysis identifying the structural, group and individual dynamics of the 'genocidal impulse'. Different to the previous perpetrator-focused contributions, however, Rafter (2016) illustrates the gendered nature of sexual violence during the Rwandan genocide and the systematic targeting of people with disabilities by the Nazi regime during the Holocaust. The ambiguousness of how violence concluded during the Guatemalan genocide (1981–93) is also observed to have left a damaging legacy rather than a conclusive end-point, despite being the first nation to convict its former leader (Ríos Montt) of genocide through its own judicial processes (UN News, 2013; see also Carrabine, 2016). Rafter's (2016) conclusion outlined a manifesto for genocide to be more fully addressed as a fundamental criminological concern (see also Friedrichs 2000). Importantly, Rafter (2016) also indicated that the study of genocide is a horizon that victimology should meaningfully pursue. This is an agenda raised by Schneider (1982b) some time ago, and most recently foregrounded in victimological research on the Cambodian genocide (see Killean, 2018).

Given the growing importance of focusing on the experiences, voices and visibility of genocide victims, we now direct attention away from the *criminal* act of genocide and look towards the *victims* of genocidal behaviour during the 21st century (we more fully address matters related to victimology and genocide in Chapter Seven).

Borders and climate change: new horizons for a 'criminology of genocide'?

In *Unstable Ground: Climate Change, Conflict and Genocide*, Alex Alvarez (2017) takes on the potential relationship between genocide, climate change and population displacement from conflict within 'border regions' across the globe. Alvarez (2017: 3) suggests that the cumulative impact of human activity on climate change has exacerbated violence and conflict in already unstable regions. He illustrates, for example, how droughts in Syria between 2006 and 2011 caused food and water insecurity, and a widespread loss of Syrian agricultural livelihoods. The rural to urban migration of many of those affected caused extensive unemployment and poverty. Come the Arab Spring during 2011, such displacement contributed – in part – to the uprising, and eventual outbreak, of civil war in Syria (Alvarez, 2017).

For Alvarez (2017), attendant to climate change are also issues related to borders. For those displaced by war and conflict – such as refugees from Syria, Afghanistan and Iraq (discussed in Chapter Three) – their treacherous journeys to other nations seeking safety and security are fraught with trauma and a high risk to their lives. In what Braithwaite and D'Costa (2018) have termed 'cascades of violence', the 'border zones' where refugee camps are located and state security forces deployed are said to be fertile spaces for existing ethnic tensions and perceived historic victimisation to re-emerge both within refugee populations or between host populations (Alvarez, 2017). Moreover, refugees displaced by conflict and genocide frequently find their arrival perceived as a threat and a source of fear, anxiety and tension by host populations (Alvarez, 2017). As Alvarez (2017: 13) suggests, claims of geographic ownership/difference by the receiving nation, the identification of refugees as either threatening, surplus or expendable 'others', and actions to forcibly remove the 'communal presence' of those seeking safety from climate change or war become identifiable as 'the essence of genocide'. The potential impacts of climate change and war – fuelled by racism, xenophobia and essentialism – appear to share a similar blueprint to the 'genocidal impulse'. Thus Alvarez (2016, 2017) brings the Global South into view in ways more akin to 'second generation' genocide scholarship (see Woolford, 2013). Here, we make use of this way of thinking and turn our attention to a contemporary example of mass atrocity and displacement in the 21st century.

'A text-book example of ethnic cleansing'

Residing in Rakhine state, the Rohingya are the largest ethnic Muslim group living in the least developed state of Myanmar (UNHRC, 2016, 2017). Since its independence in 1948, the Myanmar government has refused to recognise their status as citizens, designating the Rohingya as illegal immigrants from Bangladesh, making them the largest stateless population in the world (UNHRC, 2016, 2017). The Rohingya and Rakhine Buddhists have historic grievances relating to their national and cultural heritage in Myanmar that have 'cascaded' into the present day (Braithwaite and D'Costa, 2018). Having also faced persistent persecution from Myanmar authorities during the 20th century, the Rohingya have been frequently displaced to the surrounding regions of Bangladesh and India, and subject to further displacement, smuggling and human trafficking across the Andaman Sea towards Thailand and Malaysia (UNHRC, 2016, 2017).

Following an outbreak of violence during 2012, motivated by religious intolerance and extremism from ultra–nationalist Buddhists, thousands of Rohingya were killed, injured and internally displaced (UNHRC, 2016). The scale of this violence has increased since 2012 and intensified following an attack on Myanmar security forces allegedly conducted by Rohingya extremists on 9 October 2016 (OHCHR, 2017). Arguably this is an emblematic case of historic oppression, displacement and humiliation 'cascading' into disenfranchisement and insurgent violence (Braithwaite and D'Costa, 2018). In the wake of these attacks, the UN Human Rights Council (UNHRC, 2016) and Office of the United Nations High Commissioner for Human Rights (OHCHR, 2017) reported unprecedented levels of violence against the Rohingya, including the gruesome torture and murder of men, women and children, beatings, destruction of property and enforced disappearance. The most extensive of such violence (52%) was the raping of and sexual violence against women and girls (OHCHR, 2017: 9–10).

On 25 August 2017, claiming their violence was in response to a further Rohingya insurgent attack on security officers, the Myanmar army begun further crackdowns on the Rohingya (OHCHR, 2017). During the violence, it is reported that Myanmar soldiers burned Rohingya villages, and tortured and executed men, women and children in macabre scenes of barbarism (see Gettleman, 2017; Holmes, 2017a). Médecins Sans Frontières (MSF) conservatively reported approximately 9,400 deaths in the first month following the upsurge in violence, including 6,700 killed directly due to violence, of which 730 were children below five years of age; in addition to the widespread use of rape, and sexual and gender-based violence (MSF, 2018). Added to their existing statelessness and persecution, between August 2017 and January 2018, the UN estimated that over half a million Rohingya have been displaced by violence (UNHCR, 2018). Based in makeshift camps in Cox's Bazar at the southern tip of Bangladesh, the Rohingya have now been forced into experiencing further and continued vulnerability as a result of food and water insecurity, inadequate shelter, poor sanitation and the risk of water and airborne diseases (UNHCR, 2018).

Persistent throughout the Rohingya persecution has been what Cohen (2001) described as both 'literal' (nothing is happening) and 'implicatory' (what's happening is justified) denials. Prior to discussing the violence against the Rohingya in private with senior Association of Southeast Asian Nations (ASEAN) officials, Myanmar prime minister, Aung San Suu Kyi, had been accused of literal denial by failing to address the crisis in public until late 2017 (see Holmes, 2017b). During 2018, and following calls from UK MPs to sanction Myanmar over the violence, the Myanmar military responded with implicatory denial, restating any violence was caused by Rohingya insurgent provocation, and concluded that no Myanmar security personnel had committed killings, unlawful detention, beatings or sexual violence (Ellis-Petersen, 2018a). Such abdications of responsibility stand as profound denials of the prevailing evidence collected by the UN, MSF and other human rights organisations, typical of non-state actors participating in the globalised arena of 'new' wars (Kaldor, 2014).

Since their violent displacement to Bangladesh and surrounding regions, the Rohingya also face the perils of trauma and survival against the backdrop of the precarious environment in which they seek refuge. Rising water levels and flooding from the Bay of Bengal, coupled with the threat of drought due to less rainfall during monsoon seasons, risk causing water and food insecurity for thousands of rural citizens living in the largely agricultural areas of Bangladesh (Alvarez, 2017). These conditions add further urgent concerns for the security of the Rohingya forcibly displaced to Bangladesh as a result of persecution in Myanmar.

The intensity of the violence experienced by the Rohingya was previously reported as 'the possible commission of crimes against humanity', and that 'some of these violations could amount to war crimes' if established by a court of law (UNHRC, 2016: 13, 15). The severity of their continued persecution further escalated and, as the UN Human Rights Chief exclaimed, the violence experienced by the Rohingya appeared to be a 'textbook example of ethnic cleansing' (Al Hussein, 2017). The Special Rapporteur on human rights in Myanmar later called for the international community to map and document human rights violations in a 'master data base', with a view to establishing international criminal proceedings against Myanmar authorities (Lee, 2018: 19). As Braithwaite and D'Costa (2018: 592) state, 'time will tell whether we will look back on it as violence that was worsened by democratic populism that trumps rights. At this stage, the state of the evidence makes that likely.' At the time of writing however, a case has been forwarded to the ICC by a coalition of Bangladeshi organisations pushing for an investigation into Myanmar crimes committed in Rahkine, and a call has followed from 132 politicians from the 'ASEAN Parliamentarians for Human Rights' demanding an investigation (Ellis-Petersen, 2018b). Furthermore, the UN has formally called for Myanmar authorities (specifically the Tatmadaw armed forces) to be investigated and prosecuted for war crimes, crimes against humanity and genocide (see UNHRC, 2018). The persecution of the Rohingya by Myanmar authorities has not gone unnoticed within criminological research, however, with the International State Crime Initiative documenting at length in two separate reports the unfolding events (see Green et al, 2015, 2018). As Green et al (2015, 2018) state, the violent persecution of the Rohingya by Myanmar authorities has now fulfilled all the characteristics and processes of genocide. Akin to the positionality of critical genocide scholarship (noted earlier), they conclude:

> The parallels with other genocides are stark. In Germany, the Nazi government issued Jews with special ID cards before ghettoising them and then unleashing the Holocaust; in Myanmar, the government used special ID cards to identify the Rohingya as outsiders before unleashing the final stages of the genocide. In Rwanda, the state mobilised Hutus to slaughter Tutsi. In Myanmar, the state mobilised Buddhist and Rakhine extremists to target the Rohingya ... The

reality is that the genocide of the Rohingya in Myanmar was long in the making ... Unless the international community takes urgent and meaningful action, the Myanmar Rohingya will be eliminated. (Green et al, 2018: 18)

Herein lies a rolling horizon for the 'forgotten criminology of genocide' to keep within its sights.

Conclusion

As Woolford (2006) has pointed out, and as we have tried to illustrate throughout this chapter, a critical study of genocide requires it not to be bound by its own or any discipline, and – importantly – not merely use 'criminological' approaches as acts of redemption for the discipline's previous neglect of the topic. Here, we have endeavoured to follow such guidance while contributing to a long-standing discussion relating to criminology and genocide (see Laufer, 1999). We have made connections with the discipline's 'dark' input into the biological determinism of the Holocaust, and have made clear that – like war (discussed in Chapter Two) – the discipline has a historic relationship with the crime of genocide. We also hope to have demonstrated that abstracting genocide merely to the monumental death tolls they perpetrate, places us at an unimaginable distance from the complexities of processes and lived realities of genocide for those who experience and live through it (Woolford, 2006). As such, studies of genocide should strive to avoid value-laden judgements of how this crime *should* be studied as derivatives of any intellectual enclaves (Bauman, 1989). They should also be responsible with the information they report, and reflexive about the approaches and judgements taken (Woolford, 2006). Importantly, as Bauman (1989) and Woolford (2006) caution, we must be aware of the impossibility of studying genocide as a value-free endeavour. Foremost however, as Shaw (2003: 38) maintains, 'genocide is always and everywhere illegitimate', bringing the persecution of civilians squarely into view for criminological studies of war, and for the remainder of this book.

FIVE

From Nuclear to 'Degenerate' War

Introduction

As has become evident in previous chapters, criminological scholars have demonstrated notable engagement with the subject of war, during and in the aftermaths of the First and Second World Wars (Chapter Two), prominently in the post-9/11 era (Chapter Three), and in response to acts of genocides throughout the 20th and 21st centuries (Chapter Four). However, although capturing war and genocide at either extreme of the transition from 'old' to 'new' wars (see Kaldor, 2014, discussed in the Introduction), this is not all criminologists have had to say on the subject. They have also been active commentators on nuclear issues since the end of the Cold War era. To explore some of this commentary, in this and the following chapter we address the changing nature of war within modernity as it turned towards the disproportionate mass killing of civilians following on from the Second World War.

This chapter foregrounds previous criminological work related to nuclear issues with a specific focus on David Kauzlarich and Ronald Kramer's (1998) seminal book *Crimes of the American Nuclear State: At Home and Abroad*. This book is first used here to define nuclear weapons and armament as 'state crimes' and identify the human consequences of using nuclear weapons from a critical criminological perspective. Next, we use the work of Kauzlarich and Kramer (1998) and Kramer and Kauzlarich (2010) to identify other ways in which the 'crimes of the nuclear state' could be considered differently in relation to Shaw's (2003) concept of 'degenerate war'. In doing so, we shift the focal point for criminological analysis onto the disproportionate targeting of civilians in war during the 20th and 21st centuries. This brings war victims and the environment more fully to our attention, rather than purely focusing on 'criminals' and criminality. The chapter concludes noting the contemporary relevance of nuclear issues for criminological studies of war. It finishes by providing a platform on which aerial 'terror bombing' can be further explored (in Chapter Six) as continuing to be disproportionately directed at civilians and non-combatants as a weapon of 'new' war.

Criminology and nuclear war

During 1983, an article published by Richard Harding outlined some preliminary issues for criminology with regards to nuclear weapons and nuclear armament. Fearing that criminology was running into a 'dead-end' by not asking questions about new technologies and being confined by normative issues of crime, deviance and social control at a 'street' level, he turned attention to the importance of the 'renunciation' of nuclear energy and weapons (Harding, 1983). For Harding the key contributions criminologists could make to nuclear issues included their ability to 'vividly' illustrate that the production of nuclear energy and weapons were inherently 'deviant', insofar as no nuclear reactors – including the systems that govern them, or workers who operate them – were ever entirely safe or not prone to error, fault or corruption. These weapons should therefore be jettisoned at all costs in awareness of the destruction that they can cause to human life and the environment (Harding, 1983). In this vein, critical criminologists should work to expose corporate and state activities regarding nuclear issues to frame debates concerning what practices should be considered deviant, and how such conduct could be publicly identified (Harding, 1983). Furthermore, Harding did not consider those who worked in the nuclear industry (whom he likened to soldiers) to be exempt from the 'Nuremberg principle' (discussed in Chapter Four), inasmuch it was no excuse for them to claim they were merely passive 'victim[s] of the capitalist system' which employed them and were only following orders by virtue of their work (Harding, 1983: 89). This latter point is perhaps the least convincing of Harding's argument (we return to consider soldiers in terms of possible 'victimhood' in Chapter Six). However, in the remainder of this agenda there is much for criminologists to ponder on how and why nuclear issues should become a central part of their interests. Fundamentally, this should be to 'decrease the chances of the extinction of mankind and the destruction of the planet' (Harding, 1983: 81). It is worth noting that these sentiments were influenced by a series of articles by Jonathan Schell (1982) in *The New Yorker*, later published in his seminal book *The Fate of the Earth*.

Following Harding's (1983) early intervention, David Friedrichs (1985: 5) elaborated on the 'extreme criminological apathy to the nuclear issue'. Like Harding, he suggested that in retrospect the criminological fixation with more normative issues of 'street' crime would look like a glaring oversight of more pressing and threatening nuclear issues in the aftermath of a nuclear war (Friedrichs, 1985). Friedrichs concluded by raising a series of questions he suggested criminologists could address with regards to nuclear war. He proposed:

> law, as a mechanism of social control, is a central concern of students of criminal justice. Do our studies of criminal law provide us with any useful insights regarding the role – and limitation – of law in the nuclear realm? If we do have anything to contribute to the international law question: Is the use or threatened use – of nuclear weapons – legal? (Friedrichs, 1985: 8)

These initial forays illustrating the issues nuclear weapons raised for the criminological agenda were later developed at length by two well-known critical criminological scholars, David Kauzlarich and Ronald C. Kramer (noted in Chapter Three).

'Towards a sociology of nuclear weapons'

Like Ruth Jamieson (1998) who had advocated moving 'towards a criminology of war in Europe' (discussed in Chapter Two), Ronald Kramer also encouraged (more than a decade earlier) a move 'towards a sociology of nuclear weapons' (see Kramer and Marullo, 1985). Rather than considering the sociological study of war as hawkish (Malešević, 2010a, 2010b), and noting 'sociologists have contributed very little to this literature in comparison to other disciplines', Kramer and Marullo (1985: 279) urged their contemporaries to become active participants in researching, teaching and protesting nuclear issues. They suggested most studies focused on 'old' wars and were therefore in danger of being useless for understanding the 'new' contexts of war (Kaldor, 2014) that were emerging. However, one valuable contribution to this endeavour was highlighted: C. Wright Mills' (1959) *The Causes of World War Three*. Described as employing a similar conceptual framework to his previous work in *The Power Elite* (Mills, [1956] 2000), Mills (1959) took nuclear armament as his central issue to stage a reassessment of the concept of 'power' (Kramer and Marullo, 1985). As Kramer and Marullo observe, Mills ([1956] 2000, 1959) depicted the geopolitical power wielded by nation-states (that is, the US and Soviet Union) in the aftermath of the Second World War had become distended by, and increasingly centralised within, a small number of influential political organs (that is, government, military and so on). These 'power elites' held sway over major geopolitical decisions that could have catastrophic global consequences (such as nuclear war). Influenced by this work, Kramer and Marullo (1985) went on to identify a number of important issues sociologists could dedicate their time to in order to help progress such critical work. In addition to pointing to the psychological, economic and political effects of nuclear war, their observations included an awareness that the evolution of nuclear war could lead to an undermining of democratic institutions if left unregulated (Kramer and Marullo, 1985). This was also an acknowledgement that technology had reconfigured the ways in which wars are fought in modernity (that is, from 'old' to 'new'; see Kaldor, 2014), and recognised that a focus on nuclear issues should serve as a platform to take account of other social conflicts (Kramer and Marullo, 1985). As we will come to learn (here and in Chapter Six), this approach to these issues informed Kramer's later criminological work on nuclear war, and other forms of 'new' war (Kaldor, 2014).

Crimes of the 'American nuclear state'

Guided by Kramer's sociological approach to conceptualising nuclear issues, David Kauzlarich's (1994) later work addressing US nuclear threats during the Korean and Vietnam wars (discussed later) helped establish this aspect of criminological studies of war. In a first attempt to outline the viability for using international law as an analytic framework through which to consider state activity criminal, Kauzlarich et al (1992) depicted US nuclear armament, and US intervention in Nicaragua during the Cold War as 'organised criminal violence'. This was followed by a more focused account of the theoretical and legalistic means by which the US nuclear state could be understood to have violated the laws of war through their use, testing and threat to use nuclear weapons (Kauzlarich, 1995), later defined as 'nuclear terrorism' (Kauzlarich and Kramer, 1995). Kauzlarich (1997) then followed with an updated discussion on the technical illegality of nuclear weapons following a ruling from the International Court of Justice (that is, the 'World Court') in 1996 that their use was 'generally' contrary to international law (discussed later) as existing under the remit of the UN, before, during and after the Second World War. The zenith of this work is captured in a later formative book. During the same year as Jamieson's (1998) seminal chapter emerged advocating a 'criminology of war in Europe' (discussed in Chapter Two), Kauzlarich and Kramer's (1998) *Crimes of the American Nuclear State: At Home and Abroad* was published. Building on their previous body of work, this book established a critical criminological position to conceptually and legally address the production, threat, usage, human testing and environmental consequences of nuclear weapons by US authorities as 'state crimes'. This is achieved by situating the broad analytic framework of their argument in the historical context of the Cold War. Before exploring the analysis offered by Kauzlarich and Kramer (1998) in some detail, we provide a sketch of this era to set their argument in context.

Enter the Cold War

The first US nuclear weapons programme, known as the Manhattan Project (1942–45), was principally designed as a strategy to pursue the development of nuclear weapons for the defeat of Nazi Germany during the Second World War (see Futter, 2015). However, following Nazi Germany's surrender to Allied Forces during 1945, US attention to the production and use of nuclear weapons turned to ending the US war in the Pacific against Japan (Futter, 2015). In the first of two mass acts of violence intended to end the war, on 6 August 1945 US President Truman sanctioned the world's first use of a nuclear bomb on the Japanese city of Hiroshima. Three days later, President Truman ordered the second use of a further nuclear bomb on the Japanese city of Nagasaki. These nuclear attacks ended the war in the Pacific following the surrender of Japan to Allied Forces and ceased the hostilities of the Second World War (Futter, 2015). Whether such attacks were a necessary and proportionate means by which to end the war remain points of historical contention.

The bombs dropped on Hiroshima and Nagasaki respectively became the first and last nuclear weapons to be used against another nation as overt acts of war. However, despite the mass human devastation these weapons caused, and their use being contrary to the laws of war, their production, accumulation and testing intensified in the years following the Second World War (Futter, 2015). Between 1945 and 1989 the Cold War ensued, depicted by Kauzlarich and Kramer (1998) as a long-standing war between the US and the Soviet Union, two of the victorious forces of the Second World War. Despite comprising part of the forces that defeated Nazi Germany in Europe, both nations were ideologically divided along lines of capitalism (US) and communism (Soviet Union), and each were vying for geopolitical power in opposition of the other's sociopolitical, economic and military ideals. A fundamental part of this hostility was the continued pursuit and further development of nuclear technologies, and stockpiling of nuclear weapons. Presented with opportunities to expand their own geopolitical influences in the post–Second World War era, the US and Soviet Union's pursuit of nuclear weapons, compounded by their opposing political ideologies, witnessed both nations posturing with, rather than using, their accumulation of nuclear weapons and technology.

The Cold War era therefore sets the scene for the changing contexts of warfare in the years immediately following the Second World War. And, as Kaldor (2014: 3) observes, this 'new' type of organised violence, characterised but not defined by advancing weapons technologies, also reflected a 'new reality' of war that began to emerge before the end of the Cold War. However, these historical periods not only became the social backdrop of Kauzlarich and Kramer's (1998) work relating to nuclear war; their analysis also brought other important wars during this era into view.

The Cold War and 'nuclear extortion': from the Korean war to the Vietnam war

Building on the geopolitical issues that emerged in the aftermath of the Second World War, Kauzlarich and Kramer (1998) directed attention to the importance of understanding the contexts of both the Korean (1950–53) and Vietnam (1955–75) wars as having relevance to criminological analysis. In doing so, we learn that consecutive US presidential administrations (from Truman to Nixon) had considered the use of nuclear weapons in one form or another, influenced by their deployment in Hiroshima and Nagasaki.

Following the resolution of the Korean War in 1953 that witnessed the country split into North and South regions, we further learn from Kauzlarich and Kramer (1998) that the US's 'policy of containment' – to prevent the expansion of communism and influence of the Soviet Union – persisted throughout the Cold War era. As Kauzlarich and Kramer (1998) detail, during the McCarthy era this included: US support for the French occupation of Vietnam (1950–55) and the installation of a Vietnamese president (Ngo Diah Diam) in the South; the deployment of US troops in Lebanon in 1958 to quell the expansion of the Soviet Union in the Middle East (the Lebanon Crisis); and involvement in the Suez Crisis (1956), which effectively became the final action of colonial British imperialism. Post-McCarthyism, this continued to include: the construction of the Berlin Wall separating occupying powers in East and West Germany (1961–89); the failed attempted invasion of Fidel Castro's Cuba (which held diplomatic relations with the Soviet Union) by US-trained Cuban exiles (the

1961 Bay of Pigs); and the Cuban Missile Crisis (1962), whereby Soviet ships carrying nuclear weapons were blockaded by the US Navy from accessing Soviet missile bases in mainland Cuba (Kauzlarich and Kramer, 1998). In addition, as Kauzlarich and Kramer (1998: 82–92) note, the engagement of the US in the Vietnam war, from their point of incursion (1955) until their withdrawal (1973), reflected their ongoing 'containment policy' of communism employed throughout the Cold War, including President Nixon's plans to threaten the use of nuclear weapons against North Korea (the 'November Ultimatum' in 1969). Aided by a highly influential US anti-war movement, the use of nuclear weapons in Vietnam never transpired (see Friedrichs, 2010, for a brief overview of why US involvement in Vietnam may be considered a form of state criminality). However, although not deployed again throughout the Cold War era, for Kauzlarich and Kramer (1998: 38) the threat to use nuclear weapons by the American nuclear state is considered a form of 'nuclear extortion', a violent (and masculine) posturing informed by the previous use of nuclear weapons against civilians in Hiroshima and Nagasaki (the gendered nature of war is commented on further in Chapter Seven).

The backdrop of the Cold War outlined by Kauzlarich and Kramer (1998) demonstrates the importance of contextualizing the historical periods within which wars take place (see for example, Kramer and Marullo, 1985; Jamieson, 1998). Not only do we learn the relevance of the Korean and Vietnam wars to better situate the Cold War era (see also the historical documentary by Burns and Novick, 2017), we are also made aware of additional criminological studies exploring how war changes over time, is aided by technology, and becomes disproportionately concentrated at civilian targets (discussed further in Chapter Six). Given the uniqueness of Kauzlarich and Kramer's (1998) work, for the remainder of this chapter we use it to help illustrate, and further assemble, ways of thinking critically about war. First we address how the production, usage and stockpiling of nuclear weapons are conceptually and legally defined as a form of 'state crime', beyond the more opaque notion of 'nuclear extortion'.

Conceptualising the use and threat of nuclear weapons as 'state crime'

Kauzlarich and Kramer (1998) attempt to rectify the neglect of nuclear weapons in the social sciences by drawing them into criminological debate under the auspices of 'state crime'. Thus the (US) 'state' is depicted as a social actor capable of perpetrating 'socially injurious' acts and behaviour (Kauzlarich and Kramer, 1998: 10). More specifically Kauzlarich and Kramer's (1998) conceptualisation of the 'state' included: various political and social entities, such as government leaders, government departments with responsibility for nuclear energy and weapons development, the military, private nuclear contractors, health services, and university institutions and researchers. However, as Kauzlarich and Kramer (1998) note, at their time of writing there was no one international law or treaty that specifically outlawed the uses, threat, production or possession of nuclear weapons by the 'state' when thought of in these terms.

To overcome this problem, Kauzlarich and Kramer (1998) and later Kramer and Kauzlarich (2010) substantiated nuclear issues as 'state crimes' within a statutory framework. This included a resort to international law (that is, the laws of war) that de facto prohibit the use of nuclear weapons between states due to their known capacity to cause mass human suffering, including the Geneva Gas Protocol (1925), the Genocide Convention (1948) and the Geneva Conventions I–V (1949), all of which – in one form or another – cater for the non-proliferation of weapons of mass destruction in conventional law (Kauzlarich and Kramer, 1998). In addition, Kauzlarich and Kramer (1998) suggest customary laws may deem state actions and behaviour in their use of nuclear weapons as illegal due to being beyond the moral spirit of non-bellicose citizens, despite not being specifically codified in the laws of war.

Furthermore, the threat to use nuclear weapons (as demonstrated throughout the Cold War by the US and Soviet Union) were also considered illegal under two separate instruments. First, the UN Charter, as the key mechanism with which to identify when states are permitted to use force against one another 'legally' within international law. More specifically, Article 51 of the UN Charter (the recourse to self-defence if attacked by another nation) and Article 2(4) (the prohibition of the threat or use of force), on how states can seek recourse to war violence 'legally', and are prevented from committing acts of war 'illegally', as agreed by the UN Security Council (Kramer and Kauzlarich, 2010). As such, threats to use nuclear weapons as a means of 'nuclear extortion' by the US (or other nations) when no direct attack has occurred would make any such threat unlawful. Second, the Nuremberg Principles (1946), as derived from the Nuremberg Charter developed in the aftermath of the Holocaust, make the conspiracy, planning, and intentional use of mass violence to exterminate populations, crimes against peace, war crimes and crimes against humanity (discussed in Chapter Four) (Kauzlarich and Kramer,

1998). Therefore, the targeting of civilian populations and conspiracy to cause mass atrocity make the threat of using and possessing nuclear weapons illegal within the laws of war.

However, given that none of these instruments explicitly make nuclear weapons illegal, particularly as many were created prior to, or at the outset of, the nuclear age, their application may appear equally as opaque as the notion of 'nuclear extortion' (Kauzlarich, 1995). However following requests from the World Health Organization and the UN General Assembly for an advisory opinion on the status of nuclear weapons within international mechanisms (as noted earlier), the judicial organ of the UN, the International Court of Justice (ICJ), ruled in 1996 that the use or threat to use nuclear weapons would 'generally be illegal in international law' (Kramer and Kauzlarich, 2010: 70). As Kramer and Kauzlarich (2010: 72) note,

> All the judges [of the ICJ] agreed that there could be no doubt as to the applicability of these principles to a possible threat or use of nuclear weapons, despite the fact that these principles and rules had evolved prior to the invention of nuclear weapons.

Although not being able to *definitively* judge if the use of nuclear weapons would be illegal in the most extreme circumstances imaginable, the result of this ruling was the constitution of the Nuclear Non-Proliferation Treaty (NPT) (UNODA, 1968). As defined by the United Nations Office for Disarmament Affairs, the NPT is 'a landmark international treaty whose objective is to prevent the spread of nuclear weapons and weapons technology, to promote cooperation in the peaceful uses of nuclear energy and to further the goal of achieving nuclear disarmament and general and complete disarmament' (UNODA, n.d.a).

All five designated nuclear states (US, UK, Russia, France and China) have signed the NPT; other states, either known (India, North Korea and Pakistan) or presumed (Israel), to have nuclear weapons have not (see UNODA, n.d.b; see also Futter, 2015). Almost fifty years later during 2017, following the advocacy work of the International Committee to Abolish Nuclear Weapons (ICAN, n.d.), the Treaty on the Prohibition of Nuclear Weapons (TPNW) was adopted by the UN and opened for signatures by UN member states (see UN, 2017). If signed and ratified by 50 nations, the TPNW will become the first legally binding instrument prohibiting nuclear weapons, outlawing them alongside already prohibited biological and chemical weapons (UNODA, 2017). However, all five nuclear states objected and did not vote for the TPNW, and at the time of writing none of the states noted above, who are either known or suspected of possessing nuclear weapons, have signed or ratified the treaty (see ICAN, 2018; UNODA, 2018).

The work of Kauzlarich and Kramer (1998) therefore urges us to pay attention to both the conceptual and legal conditions (past and present) under which nuclear issues resemble 'state crimes' and may be considered internationally illegal. However, it is at this point we are compelled to question the limitations that such a legal framework places on our capacity for further critical analysis. Indeed, what is perhaps most evident from the discussion earlier are the discrepancies between the ongoing irresponsibility of nuclear states not to ban nuclear weapons via international treaties, and the continued possession of nuclear armaments by these 'power elites' (Mills, 1959), despite such actions being contrary to the essence of the laws of war.

Nuclear proliferation

As Futter (2015) points out, the stockpiling of nuclear weapons since the Manhattan Project in 1945 has occurred vertically (that is, via expansion from existing nuclear armed states) and horizontally (that is, via the establishment and expansion of newly armed nuclear states). At the time of Futter's (2015) analysis, estimates of these stockpiles ranged from between 8,000 (Russia) to 225 (UK) warheads within signatory nuclear states to the NPT (that is, vertical proliferation), and between 100 (India) to fewer than 10 (North Korea) in nuclear states who are not signatories of the NPT. Israel is also suspected of possessing approximately 80 nuclear warheads (that is, horizontal proliferation) (Futter, 2015). Explanations for such proliferation vary from political disagreements on the levels and processes of nuclear weapons reduction, their geopolitical value to establish or maintain geopolitical status between nations within modernity, and their production being the inevitable consequence of technological advancements in modernity (Futter, 2015). Perhaps the most prevalent explanation for nuclear weapons proliferation is distrust between nuclear states, and their production as a deterrence against the threat of nuclear attack from other nuclear states (Futter, 2015). Nevertheless, despite the well-founded conceptual and legal frameworks for designating the possession, threat and use of nuclear weapons as illegal 'state crimes' within international law, such justifications for their continued production and possession further illuminate the paradox that exists between the proliferation and illegality of nuclear weapons. How, then, might we explain why nuclear armament persists, and how could we approach nuclear issues differently to further our critical understanding? One answer to this first question lies in thinking a little differently about the matter of 'deterrence'; an answer to the second rests on how such war is defined conceptually.

Deterrence and nuclear weapons

Although vertical and horizontal proliferation of nuclear weapons has significantly declined since the end of the Cold War (at its peak estimated at 63,632 nuclear stockpiles globally in 1985), current stockpiles of nuclear warheads worldwide are still substantial (estimated at 16,300 in total) (Futter, 2015: 3). As such, it is possible to question the value of the laws and treaties established to govern their proliferation (including the potential impact of the TPNW, if ratified), and – importantly – the ways in which both nuclear and non-nuclear states respond to such governance. With regards to international criminal justice, Rothe and Mullins (2010) suggest the efficacy of international laws (such as those noted earlier) need to be considered in relation to both the ways in which state entities and state officials regard them in terms of deterrence and legitimacy. They suggest the presumption that international laws are de facto effective in deterring states from violating treaties, committing atrocities and perpetrating war crimes is 'premature' (Rothe and Mullins, 2010). Indeed,

> most committers of atrocities do not *perceive* international law or a given country's law as a threat for prosecuting their behavior, especially given the history of impunity and common tactics which are employed to ensure deniability (e.g., propaganda, political pressures, plausible deniability, and techniques of neutralization). (Rothe and Mullins, 2010: 102, emphasis in original)

In brief, if international laws and treaties are not perceived as a threat at both structural (that is, public) and interactional (that is, individual) levels of society, their 'general deterrence is negated' (Rothe and Mullins, 2010: 102). Furthermore, if not considered legitimate (that is, are not ratified such as the TPNW currently, or are considered outmoded by UN member states or go unacknowledged by non-UN member states), then they are unlikely to be considered as legitimate governance, rendering their deterrent effects nonexistent (Rothe and

Mullins, 2010). As Kramer and Michalowski (2005, 2006) have well evidenced, the 2003 invasion of Iraq stands as an enduring example of how international law (that is, the UN Charter) failed to have any deterrent effects against illegitimate war violence by the US against Iraq (discussed in Chapter Three). As Mullins (2011: 933) illustrates, during the 2008 Georgia–Russia conflict it was not only the Russian state that failed to enforce the Geneva Conventions to moderate war violence, 'the worst of the crimes were committed by non-state actors, the South Ossetian militia'. Taking Rothe and Mullins' (2010) argument as apposite to nuclear armament, we might therefore suggest that those who do not consider international law as a deterrent due to their capacity to practise realpolitik regarding nuclear issues, they are also unlikely to consider them threatening or adhere to their governance (that is, those designated nuclear states who are signatory states of the NPT). Whereas, those who do not consider international law as a legitimate authority are likely to find rationalist ways to construct international law as invalid, and not adhere to its principles (that is, states known and presumed to have nuclear weapons but are not signatory states of the NPT) (Rothe and Mullins, 2010). Indeed, the current non-ratification of the TPNW aligns both signatories and non-signatories of the NPT into the same position of defiance vis-à-vis nuclear disarmament and prohibition.

Therefore, despite criminological work assisting in conceptually and legally denoting the use and threat of nuclear weapons as a state crime, perhaps the recourse to yet further codified international definitions of crime does put limitations on the type of analysis that can be gleaned from this way of thinking. To pivot towards other ways of exploring nuclear issues, we turn our attention back to the original analysis of Kauzlarich and Kramer (1998) to ask *what about the victims of nuclear state crimes?*

Victimisation and the nuclear state

Kauzlarich and Kramer (1998) illustrate how the crimes of the nuclear state extended to harms caused to both human subjects and the environment through the production and testing of nuclear materials. In their analysis, they foreground the practice of the US government conducting human radiation experiments on both members of the public and prisoners. In events that only surfaced during the late 1990s, it is clear that members of the public suffering from health problems such as cancer were injected with plutonium under the premise of 'treatment', but without their consent (Kauzlarich and Kramer,

1998). Testicular irradiation experiments were also carried out on prisoners incarcerated in several US penitentiaries and, although some are evidenced as having given basic forms of consent, details of this, and an awareness of the consequences, were questionable (Kauzlarich and Kramer, 1998). Here not only is the wanton behaviour of the US in flouting international law and international humanitarian law identified, but we are made aware that despite such non-consensual experimentation on human subjects being prohibited by the Nuremberg Code (1947), it continued to be practised in secret by the US nuclear state throughout the Cold War era (Kauzlarich and Kramer, 1998). However, although partially bringing victimisation into view, Kauzlarich and Kramer (1998) never fully pursued farther-reaching matters of victimising state practices in significant detail, such as the consequences of nuclear deaths and harms that occurred 'abroad' (as the subtitle of their book suggests). However, it is possible to excavate this further to consider the effects of such war making and victimisation (consequences which the TPNW aims to recognise and address). In order to do so we must reconceptualise our understanding of this type of 'new' war (Kaldor, 2014).

Reconceptualising war as 'degenerate'

As Martin Shaw (2003) argued, the mass slaughter of civilians has been witnessed on an unimaginable scale during the 20th and 21st centuries. Shaw (2003) makes the distinction between three notions of such mass victimisation. First, as Kaldor (2014) has done (discussed in Chapter One), Shaw (2003) draws on the general rationalist model of warfare offered by Clausewitz ([1832] 1997). Next, as discussed in Chapter Four, he defines the notion of genocide, understood as the intentional mass execution, persecution, displacement and dehumanisation of civilian groups, targeted by state and military entities via mass violent racist acts and social ordering processes (Shaw, 2003). The third notion of mass violence discussed by Shaw (2003) nestles between these two concepts of war and genocide. In brief, given that genocides have disproportionately occurred throughout history during times of war, Shaw (2003) suggests the term 'degenerate war' is perhaps more useful conceptually to demarcate and analyse the destructive capacity and consequences of modern war, particularly in an era characterised by 'new' forms of war (Kaldor, 2014). This concept is informed by an awareness that a Clausewitzean definition of 'old' war should not be considered as an unchanging or unchanged phenomenon in modernity (see for example, Giddens, 1985; Kaldor, 2014). The ways in which this becomes analytically useful for our purposes is that it helps foreground not only how wars are now fought, but who disproportionately suffers as a result of war violence: civilians.

Defining 'degenerate' war

As Kaldor (2014) describes, in the shift between 'old' and 'new' wars during the 20th and 21st centuries, war violence has changed, and been changed by not only geopolitical developments and social relations, but also technological advancements and a change in the actors and organisations who enact such violence. Each has come to disproportionately target civilians. Although Kaldor (2014) only considered advanced weapons technologies to have aided the emergence of 'new' wars rather than characterising them, Shaw (2003) implies that the decimation of civilians via 'degenerate' war violence is the foremost consequence of such technological developments (such as nuclear and 'precision' weapons). As he describes,

> The dialectic between discriminating aims and indiscriminate results is the key to the meaning of *degeneration* in modern war. It involves simultaneously:
>
> 1. the extended definition of the enemy as civilian as well as military;
> 2. the deliberate targeting of elements of the civilian population as well as military forces;
> 3. intensified means of destruction which killed more people more speedily and efficiently;
> 4. but also increasingly indiscriminate slaughter which killed people across broader areas with little precision as to their membership of an enemy group. (Shaw, 2003: 25, emphasis in original)

In view of our previous discussion of nuclear state crimes (see Kauzlarich and Kramer, 1998), reconceptualising war as 'degenerate' is emblematic of how the targets of war violence changed with the ascension of the nuclear bomb. In making this distinction, and putting the civilian targets in the foreground of how war is waged in modernity, our attentions are firmly shifted from the realm of the *criminal* nuclear state to those pertaining to the *victimising* nuclear state.

From nuclear state crime to nuclear state victimisation

The later work of Kauzlarich et al (2001) and Rothe and Kauzlarich (2014) provides ways to advance conceptualising state crime similar to our previous observations. The stated intention within this body of work is to emphasise and study the victimisation *caused* as a result of state crime as a far-reaching endeavor of critical criminology and (radical) victimology. An exemplar of this can be found in a later update to Kauzlarich and Kramer's (1998) *Crimes of the American Nuclear State*. In a rejoinder, Kramer and Kauzlarich (2010) more fully addressed a notable omission from their original analysis: the 'degenerate' bombings of Hiroshima and Nagasaki, and the human costs of detonating nuclear weapons against civilians. It is to this pivotal moment in history during the transition from old to new wars (Kaldor, 2014) that we now turn to illustrate how nuclear state victimisation might be envisaged.

Human nuclear annihilation

As Kramer and Kauzlarich (2010: 74) point out, '[t]he basic facts concerning the atomic bombings of Hiroshima and Nagasaki are clear.' The first detonation of a five-ton uranium bomb above a hospital in Hiroshima (a city of approximately 350,000 people) had utterly devastating human consequences. 'Little Boy', as the bomb was known, killed an estimated 70,000–100,000 people in its initial blast, causing a further estimated 100,000 deaths in the years that followed through radiation-related sickness and disease (Kramer and Kauzlarich, 2010). The detonation of a second (plutonium) bomb, known as the 'Fat Boy', dropped over the city of Nagasaki (with an estimated population of 270,000 people) initially killed between 40,000–70,000 people, mounting to an eventual total estimate of 140,000 people (Kramer and Kauzlarich, 2010). As such, the *estimated* cost to human lives caused by the US detonating these two nuclear bombs is well over 300,000 people; significantly more than the population of Nagasaki at the time, and almost equal to the total population of Hiroshima during 1945 (see for example, Futter 2015).

Citing large death tolls, however, abstracts the factual occurrences of these nuclear bombs from their lived consequences. Harnessing the personal testimonies of survivors from Hiroshima and Nagasaki, Paul Ham (2013) provides biographical accounts of the utterly macabre scenes of the aftermath of these nuclear weapons. From survivor accounts we learn that the blasts and their aftermath created myriad death, destruction and misery: from the initial melting and burning of skin, flesh, bone and steel alike, to the instant boiling of rivers and lakes; from blindness, decapitation and amputation to the helplessness of scorched human organs; from the immediate decimation of non-human animals, plants, trees and physical infrastructure to bodies instantly turned to ash or made literally into shadowy imprints; from the instant or slow and painful loss of loved ones to long-term emotional, physical and health consequences of living in the aftermath with psychological or physical trauma; from sickness and death induced by radiation at the time of the blasts to radiation-related illnesses passed on through generations (see Ham, 2013, chapters 17 and 19 for detailed survivor accounts of Hiroshima and Nagasaki, respectively). The accounts provided by Ham (2013) are almost too inconceivable to qualify with words, images or even video footage (see for example, Barnouw, 1970). Suffice to say, there is no doubt that the consequences of detonating nuclear weapons are devastatingly violent, bluntly undiscriminating, utterly morbid, and mercilessly victimising. Indeed, like genocides, they epitomise state victimisation in its most extreme form (Jamieson, 1998).

When considered as victimisation this form of degenerate war can never be conceptualised as a rationalist instrument of state violence (contra to Clausewitz, [1832] 1997). However, what perhaps deepens such disturbing consequences is that the primitiveness of these nuclear weapons meant they were only operating at a fraction of their full deadly potential:

> The destructive capacity of these bombs shocked the world as two bombs inflicted the equivalent damage of several hundred aircraft each dropping thousands of pounds of conventional bombs. However, compared with modern nuclear weapons, these bombs [Little Boy and Fat Man] – with yields of between 15 and 20 kilotons – look disturbingly mild. (Futter, 2015: 25)

Futter (2015) continues to note that if more advanced technology of the hydrogen bomb (or thermonuclear bomb, with a yield of more than 50 megatons) were dropped in densely populated areas today, the destruction would *exceed* that inflicted on Hiroshima and Nagasaki. Indeed, it could result in the annihilation of entire countries, or 'even life as we know it' (Futter, 2015: 25). Yet there has been a continued desire by nuclear states to advance this deadly technology further, and here we find other – more hidden – civilian consequences of this form of degenerate war. Although not addressed in Shaw's (2003) earlier definition, it is through studying the degenerate consequences of nuclear issues that we are made aware the environment also suffers the victimisation of war violence.

From human destruction to environmental despoliation

As noted earlier, although not addressing the impact of nuclear testing 'abroad' in their analysis, Kauzlarich and Kramer (1998) did identify at length how the production of nuclear materials contaminated the environment at 'home'. They acknowledged the management of nuclear energy production in the US was driven by both secrecy (established by the Manhattan Project), and an 'organisational' imperative to deliver privately funded contracts on behalf of the Department of Energy and Department of Defense (Kauzlarich and Kramer, 1998). In addition to a lack of interdepartmental oversight of production and disposal of nuclear (waste) materials, Kauzlarich and Kramer (1998: 116) suggest this led to a 'weapons culture complex'. This 'culture' resulted in the careless contamination of the environment, in violation of environmental and health and safety regulations, and operated anonymously for decades without external and independent checks and balances (Kauzlarich and Kramer, 1998, 2006). Deviance in the production of nuclear materials was thereby institutionally 'normalised' and, although not being detonated – as Harding (1983) also made abundantly clear – the domestic production and proliferation of nuclear weapons are core aspects of criminological concerns, to study and protest nuclear armament as forms of organisational deviance and state victimisation.

Nuclear weapons have, of course, not been deployed as weapons of war since 1945. However, as Futter (2015) points out, since then there have been more than 2,000 nuclear tests conducted worldwide by nuclear states. Although now completely banned under the Comprehensive Nuclear-Test-Ban Treaty (CTBT), many states (China, North Korea, India, Israel, Egypt, Iran and Pakistan) including the US have still to ratify this treaty (see UNODA, 1996). As noted earlier, although not principally addressing this in their original analysis, instead choosing to discuss the testing of nuclear materials on human subjects, Kauzlarich and Kramer (1995) and Kauzlarich (1997) did make brief mention of this in previous work in relation to US-occupied islands in the Pacific. Throughout the Cold War era, Pacific territories inhabited by the US military were frequently used as the testing sites for hydrogen bombs. More specifically, as Kauzlarich and Kramer (1995), Kauzlarich (1997) and McGarry and Walklate (2018) point out, the inhabited Marshall Islands of Bikini Atoll became the testing sites for 23 nuclear and hydrogen bombs (between 1945 and 1958), weapons significantly more powerful than those dropped on Hiroshima and Nagasaki.

Similar to the US human test subjects of plutonium and uranium experiments identified by Kauzlarich and Kramer (1998), the Marshall Islanders not only unknowingly participated in the testing of US nuclear weapons technologies long after the Nuremberg Code (1947) was established, but the environment within which they lived was also exposed to the toxic impacts of nuclear radiation which has made many of the Marshall Islands uninhabitable ever since (Center for Political Ecology, 2014). In acts resulting from the 'violence(s) of militarism' (McGarry and Walklate, 2018), the impacts of this nuclear testing had devastating physical and structural consequences for the Marshall Islanders and the Atoll islands, including radiation sickness, skin conditions, cancers and physical disabilities. This is in addition to the decimation of their cultural livelihoods and practices through forced displacement, and the toxic contamination of the soil, marine life, air and water (Center for Political Ecology, 2014). This victimisation remains an enduring legacy imposed on the habitat of the Marshall Islands, its residents and their future generations (McGarry and Walklate, 2018). As the Center for Political Ecology documented for the UN Human Rights Council:

> The RMI [Republic of the Marshall Islands] Islands Nuclear Claims Tribunal recognizes some 36 forms of radiogenic cancers and disease as resulting from nuclear weapons test exposures. A review of Tribunal awards in 2007 found that most awards were for thyroid cancers and disease, pulmonary and lung cancer, cancers of the blood, bone marrow, and lymph nodes, breast cancer, and cancers of the ovary. Chronic and acute radiogenic exposure creates documented impact on cardiovascular system function, impacts immune system response, and creates a population-wide vulnerability to infectious and non-communicable disease. For example, worldwide some 1/3 of the human population carries the bacterium for tuberculosis; but most people do not become sick as their immune systems fight off infection. In 2005, the Marshall Islands the tuberculosis rate was some 23 times the rate of the US. In 2011, Marshallese mortality rates for TB were the highest rate in the Pacific, and fourth highest in the world. Other infectious disease runs rampant. (Center for Political Ecology, 2014: 6)

We must therefore also remain cognisant of the testing of nuclear weapons 'abroad' as it were (see Kauzlarich and Kramer, 1998), and the consequences that this can bring to both humans and non-human animals, the environment and – as crucially witnessed in the Marshall Islands – the indigenous rights of Indigenous peoples (see for example Cunneen and Tauri, 2016, returned to in our concluding Chapter Eight).

New 'green' horizons?

Of course, these final observations are far from original. Put to the fore within Harding's (1983) first criminological concerns for nuclear issues, was not so much the mass scale of human loss due to a nuclear detonation, but how the earth would be irreversibly damaged to no longer sustain human life (see also Schell, 1982). It was therefore the harmful (read victimising) effects to the environment that was initially foregrounded as a key problem for criminologists to grapple with regarding nuclear issues, and not international legal matters related to 'state crimes', as Kauzlarich and Kramer (1998) outlined. As O'Sullivan and Walters (2016) have pointed out, it is harms such the despoliation of the environment – whereby land, air, water systems and marine life come to be destroyed by violent human behaviour – that are frequently overlooked as being part of the victimising consequences of war violence. Inversely, the oversight of war continues to be found, for example, in other more recent calls for 'cultural' developments in victimology to take account of 'green' issues, including harms to the ecosystem and non-human animals (see Hall, 2017; although see Hediger, 2017, on the uses of animals in war as a form of abuse). However, it would be incorrect to suggest that criminological scholars concerned with 'green' issues have been ignorant to the importance of considering war as part of their concerns. For example, in the same year as Kauzlarich and Kramer (1998) published *Crimes of the American Nuclear State*, Nigel South (1998) directly appealed for war to be considered one of the 'ten connections' criminologists could make vis-à-vis 'green' issues. Citing Jamieson's (1998) move 'towards a criminology of war in Europe' as *the* connection point for such work, he observed that 'Green issues are also relevant to the emerging criminological study of other 'new' topics of international global importance, notably war crimes … and violations of human rights' (South, 1998: 226).

McClanahan and Brisman (2015) later reconnected 'green' issues with war: addressing war in its metaphorical form (discussed in Chapter Three), they object to waging a 'war on climate change' as policy makers, politicians and industry leaders advocate. Doing so merely assumes the utility of 'war-making' and 'weaponised' solutions to environmental issues which separate humanity from the environment itself and can only cause more damage in the process (McClanahan and Brisman, 2015). Instead, they propose that by 'recognizing humanity's place *in* nature, rather than *above* nature, we can in effect sign a peace treaty with the natural world' (McClanahan and Brisman, 2015: 425, emphasis in original). While remaining hopeful of this being achieved, the continued non-ratification of nuclear proliferation treaties from influential global nations (noted earlier) keeps us sceptical of the outcome.

Returning to the specific concerns of this chapter, there are indeed green connections to be made with nuclear issues which should be considered in tandem with the human consequences of war. As passionately noted by Sagan (1983), the longer-term environmental consequences of detonating nuclear weapons, such as occurred in Hiroshima and Nagasaki, was a 'nuclear winter' whereby a 'climate catastrophe' would ensue from the heat, fire, soot/ash and light radiation created by nuclear blasts. Foregrounding the environment as the first in a cascade of health, agricultural, meteorological, structural and policy consequences that would quickly unravel in the aftermath of detonating nuclear weapons, Sagan's solution, like others of his generation (see for example, Schell, 1982; Harding, 1983; Shaw, 1984; Kramer and Marullo, 1985), and as we advocate here, was the decommissioning of nuclear arsenals worldwide, to avert the 'real danger of the extinction of humanity' (Sagan, 1983: 292).

Conclusion

In this chapter we have endeavoured to provide a thorough review, critique and development of extant criminological work relating to nuclear war. By primarily using Kauzlarich and Kramer's (1998) seminal book, *Crimes of the American Nuclear State*, we have sought to illustrate how nuclear issues can be considered as state crimes within international law. In presenting this, we have identified a fixation with matters of prescribed law that may conceptually obscure ways of thinking about war, thereby preventing more far-reaching consideration of the victimising consequences of using and proliferating nuclear weapons and materials. To navigate this problem, we introduced the notion of 'degenerate' war (Shaw, 2003) to help redirect analytical attention from the *crimes* of the nuclear state (which remain important) to *victimisation* from the nuclear state (which we have prioritised).

However, one way of ensuring this agenda is of sustained importance for criminological studies of war is to ensure *both* of these analytical frameworks remain closely interconnected. In doing so, what will always be clear is that it is civilians and the environment who are disproportionately the victims of (criminal) war violence. Next, in Chapter Six, we explore other sociological and criminological work related to 'new' forms of war (Kaldor, 2014) to institute further ways of thinking about war violence as a changing social and gendered phenomenon disproportionately targeted at civilians. We do so by using the discussion here as a platform from which to draw attention to a further prolific and routinised practice of war violence against civilians, ongoing since the Second World War and the Cold War era: the state practice of aerial 'terror bombings'.

SIX

The 'Dialectics of War' in Criminology

Introduction

In the Introduction it was noted that the work of Clausewitz ([1832]1997) depicted war in rationalist terms as a violent entitlement of the state, to be used without limit against an 'enemy' for political ends. However, in what has followed Kaldor's (2014) interpretation of this as an old mode of warfare has been reinterpreted to illustrate that throughout the 20th and 21st centuries war can be understood as a dynamic social phenomenon which has changed into new forms. Importantly, from the Second World War onwards, these 'new' wars disproportionately targeted non-combatant civilian populations during the 'war on terrorism' (Chapter Three), via atrocity and genocide (Chapter Four), during the production, use and proliferation of nuclear weapons (Chapter Five); and, as we will come to learn (in Chapter Seven) through the perpetration of sexual and gender-based violence. In this chapter, we shall problematise further the disproportionate targeting of civilians by concentrating on their continued victimisation through aerial terror bombing. As Ruggiero (2015: 33) points out:

> Estimates suggest that, throughout the nineteenth century, apart from the American civil war, 90 per cent of losses were among fighting troops. In World War I (WWI) deaths of civilians still accounted for 10–15 per cent, becoming around 40 per cent in World War II (WWII).

Contemporarily, civilians are now estimated to total some ninety per cent of all war deaths (Ruggiero, 2015). Indeed, as Steinert (2003: 276) further suggests, the asymmetry of this victimisation meant that 'from the Second World War on, it became safer to be a soldier than a civilian' during war. By exposing this dilemma to sociological analysis, here we argue that the social phenomenon of war comes to form multiple dialogues within civic and intellectual life. Drawing on further work of Martin Shaw (1988a), we outline two interconnected 'dialectics of war' within criminology: first between civilian war victims and the 'deviant' soldier; second between what we have termed the politics of remembering and 'forgetting' war violence. The purposes of examining these two interconnected dialectics are to illustrate that the 'risk-transfer' wars of the 20th and 21st centuries (Shaw, 2005) have come strategically to prioritise the lives of soldiers over the deaths of civilians, and that war making is a relational process. Before undertaking this discussion however, terror bombing is foregrounded as a state crime to set this chapter in context and to offer a point of departure for the analysis which follows.

Terror bombing of civilians: moving beyond state crime

The military strategy of aerial terror bombing, that is the intentional killing of civilians as part of airborne military efforts to defeat 'enemy' states and/or forces, is an enduring facet of contemporary warmaking (Kramer, 2010a). Kramer (2010a) evidences such bombing occurring prior to the Second World War by the Italian and German strafe bombings of the Basque town of Guernica during 1937. Although not the first aerial bombing of civilians, Kramer (2010a) states it was the first time that an undefended European town was attacked by heavy military airpower. It was also the 'first glimpse of the warfare of the future' (Kramer, 2010a: 119). Throughout the Second World War, this strategy became normalised as 'total war' (Kramer and Smith, 2014) and reached its pinnacle with the nuclear bombings of Hiroshima and Nagasaki (discussed in Chapter Five) (Kramer and Kauzlarich, 2010). Understood as a form of 'degenerate war' (Shaw, 2003; also discussed in Chapter Five), this strategy of 'total war' was rationalised as being in the moral public interest of ending war violence and saving further lives (Kramer and Kauzlarich, 2010). Then, during the Cold War era, Kauzlarich and Kramer (1998) suggest a political reluctance to use nuclear weapons again as acts of 'hot' war became superseded by the use of 'precision weapons' against civilians (as demonstrated throughout the Vietnam War). As we will learn, this exacerbated and further developed 'degenerate' war making (Shaw, 2003).

With the complete 'redundancy' of nuclear war, military strategists therefore faced a crisis: how to facilitate warfare that did not constitute 'total war' (Shaw, 2005). During the post-Cold War era, the development and use of non-nuclear weapons capitalised on existing deadly weapons technologies to continue bombing civilians indiscriminately in seemingly less malicious ways than via nuclear violence. This is illustrated by the 'conventional' aerial bombings of Syria, Iraq and Afghanistan (discussed later) during the 'war on terrorism' (discussed in Chapter Three). Although not the focus of this chapter, this can also be further evidenced in the use of (un)piloted weaponised drones across these geopolitical spaces, including Pakistan (see, for example, Wall and Monahan, 2011).

Kramer (2010a, 2010b) suggests that during the Second World War the normalisation of aerial bombing as 'degenerate' warfare (Shaw, 2003) was facilitated by its social and cultural construction as a strategy of conducting a morally 'good war'. Killing civilians *and* military targets became moral justifications to end war quickly and save more (Allied military) lives. This strategy was driven by organisational rather than military imperatives; namely pressure to use advances in weapons technologies (Kramer, 2010a, 2010b). For Kramer, however, 'The terror bombing of a civilian population is a moral and legal *state crime* because it violates the "long standing and widespread" moral principle and international legal norm of "noncombatant immunity"' (Kramer, 2010a: 118, emphasis in original).

Indeed, Kramer and Smith (2014) suggest the military practice of aerial terror bombing across history has been a crime facilitated within a paradox created by the laws of war. While the killing of civilians at war has always been illegal within international humanitarian law, such terror bombing was not prosecuted at either the Nuremberg or Tokyo trials in the aftermath of the Second World War and thus de facto legitimised Allied terror bombing of civilians during that war (Kramer and Smith, 2014). Added to the 'elasticity' of how the term 'military necessity' is permitted, past and present, by war-making states such as the US (demonstrated during the 2003 invasion of Iraq, discussed in Chapter Three), as Kaldor (2014) also noted the laws of war have inadvertently served to permit such war violence as rational and 'legitimate' state activity. The practice of bombing civilians has therefore been an enduring facet of war-making from the Second World War onwards. However, its establishment as the *raison d'*être of 'new war' has a specific historical moment. As Kaldor (2014: 32) observes in some detail, the 'war in Bosnia-Herzegovina became the archetypal example, the paradigm of the new post-Cold War type of warfare'.

Beginning in the Balkans: Bosnia-Herzegovina as a 'new paradigm' of war?

Occurring after the dissolution of the former Yugoslavia (as the Cold War came to an end) into five provinces (Serbia, Montenegro,

Kosovo, Bosnia-Herzegovina and Croatia), each 'balanced' so no one ethnic group (Serb, Croat or Muslim) dominated a region, the war in Bosnia-Herzegovina is described by Kaldor (2014: 44) as a 'new nationalist war'. This war was led by aggression from former Serbian president Slobodan Milošević and former Bosnian Serb leader Radovan Karadžic, intent on dividing the regions into distinct ethnic territories and establishing a central state of Serbia by co-opting Croatia and Bosnia-Herzegovina into its sovereignty (Hagan, 2003). Developing from an amalgam of economic insecurity throughout the regions, and corrupt elites struggling to control the 'remnants of the state' (Kaldor, 2014: 36), nationalist identities were reconstructed by Milošević and Karadžic to facilitate war and expand the sovereignty of Serbian territory in Croatia, Bosnia-Herzegovina and Kosovo (discussed later) (Hagan, 2003).

Following Muslims and Croats in Bosnia-Herzegovina voting to leave the former Yugoslavia in 1992, '[d]uring the three years which followed, the country experienced a particularly brutal interethnic conflict that prompted the international community to intervene and broker the Dayton Peace Agreement in December 1995' (Blaustein, 2015: 5).

Supported by Milošević, Karadžic declared an independent Serbian Republic of Bosnia (Republika Srpska) and reconstituted the Yugoslav People's Army into the Bosnia Serb Army (VRS), led by his military chief Ratko Mladić (Hagan, 2003). The war was fought between regular military forces including: the Bosnian Serb Army (VRS), the Croatian Defence Council (HVO) and the Army of Bosnia-Herzegovina (ABiH), in addition to non-regular actors typical of those participating in 'new wars', such as: Serb militia (Tigers and Chetniks, coordinated by the VRS), Croat paramilitary (Croatian Party of Rights and the Wolves, both working with HVO), and Bosnian paramilitary (Green Berets or Muslim Armed Forces, reportedly operating under ABiH) (Kaldor, 2014). Other groups, including the mujahideen, organised criminals and former British soldiers (who trained Bosnian and Croat forces) also participated (Kaldor, 2014). Fundamentally, the strategies of both regular and non-regular actors during this war were to use 'violence to control populations rather than capture territory' (Kaldor, 2014: 51). As we learn from criminological work on this war, such violence included myriad forms of brutal victimisation. In particular, as Hagan (2003: 13) depicts in considerable detail,

> [t]he ethnic cleansing of Prijedor, the siege of Sarajevo, and the massacre at Srebrenica were three of the most devastating of the Bosnia Serbian aggressions against the Bosnian Muslims. Prijedor set a standard for barbarity. Men, women and children were forced from their homes and into detention camps. The Keraterm and Omarska detention facilities in Prijedor became death camps.

A key feature of these genocides and mass population displacements was the perpetration of rape as a weapon of war (Kaldor, 2014), most notably occurring in the mass rape and sexual violence perpetrated in Foca (see Hagan, 2003, chapter 6). As Hagan (2003: 176) continues, both the genocide in Srebrenica and mass rapes in Foca,

> combined to reflect the gendered realities of war, namely, that whereas men tend to get killed, women and children more often are forcibly detained and deported, and young women in particular are at risk of sexual assault and rape. Women are also often left with the challenges of rebuilding the lives of their devastated families.

We return to discuss in detail the gendered nature of war in Chapter Seven (however, see also Nikolic-Ristanovic, 1999, regarding violence against women in the former Yugoslavia).

The 'international community' (that is, UN, NATO and so on) appears to have been reluctant to be drawn into the war in any more than a peacekeeping capacity. This judgement was indicative of the prolonged nature of this war since it became the most continuous European conflict in the post-Second World War era (Kaldor, 2014). Kaldor (2014) suggest this was an error made by a deep conceptual misunderstanding that this war was *not* being fought in traditional Clausewitzean terms (that is, between warring parties for the capture of territory). Indeed, '[h]ad the war been understood as, first and foremost, a war of genocide then the first priority would have been the protection of the civilian population' (Kaldor, 2014: 65).

However, as we learn from Hagan (2003: 14), soon after the Srebrenica genocide occurred, during 1995 'the Clinton administration gave support to NATO bombing of the Bosnian Serbs'. Between 29 August and 14 September 1995 NATO conducted Operation Deliberate Force via the use of airstrikes, flying more than 3,000 sorties and dropping 1,000 bombs on Serbian forces; coupled with the Dayton Settlement (1996–98) to enforce humanitarian interventions a ceasefire was reached and the war ended (Kaldor, 2014). However, as Kaldor (2014: 67) continues, 'airstrikes are a cumbersome instrument for protecting civilians on the ground, and it was the protection of civilians that was needed above all else'.

Civilians during the war in Bosnia-Herzegovina, particularly those who opposed the onslaught of nationalism (Serb, Croat and Bosnian alike; Kaldor, 2014), were victimised twofold: first from being purposefully targeted mainly by hostile Serbian forces on the ground; and second, through the indiscriminate targeting of them from NATO airstrikes from the skies.

The early work of Nikolic-Ristanovic (1998) – published in the same edited volume as Jamieson's (1998) manifesto for a 'criminology of war' – is pioneering in documenting the wider impacts of the gendered nature of this war in relation to domestically occurring crimes (that is, theft, assault and rape), and the involvement of organised criminals in war-making activities (see also Parmantier and Weitekamp, 2014). Most recently, some twenty years later, DiPietro (2019) has presented the impacts of the violence of this war and genocide via biographical research exploring violent offending, masculinity and socio-cultural issues as experienced during the lives of male Bosnian war refugees in the US and Bosnia. Such work allows an appreciation of the violence(s) of this war 'cascading' from the state to civic life (Braithwaite and D'Costa, 2018).

Echoing the words of Ruggiero (2015) earlier, contemporary war-making in Bosnia-Herzegovina had indeed come to be waged against civilians in multiple ways. Moreover, as Kaldor (2014) points out, this 'new' war stands as a historical landmark in the evolution of asymmetrical aerial warfare. Set against this example, and foregrounding the intentional targeting of civilians, for the remainder of this chapter we present a different view of how the violence of new war can differently 'cascade' to become relational within intellectual and civic life. To do so we begin with a sociological view of the deeper conceptual problem of transcending the notion of 'terror bombings' as purely a matter of state crime.

Dialectics of war

Writing prior to the end of the Cold War, in *The Dialectics of War* Shaw (1988a) suggests war endures as a social phenomenon as a contradistinction within society. Not only did war-making derive from social activity (as Clausewitz, [1832] 1997, was clear to point out), the violence it produced would also return to society either directly through killing and brutality, or indirectly though militarism and modalities of social control and surveillance (Shaw, 1988a). Several key features of Shaw's (1988a) analysis offer connections between war and society that reach beyond the killing of civilians via terror bombing as state crime alone. First, the weapons produced by the modern world to facilitate 'new' wars (Kaldor, 2014) would eventually return and destroy it. Second, war and its preparedness (that is, militarism, discussed in Chapter Two) need to be better understood as related social issues providing insight into the impact war has on society. Third, if destruction as a result of war violence is to be avoided, Shaw (1988a) suggests alternative demilitarising perspectives are needed that do not constitute war-making and militarism by other means. For Shaw (1988a), these 'dialectics of war' therefore emerge out of contradictory relationships within society produced by the presence and perpetration of war in the use of advanced technologies (such as nuclear weapons). In other words, they harbour the potential to have impacts on social change, social structures and, ultimately, the outcome of history (Shaw, 1988a).

Although making his argument with reference to nuclear armament (discussed in Chapter Five), the 'dialectics of war' still has conceptual use and contemporary relevance to better understand the 'new' wars of the 20th and 21st centuries (Kaldor, 2014), and those which Shaw (2003, 2005) later termed as 'degenerate' and 'risk-transfer' wars (discussed later). Moreover, by making evident that it is the presence and perpetration of war which creates tensions, divisions and contradictions within society, it is possible to meld this sociological reasoning with a criminological commentary on war.

Civilian war victims and the 'deviant' soldier

Shaw (1988a) acknowledges that the sophistication of weapons technologies (that is, nuclear weapons at his time of writing) are produced by advanced technologies of the industrialised world. Yet, not only are these weapons of war simultaneously hidden out of sight, when used they are returned to societies with 'a most terrible vengeance' (Shaw, 1988a: 10). This predicament, Shaw (1988a) suggests, is an 'arch' over (Western) societies which members of the public are generally unaware of since the realities of war violence are abstracted from social life. As Shaw (1988a) further notes, it is only when extraordinary events occur within societies (that is, a nuclear attack, terrorist attack, or military deaths caused by war) that members of the public become (temporarily) aware of this 'dialectic'. However, when considered in context of new wars such as experienced in Bosnia-Herzegovina (noted earlier), this 'dialectic of war' appears as a lopsided view of the impacts of war violence. To make this conversant with 'new' wars, Shaw's (1988a) analysis requires some reinterpretation with reference to two common actors for criminology: victims and offenders. For the purposes of our argument, discussing these actors helps us to identify the normative logics of the ways in which criminological studies of war have often prioritised the latter, and routinely overlooked the former. This is the crux of the first 'dialectic of war' for criminology.

Civilian victims of war

As Shaw (2005: 5) observed and Kaldor (2014) also pointed out, wars occurring in modernity should not necessarily be defined only by the use of advanced weapons technologies. Instead, the practice of bombing civilians can be understood as a 'new Western way of war', conceptualised in relation to social, political and militarised contexts, and understood as a development from the advent of 'degenerate war' (Shaw, 2005). A crucial distinction between this notion of contemporary war and that of terror bombing (Kramer, 2010a, 2010b) is that the 'new Western way of war' (Shaw, 2005) does not simply target civilians indiscriminately as part of an attack on an 'enemy'. Civilians are instead targeted as part of contemporary risk-taking military strategies, wilfully situated at the centre of war planning rather than indiscriminate and peripheral 'collateral' (Shaw, 2005).

This 'new' Western approach to war fighting has changed gradually from the Cold War era to date. For example, Shaw (2005) illustrates that during the Falklands War (1982) no civilians were killed by NATO forces, against the war deaths of approximately 1,000 Western military and 'enemy' forces (252 and 655 respectively). Contemporarily however, although conducted under different auspices and over a much shorter period, when contrasted with war fighting in Afghanistan (2001 to present), the extent and advancement of a 'new Western way of war' established in the Falklands is sharply revealed (Shaw, 2005). Since the initial US and coalition military invasion of Afghanistan, and subsequent war fighting by the International Security Assistance Force (ISAF) and NATO during 'Operation Enduring Freedom' (2001–14), the civilian casualties in Afghanistan are an entrenched feature of this war. Following the dissolution of ISAF during 2014, fighting has persisted to date, led by Afghan National Security Forces, supported by NATO's 'Resolute Support Mission' and the US's 'Operation Freedom's

Sentinel' (2015 onwards). Crucially, during 2017 the UN once again declared Afghanistan was no longer a post-conflict environment.

The annual report of the United Nations Assistance Mission in Afghanistan (UNAMA, 2018a) documents that between 2009 and 2017, over 28,000 civilians have been killed and more than 50,000 injured. In addition, for the fourth consecutive year more than 10,000 civilians have suffered injuries and death as a result of the ongoing internal conflict (UNAMA, 2018a). During 2017, 65% of all 10,453 civilian casualties were attributed to anti-government forces, including the Taliban (65%), Daesh/ISIL (15%), and those either undetermined or carried out by 'other' anti-government activities (20%) (UNAMA, 2018a). The casualties directly caused by these actors included the use of suicide attacks (22%) and improvised explosive devices (18%) (totalling 40% combined as the leading cause of civilian casualties), and targeted deliberate killings (11%) (UNAMA, 2018a). Responsibility for other deaths and injuries were caused by pro-government forces (20%), including Afghan National Security Forces (80%), international military forces (that is, NATO) (12%), and pro-government armed groups (4%, plus 4% 'other' pro-government groups) (UNAMA, 2018a). The casualties directly caused by these actors primarily came from ground engagements with/against anti-government forces (33%, the second leading cause of civilian casualties) causing 823 deaths and 2,661 injuries; in addition to aerial operations (6%) which accounted for 295 deaths and 336 injuries, a 7% increase from 2016 (UNAMA, 2018a). Finally, what is known as the 'explosive remnants of war' caused by unexploded munitions and landmines, accounted for a further 6% of civilian casualties (164 deaths and 475 injuries), most of whom were children (81% or 142 deaths and 376 injuries) (UNAMA, 2018a). Since 2017 UNAMA (2018b) further reported that on 2 April 2018 Afghan Air Forces conducted airstrikes on Laghmani village, Dasht-e-Archi district of Kunduz province, targeting senior Taliban leaders. During this strike, rockets and heavy machine guns were used during an open-air religious ceremony (*dashtar bandi*) and killed (36) and injured (51) 107 people; most of those killed (30) and injured (51) were confirmed as children (UNAMA, 2018b).

At the time of writing, then, the 'arch' (Shaw, 1988a) of this 'war/crime nexus' (Jamieson, 1998; see also Chapter Three) has been a persistent and unavoidable feature for the people of Afghanistan for almost two decades. As we further learn from Shaw (2005), within this 'new Western' mode of warfare 'degenerate' war is reconceptualised as 'risk-transfer' war wherein political risks are weighed against 'life risks' in which the lives of civilians killed at war come to matter less in terms of their (high) expendability, (low) visibility and lack of sentiment with the public. The priorities in the 'new Western way of war' instead include keeping war-making short and ensuring wars are fought at a proximate and temporal distance to the public (Shaw, 2005). So too must Western forces attempt to minimise civilian casualties as far as practicable, while framing 'small massacres' as the inevitable consequence of war (Shaw, 2005: 84). However, above all else, 'new Western wars' tend to minimise military casualties primarily by relying on the advanced technologies of airpower (Shaw, 2005). The risk of war-making is therefore strategically rather than indiscriminately transferred onto the (dead) bodies of civilians and dictated by 'contemporary forms of subjugation of life to the power of death (necropolitics) [which] profoundly reconfigure the relations among resistance, sacrifice, and terror' (Mbembe, 2003: 39).

Discussing the deaths of civilians at war, such as those documented above, has further depth and complexity. As Zehfuss (2012) details, this complexity is reflected in ideas distinguishing between combatants and non-combatants during war fighting. Thus the nuances of 'non-combatant immunity' is a term which may – like the laws of war – unintentionally afford war as rational and legitimate (Zehfuss, 2012). In addition, the contested notion of 'intent' (also discussed in Chapter Four) demonstrates the conceptual messiness of understanding civilian deaths at war (Zehfuss, 2012). We unfortunately do not have the space to explore these debates in more detail here. In their place, we point out that during the wars in Afghanistan and Iraq, while the biopolitics of military risks (MacLeish, 2015) were being transferred away from the bodies of military personnel and towards the necropolitics of civilian bodies (Mbembe, 2003), the 'self-referential' preoccupations of criminology (Jamieson, 1998) diverted attention towards 'deviant' soldiers and military veterans vis-à-vis locally occurring matters of crime and disorder. In doing so, civilian victims once again became far abstracted from 'thinking the practice of war' (Zehfuss, 2012) within criminology.

The 'deviant' soldier

The depiction of soldiers as 'criminals' and 'deviants' in the post-9/11 era (re)emerged as one of the most prevailing concerns of the discipline. Indeed, myriad studies addressing military veterans' issues now exist in the post-9/11 contexts of 'criminology's third war' (discussed in Chapter Three). This includes, for example: the psychological impacts of war violence as affecting the criminality of ex-military personnel (for example, MacManus et al, 2012, 2013, 2015); substance misuse as contributing risk factors to offending (for example, Albertson et al, 2016, 2017); and the transferability (or not) of militarised institutionalisation between military and prison contexts (for example, Logan and Pare, 2017; May et al, 2017); all of which require treatment, intervention and prevention. Other policy-derived research has more squarely addressed the management of military veterans within criminal justice processes (for example, Kelly, J., 2014; Phillips, 2014; Ford et al, 2016; Fossey et al, 2017). With some exceptions, including those concerned with reintegration between military and civic life as an aggravating element of offending behaviour (for example, Brown W.B., 2008, 2010, 2011, 2015), high-profile policy research (as mentioned above) has been more reluctant to consider the institutionalised context of the military as problematic in respect of subsequent offending. Instead, (in contrast to Bonger, 1916) military experience is considered to have limited influence on the 'deviant' and criminal post-service behaviour of ex-military personnel (for example, Howard League for Penal Reform, 2011; see Treadwell, 2016, for a critical review of these policy-related matters). The most recent of this research has returned to document biographically the normative 'violent veteran' in relation to the social, economic and structural contexts from which they derive, intersecting with military institutionalisation: a process suggested to stagnate an individual's capacity to keep pace with cultural and economic changes of late modernity (see Banks and Albertson, 2018).

Such concerns are among the most prescient contemporary issues within criminology with regards to war (see for example, Murray, 2015, 2016). Their focus on soldiers and military veterans (rather than civilians) is also one of the most enduring within the literature. This is evidenced by previous scholarship which has historically considered war and military service as reducing, or at least not adversely affecting or exacerbating, crime in a domestic context (see for example, Bromberg, 1943; Willbach, 1948; Lunden, 1952; Sampson and Laub, 1993, 1996). Mannheim's (1965) remarks are emblematic of this tradition within criminology. His concerns were directed at the home front in the aftermath of the Second World War, with specific reference to returning (male) soldiers as deviants and criminals, and how the criminogenic and social consequences of their return may be latently, rather than immediately, felt following war (Mannheim, 1965). As noted earlier, such matters were, of course, first raised many years prior by Willem Bonger (1916) and other scholars with concurring views throughout history (see also Gault, 1918; Wagley, 1943).

It is not our interest to unpack the contemporary or historical literature regarding the 'deviant soldier' in further detail here; its modern reinterpretation has indeed been afforded considerable attention within the ongoing interests of the crime/security nexus of 'criminology's third war' (discussed in Chapter Three). Instead, following Tham (1990: 415) we wish to indicate that, '[f]or criminology, war has been seen as a large pseudo-experiment' in respect to these aforementioned concerns, by regarding crime as a social indicator of a well-functioning (that is, non-deviant) society. As Tham (1990) goes on to observe, criminological studies (such as those indicted earlier) reflect significant conceptual constraints within the discipline since they are entirely predicated on legal definitions of crime; classifications that are dependent on power relations (that is, state authority), legitimacy and legality (that is, criminal law) and notions of normalcy (that is, non-offending) at a 'street' level. The returning criminogenic 'military veteran' – both past and present – can therefore be regarded as a perennial negative influence on social (dis)organisation, crime and (dis)order. Under these normative interests, the 'arch' of violent war technologies – this time soldiers operating as 'good machines' (MacLeish, 2015) come into view differently for a public situated at a greater proximity to war violence.

For Bonger (1916) and Tham (1990), such attention to military 'veteran' criminality obscured a detailed insight into the crimes and abuses committed at war that remain unseen and unknown, such as those disproportionately experienced by civilians (discussed in Chapters Four to Six, and herein). Bonger (1916) and Tham (1990) may also have acknowledged within their critiques that preoccupations with soldiers and military veterans have served to render a long-standing and dominant aspect of the criminological study of war as being centred on problems experienced or caused by *men*, largely – but not exclusively – against other men vis-à-vis interpersonal violence. As a result, the gendered nature of war and its violence(s) (discussed in Chapter Seven) becomes assumed as unproblematic and normative, and as a result a contentious issue for a 'criminology of war'. However, in the post-9/11 era these matters have perhaps been further obscured by work not only addressing 'deviant' soldiers as an old concern with renewed focus, but also relating to soldiers – rather than civilians – as victims of war violence (see for example, McGarry and Walklate, 2011). It is this previous work of our own which introduces our second 'dialectic of war'.

Politics of remembering and 'forgetting'

As Shaw (1988a) observed, and as detailed above, the proximity of the production and execution of war violence to everyday life can dictate how the threat of war is known and experienced. To this end, we suggest that long-standing criminological preoccupations with the 'deviant' soldier, and newly identifying the 'soldier as victim' permitted war to become knowable for Western publics through the social construction of their own soldiers. First, by way of their professed 'deviance' (as noted above), and second, through the 'biopolitics' (Foucault, 2004) of their perceived vulnerability as 'victims', or as MacLeish (2015: 15–16) describes, 'good machines':

> The soldier is at once the agent, instrument, and object of state violence. He is coerced and empowered by discipline, made productive by being subject to countless minute and technical compulsions ... The soldier is permitted the sovereign power to kill in the name of upholding the law but also allowed to be killed, placed outside the law's protection as he is sent into harm's way ... And he is the subject of extensive measures to protect and maintain life, to keep him alive and able to continue working, fighting, and killing effectively, a biopolitical subject not merely kept from dying but also made to live.

Hence the second 'dialectic of war' for criminology comes into view.

To illustrate the long-standing normative concerns with the 'deviant' soldier noted above, an intervention in the literature sought to mark a break with 'self-referential' scholarship within criminological studies of war (Jamieson, 1998). By shifting attention onto the harms that soldiers may experience during war, the personal testimonies of British soldiers – many of whom had served in Iraq since 2003 – were presented to conceptualise the 'soldier as victim' (see McGarry and Walklate, 2011). This principally sought to highlight the theoretical inefficacy of victimology as incapable of conceptualising violent victimisation in an extreme (masculine) form. In doing so, an alternative view of the experience of soldiering became evident, one that showed the permeability of boundaries between experiencing, witnessing and perpetrating war and war violence, and sought to challenge the normativity of hegemonic masculine perceptions of soldiering by pointing out some of the vulnerabilities (and mundanity) inherent within warfighting (McGarry and Walklate, 2011). In a further addition, these concerns were situated within a framework of human rights to suggest through inadequate state provision and protection at war the lives of soldiers had been placed in a 'state of exception' (Agamben, 2005) from other legitimate legal (and moral) claims to the right to life (McGarry et al, 2012). It was later proposed that the psychological and physical injuries sustained by soldiers returned from war were illustrative of the 'traces' (Fassin, 2011) of state-enacted war violence (Walklate and McGarry, 2015).

While these issues remain socially, culturally and politically important, we also consider them to be conceptually problematic and recognise their potential to generate a further 'dialectic of war' within criminology. When the 'arch' of war (Shaw, 1988a) becomes recognisable in what has been described as 'military victimhood' (see McGarry, 2015), the ongoing presence of war in society creates tension between who and what is 'remembered' via commemorative practices, and who or what is systematically 'forgotten' through their enactment.

Politics of remembrance

Contemporarily, while war remembrance is situated more closely to our own personal lives (Martinsen, 2013), it no longer relies on being associated with stone structures symbolic of war memorialisation (as depicted on the cover of this book and in Figure 6.1 below). For King (2010: 3), although individual motifs of the war dead have remained a consistent feature of national commemorative practices in the UK, the material practice of war remembrance has been 'continually revised' during the new wars of the 20th and 21st centuries (Shaw, 2005; Kaldor, 2014). For example, as Danilova (2015a) points out, the remembrance of UK soldiers killed at war are indicative of an 'inclusive heroism' in which the war dead become afforded the status of 'hero' as an undifferentiated collective, regardless of how their deaths occurred. Yet even the inclusivity of attributing death 'heroic' status requires distinctions to be made in how it revises the practice of remembrance.

In contrast to our previous observations of civilians killed in Iraq (discussed in Chapter Three) and Afghanistan (discussed earlier) from 2001 onwards, both Zehfuss (2009) and King (2010) have made parallel observations on the commemoration of British military personnel killed in both wars and their memorialisation on Ministry of Defence (2015) obituary web pages (see also Danilova, 2015b, for a further similar study of digital commemorative spaces for military deaths during these wars; and Hamourtziadou, 2016, for an alternative appreciation of the adage 'lest we forget' in relation to civilian victims of the 2003 war in Iraq). For King (2010), a 'postmodern' memory has been established through this contemporary commemorative practice for the 456 British soldiers killed during the war in Afghanistan. As he observes, the digital memorialisation of British soldiers provided

Figure 6.1: Liverpool cenotaph, St George's Hall

© Ross McGarry 2019

textual narratives depicting the deceased not as soldiers in the service of national war-making activities, but in relation to their personal character as professionals; embracing the dangers of war for its virtue as a vocation (King, 2010). Accompanied by images intentionally presented to demilitarise the deceased (that is, depicting them in civilian clothing, or without visible military accoutrements) this digital visualisation of deceased soldiers emerged in lieu of a fixed public Afghanistan war memorial and reconstructed them relationally as fathers, brothers, sons, friends and colleagues (King, 2010).

This form of remembering was not only materially different from the 'lapidary conventions' (King, 2010) of traditional war remembrance practices (depicted in Figure 6.1 above), it also put into relief how depersonalised traditional representations of soldiers on war memorials and cenotaphs had previously been presented. Indeed, as can be seen in Figure 6.1, 'the faces are not of specifically identified soldiers but generic warriors, with fixed expressions and firm chins' (King, 2010: 10). The digital images and text used to account for the (military) 'dead of Helmand' were instead given distinct personalities, deinstitutionalising them from the military and re-socialising them relationally with our own private, professional and civic lives: the British military dead therefore became 'domesticated' (King, 2010). Their remembrance also merged into commemorative practices that existed between and across digital and 'lapidary' spaces of war memorialisation (King, 2010). The crux of this 'domesticating' transformation was its failure to define military deaths in relation to wider national and geopolitical purposes of the wars being fought, instead articulating them in relation to expressions of masculinity and professional soldiering (King, 2010; Danilova, 2015a). Crucially, it is within this process of domesticating the 'professional' war dead as relational subjects that the 'soldier as victim' emerges (for us at least) as problematic.

Danilova (2015a) points out that repackaging the identities of military personnel serving (and killed) at war via their personalities permitted them to be received as vulnerable subjects whose lives required adequate protection by the state from unnecessary harm. Although casting the 'soldier as victim' has been perceived as threatening to the recruitment, retention and practices of the military institution (see McCartney, 2011), their elevation as vulnerable subjects who do not operate in exception of human rights entitlements, King (2010) suggests, potentially undermines social solidarity and/or introduces new ways of arranging solidarity between soldiers, citizens and government (in the manner of Clausewitz's [1832] 1997 'trinity' to facilitate war-making). Herein, the potential arises for 'postmodern memory' to renegotiate war commemoration with the state (King, 2010). The government thereby becomes less free to lose its soldiers at war, particularly if doing so needlessly as a result of inadequate support, equipment and preparation (McGarry, et al, 2012) and renders soldiers' deaths more easily assimilated – and therefore increasingly valued – within public life (King, 2010). Put differently, for Danilova (2015a, 2015b) the acceptance of soldiers as vulnerable subjects transforms their identities (in life and death) from heroes, to 'victims', to 'hero-victims'. This reconceptualisation underpins public perceptions that Western soldiers' lives should be prioritised over those of non-Western civilians (Danilova, 2015a, 2015b). As Carruthers (2014) notes, 'casualty aversion' for civilian *and* military fatalities at war are therefore paradoxical matters.

Politics of 'forgetting'

As Winter (2014) notes, however, the paradoxical relationship of commemorating the war dead as originally established through war memorials and the practices they give affordance to are predicated on the juxtaposition between remembering *and* forgetting. The same may also be inferred from the more contemporary digital spaces where war is commemorated. Indeed, as Lowe and Joel (2013: 13) point out, '[c]ompetition over what is to be remembered and what is to be discarded, of course, is one of the hallmarks of the politics of memory'.

Like remembrance, the notion of 'forgetting' with regards to war commemoration is open to interpretation. Perhaps in its simplest explanation it has been related to the eventual disuse of certain war memorials over time, or wars (and those who fought in them) that are 'unjustly forgotten' during national days of war commemoration by not being offered recognition (Martinsen, 2013: 100). However, the 'dialectic' between remembering and forgetting war commemoration has a deeper complexity. As Winter (2014) further suggests, remembering requires us to feel and/or recognise sacrifice by urging that the violence of war should be neither repeated nor 'forgotten', and by foregrounding the human sacrifice of soldiers to which the nation is indebted and duty-bound not to repeat. Simultaneously, however, the repetition of messages conveyed within commemorative practices and events not only has continuity over time (King, 2010; Martinsen, 2013), it also institutes an 'ignorance' for the realities and awfulness of war (Winter, 2014). It may be argued of course that such an 'encounter with the real' is not possible and cannot be reduced to words and actions, but only operates as a form of memory 'outside the symbolic or social order' of how war is to be recounted (Edkins, 2003: 213–14). For both King (2010) and Danilova (2015a) however, the prioritisation of 'military-centric' forms of commemoration for professional individual soldier personalities (as discussed earlier) decouple commemorative processes from the geopolitical context of war, and thereby depoliticise war-making within public debate. The question here of course is how might this be challenged or overcome? One answer to this from Wimmer (2014: 184) is the acknowledgment rather than exclusion of known war crimes within public remembrance practices (such as accomplished in Berlin). This is a critical form of remembering with the intention not to disremember (or 'forget') the atrocities of war violence. Another answer is to use military commemoration as a means to remember all war deaths. However, this too has its constraints.

In an ethnographic account of a 'military pilgrimage' to the Vietnam Wall war memorial in Washington, the dialectics of 'remembering' and 'forgetting' are terms adopted in the concluding chapter of Michalowski and Dubisch's (2001) *Run for the Wall: Remembering Vietnam on a Motorcycle Pilgrimage*. As they acknowledge, their account contained little discussion of the civilian Vietnamese who were disproportionately killed during the Vietnam War. They nonetheless suggest it is through remembering the military war dead that we should come to not 'forget' and fully remember all who suffer as a consequence of war (Michalowski and Dubisch, 2001). Michalowski and Dubisch (2001) suggest the importance of 'remembering' the past to inform the present through war commemoration is to ensure we do good in the present and not repeat the horrors of the past. This framing of not 'forgetting' as a means of learning from past encounters with war is resonant of Shaw's advocacy for a 'historical pacifism' within *The Dialectics of War*, which, as he suggests, 'will lead us to ask, even of warfare which seems wholly non-nuclear [such as 'new' wars], whether the mass killing involved can seriously be justified by the political goals or state interests which it purports to further (Shaw, 1988a: 133).

However, if the importance of not 'forgetting' all who have suffered at war is to be facilitated by the remembrance practices inherent in war commemoration (note that Shaw, 1988a, did not advocate this), a further constraint is added to the politics of 'remembering' and 'forgetting'. Michalowski and Dubisch's (2001) suggestion of how not to 'forget' civilian war victims appears contingent on the biopolitics of deceased military bodies (MacLeish, 2015). More specifically, the approach they advocated requires the presence of military bodies to mourn and be mourned for in order for recognition of the civilian dead to be facilitated. However, under the conditions of the 'new' (Kaldor, 2014), 'degenerate' (Shaw, 2003) or 'risk-transfer' (Shaw, 2005) wars of the 20th and 21st centuries, such domesticated military bodies have become fewer to mourn. At the same time, as we have established throughout this chapter (and for the greater part of this book), the loss of civilian lives at war have been increasingly asymmetrical to the deaths of (Western) soldiers. We are therefore left to question how such lives can be conceptualised so as not to be disremembered.

'Non-grievable' victims of war

The asymmetry of military lives prioritised over those of civilians underpins the geopolitical logics of what Shaw (2005) defines as 'risk-transfer wars', namely minimising the deaths of 'professional' military personnel at the expense of killing (distant) civilians. It is said that soldiers' lives matter more (socially, politically and culturally) than those of civilians when Western governments contemplate war-making (Shaw, 2005). Judith Butler (2006) articulates this as a cultural acceptance that Western military lives are perceived as 'grievable', and civilian non-Western lives are not. For Zehfuss (2009) this distinction offers a meaningful and critical view of whose war deaths are prioritised as worthy of attention and sympathy during the 'war on terrorism'.

However, for Zehfuss (2009), Butler's (2006) account of the prioritised grievable lives of military personnel via their commemoration does not prevent them from being put at risk (as 'good machines'; see MacLeish, 2015); nor has this distinction engendered a more far-reaching public or political distaste or critique of Western war-making. In this regard, and akin to our previous observations of the soldier's right to life (McGarry et al, 2012), Zehfuss indirectly raises the 'soldier as victim' as an unresolved problem within Butler's (2006) analysis 'in not considering the lives of Western service personnel who are grievable and yet not given the sort of protection that other Western lives may expect' (Zehfuss, 2009: 440). The public's ability to recognise military lives as grievable (Butler, 2004) does not counteract them as being tolerably sacrificed at war (Zehfuss, 2009). Importantly, for Zehfuss (2009) the inverse of this is also implied: being able to conceive of non-Western military lives as 'grievable' does not preclude an end to war violence enacted against non-Western nations. In sum, personalising and mourning the contemporary military war dead does not prevent either military or civilian lives being viewed as expendable via contemporary 'rational' acts of war-making. War therefore remains an illogical act rather than a rational political end (Shaw, 1988a).

However, given that we can only forget what we once knew we return to the comments of Ruggiero (2015) and Steinert (2003) with which we began this chapter. Their maxims are clear: modern warfare is waged against civilians and it is indeed (statistically) safer to be a member of the military during war. No more was this evident than during the war in Kosovo (1999).

Back to the Balkans: Kosovo and the 'bare life' of civilian war victims

Reconnecting with our opening example of the war in Bosnia-Herzegovina, as we further learn from Hagan (2003: 14), 'the Dayton Accords unintentionally entrenched Republika Srpska as a separate part of Bosnia', which for Kaldor (2014) de facto supported and helped continue the nationalist interests of Milošević and Karadžic. The war in Kosovo occurred subsequent to the collapse of the Dayton Settlement (1996–98) following the election of Milošević as the president and commander-in-chief of the newly named Federal Republic of Yugoslavia during 1997, resulting in the continued persecution of Albanian Kosovans by Serbian forces in Kosovo under his command (Hagan, 2003: 15). As we learn from Shaw (2005), during this war although civilian deaths were experienced at a much lower magnitude than the later war in Afghanistan (discussed earlier), the asymmetry of 'new' war (Kaldor, 2014) presented itself as much more one sided.

A common trope of how this war was brought to a 'successful' conclusion is through the perceived effectiveness of the NATO-led 'humanitarian intervention' by bombing Serbian forces in Kosovo from the air (see, for example, Marsavelski et al, 2017). However, as a form of 'risk-transfer' war, strategically this approach resulted in *no Western military forces being killed* at the expense of 500 civilian and 1,000 'enemy' deaths by Western military forces, in addition to hundreds of local allies (Kosovo Liberation Army) killed by Serbian forces (Shaw, 2005). Furthermore, this war not only caused mass civilian deaths, both directly and indirectly, it also witnessed thousands of Kosovan Albanians displaced into refugee camps as a result of a combination of Serbian violence and NATO airstrikes (Edkins, 2003), and Serbian forces using these bombings 'as an excuse to explain the deportation of one-third of the Kosovan Albanian population' (Hagan, 2003: 15). As Edkins (2003) points out, subsequently thousands more Serbian civilians became refugees in an 'ethnic cleansing in reverse' once Serbian forces were defeated by NATO. This final example provides an insight into a war that we are undoubtedly aware of, but whose victims are easily forgotten under the conditions of 'new' war (Kaldor, 2014). In view of our above discussion it therefore urges us to question how civilian deaths at war may be considered other than non-grievable (Butler, 2006) if unable to be 'remembered' via the (absent) biopolitics of (Western) military bodies.

Following Edkins' (2003) use of the concept of 'bare life' (Agamben, 1995), the war in Kosovo is understood as not only being characterised by the absence of Western military deaths; the necropolitics of civilians also featured (Mbembe, 2003). Yet they were only subject to inclusion in this war as a result of their exclusion from its geopolitics (Edkins, 2003). Like victims of the war in Bosnia-Herzegovina, civilian victims of the Kosovo war were subject to persecution on the ground from Serbian forces and simultaneous victimisation from the air by NATO. However, they were also the subject of displacement via the necropolitics of 'humanitarian' intervention (Mbembe, 2003). As Edkins (2003: 203) states,

> The bombing campaign that accompanied the constitution of the Kosovan refugee as bare life or *homo sacer* inaugurates Nato as sovereign power and at the same time legitimates its assumption of the monopoly of legitimate violence. It is only with the refugee crisis that the bombing campaign

becomes justifiable and Nato emerges as a new 'state' with a claim to sovereign force and the sovereign ban.

As Mbembe (2003: 27, emphasis in original) points out, 'sovereignty means the capacity to define who matters and who does not, who is *disposable* and who is not.' NATO's humanitarian intervention and bombing campaign in Kosovo therefore rendered civilian war victims as 'bare life' in Agamben's (1995) terms (Edkins 2003): both sacrificial and saveable by the state, but in exception of sovereign protection and without claim to political agency or autonomy. Hence their exposure to necropolitics (Mbembe, 2003). Once they returned to their homes no law and order was restored, and as refugees the Albanian Kosovans had involuntarily surrendered their political agency and status as citizens through being conceptualised by the initial military sovereignty of NATO (and later sovereignty of the UN) as in need of temporary intervention (Edkins, 2003). As Edkins (2003: 204) continues, for refugees of this war: '[i]n their victimhood they had no voice'.

What this serves to illustrate for the purpose of our argument is for those not proximate to war violence, returning the 'political' to memory politics, as we have done throughout this chapter, is to actively engage in not disremembering (Edkins, 2003). Moreover, for those civilians frequently under the noticeable 'arch' of the violence of 'new' wars, ensuring they are not forgotten is to afford agency and primacy to their witnessing and personal testimony which of course may be evidenced in the continuing presence of 'ordinary' members of the public at remembrance ceremonies across the globe, with the question of what it is they are remembering remaining open ended. Situating their experiences is a crucial and hearable dialogic component of the 'dialectics of war' (Shaw, 1988a) within criminology, to ensure they are not silenced by other long-standing normative interests of the discipline.

Conclusion

As discussed throughout this chapter, the 'dialectics of war' assist us in seeing the contemporary war-making of terror bombing as other than merely a matter of state facilitated crime. Here, we have intentionally departed from previous ways of conceptualising offenders and victims as criminological subjects by exposing them to sociological analysis using Shaw's (1988a) conception of the 'dialectics of war'. First, we have displaced attention from the 'deviant' soldier (at home and at war) as the normative focus of criminological analyses of war. This permitted us to bring into view their conceptualisation as 'victims' of war and helped illustrate the deprioritisation of civilians from within this imagining. In doing so, we have been able to identify the conceptualisation of soldiers as 'victims' as a means of giving affordance to war publicly and culturally within societies situated far from the execution of war making. The problem of reconfiguring the war dead via remembrance practices as domesticated subjects may, as King (2010) suggests, have 'stealthily encouraged' war to become supported by the public as a normative state activity (see also Danilova, 2015b). Indeed Kramer (2010a: 123) suggests that a long-standing masculine hawkishness engendered within the (Western) public to fixate on saving 'our boys in uniform' – between 'lapidary' and digital spaces (King, 2010) – has historically prevented attempts to critically and morally evaluate the killing of civilians at war. For Danilova (2015b), this is also true for both military-centric and community-driven memorial practices contemporarily.

To conclude, when considered as a form of nationalistic valorisation (which we did not and do not) it is possible to suggest that the notion of the 'soldier as victim' serves to complement the study of the 'deviant' soldier by further stifling a wider critical appreciation of state (and non-state) perpetrated war violence. By contrast, with regards to the politics of forgetting we are also faced with a further problem: forgetting civilian war victims becomes increasingly likely if there are fewer 'hero-victims' of a war to valorise (Danilova, 2015a). Moreover, when the limited presence of the 'soldier as victim' does emerge, the cultural and political imagination with which they come to be 'domesticated' as relational subjects to the public (King, 2010) risks civilian victims being even further obscured from 'thinking the practice of war' (Zehfuss, 2012). With the main tenets of our argument now fully outlined up to this point, in the following penultimate chapter we return to reconsider the crime of genocide to begin introducing some initial ways of reflecting critically on previous chapters. We do so next by foregrounding the issue of gender.

SEVEN

Criminology's 'Fourth War'? Gendering War and Its Violence(s)

Introduction

So far this book has been preoccupied with the fixations of extant criminological studies of war and their relative strengths and weaknesses in making sense of war and its consequences. In this penultimate chapter, we take a noticeably different view of how war has been generally studied within criminology (and sociology). By drawing out some key themes relating to the violence(s) of war more broadly understood throughout the literature covered so far, in this chapter we foreground two perspectives that have been understated up to this point: on the one hand, victimology (aspects of which have been discussed elsewhere in this book), and on the other hand, feminism. In so doing, and following Barberet (2014), this chapter focuses attention on interconnections between war-time, peace-time and post-conflict contexts in the experience of war and its violence(s). The substantive topics of concern in exploring such interconnections are twofold: the repositioning of war as a gendered activity predicated on hegemonic forms of masculinity and masculine posturing; and the nature and extent of sexual violence(s) and their varying expression across the domains of war, peace and post-conflict when understood as gendered crimes. These, we believe, offer a corrective to how the normalcy of war violence has been assumed and understood so far in our discussions in this book. However, in the interests of providing a coherent and focussed illustration of this reconceptualisation of war our example in this chapter draws primarily from the nature and impact of genocide.

As will become evident, drawing clear boundaries between some aspects of the issues addressed here is highly contentious and they are drawn as a heuristic device only. This is to help illustrate how war violence is normatively considered in criminological and sociological literature more generally, and as a means by which to be critically reflective on what has been presented throughout the previous chapters. Moreover, as earlier chapters have been concerned to demonstrate, it is the case that there have always been criminologists and, for the purposes of this chapter, victimologists and feminists, concerned with the practices and consequences of war. To begin our discussion, we first return to reconsider genocidal violence (discussed in Chapter Four), this time from the view of victimology.

Victimology, 'monstrosity' and war

The interconnections between the development of victimology and the violence(s) of war are to be found in the work of Benjamin Mendelsohn (among others). Considered to be one of the 'founding fathers' of this area of investigation, like many of his contemporaries such as Mannheim and Radzinowicz (noted in Chapter Two), Mendelsohn was one of a number of émigré lawyers along with other intellectuals who were either exiled or fled from Nazi Germany prior to, during, and just after the Second World War. Having spent some considerable time trying to make sense of why the events of the Second World War unfolded as they did, writing in 1992 Hoffman makes the links between Mendelsohn's concern with victims and the experience of war explicit. He states, '[h]aving been a Jew in Rumania, before and during the Second World War Mendelsohn personally experienced the severe results of anti-Semitism, then prevailing in that country' (Hoffman, 1992: 91). In his later work these experiences were evident in his thinking in relation to the theoretical and empirical study of 'victims'. Indeed, Mendelsohn invented the term 'victimology' and went on to delineate a wide range of victimising contexts including 'individual or collective oppression, [by] caste, social class or political parties, up to and including genocide or war crimes' (Mendelsohn, 1976: 17). By 1982 Mendelsohn had decided that victimisation was attributable to 'six fundamental factors', including 'nature, *society*, energy supply, motorization, criminality, and sometimes the victim itself' (Mendelsohn, 1982: 60, our emphasis). Within this broad gamut of victimisation, included within the attribution of 'socially determined victimity', was 'a collective potential for starting mass conflicts that may escalate to pogroms and genocide' (Mendelsohn, 1982: 60). He continues,

> On the issue of genocide, the position of victimology is as follows: While ordinary crime always involves deviant behaviour, which is always and everywhere subject to public prosecution, genocide is a crime tolerated or even ordered by the state, with an utter disregard for justice and humanity. In the case of genocide large numbers of

persons show willingness to exterminate entire peoples or ethnic groups that have been outlawed by the state and are officially denied all human rights including the right to live. It is imperative that a specific term be introduced adequate to the seriousness of that crime: 'monstrosity' appears to be appropriate. (Mendelsohn, 1982: 63)

For Mendelsohn (1982), there should be no abdication of culpability for genocidists, and no space for reintegration or lenience in their sentencing. So, much like the connections made by Laufer (1999) with regards to criminology (discussed in Chapter Four), it is possible to see that war and genocide were not 'forgotten' issues for victimology or victimologists. Indeed, it is the birth of victimology and its connections with the Second World War, and particularly one feature of that war, The Holocaust, which gave this area of investigation a relatively unique, if somewhat understated, relationship with the most extreme form of war violence: the 'monstrosity' of genocide (Mendelsohn, 1982).

Whether acknowledging his work and influence within victimology or not however, others have followed in the wake of Mendelsohn in attempting to place genocide at the forefront of criminological and victimological concerns. Notably, and as discussed in chapter two, Hagan and Greer (2002) point to the role played by Sheldon Glueck in ensuring that genocide was punished as a crime in the Nuremberg Trials. Decades later (as noted in Chapter Four), employing 'The Atrocities Documentation Survey' – a variation on a mainstream method of empirically studying 'victims' of domestic crime (via criminal victimisation surveys) – the work by Hagan and Rymond-Richmond (2009) ensured that genocide as a feature of the civil war in Darfur was centred as an issue for serious attention (see also the work of Letschert et al, 2011, and Smeulers and Haveman, 2008, on victimology and genocide more generally). However, while the Holocaust and further genocides throughout the 20th and 21st centuries cast an important shadow over the framing of victimology (as it does with criminology, discussed in Chapter Four), this was not the only area of investigation pointing to the violence(s) of war and its consequences pertinent to the victimological agenda. The later seminal work of Fassin and Rechtman (2009) offered a different victimological perspective through which to appreciate the nature of war violence.

Victimology and wartime trauma of soldiers and civilians

Within *The Empire of Trauma,* Fassin and Rechtman (2009) trace the emergence of what they have called 'psychiatric victimology'. This interpretation of victimology, while having its origins in the incipient understandings of workplace related physical trauma of the mid-19th century, secured a strong and significant presence during the First World War. In so doing, as criminology did with regards to the 'deviant soldier' (discussed in Chapter Six), the attention of 'psychiatric victimology' focused on the faltering soldier: those who, as a result of what came to be called 'shell shock', were deemed cowardly and dealt with accordingly. Sometimes these *men* were shot for cowardice (which happened in the British military) or subjected to electric shock treatment (which occurred in the French military). In both cases, many men suffered not only as a result of the brutality of the treatment they received but also because of their exposure to war. Thus, in Fassin and Rechtman's (2009) analysis, the role of this version of victimology was central to the recognition of the consequences of war for military personnel. This recognition reached its peak in the early 1980s with the identification of post-traumatic stress disorder (PTSD, not to be conflated with shell shock) in the aftermath of events associated with the Vietnam War, with the Mai Lai atrocity of 1968 being a significant turning point: events later frequently understood through the moniker of PTSD (see, for example, Collins, 2008).

Of course, it is not only the military who suffer health consequences in the aftermath of war. As we have endeavoured to make clear in previous chapters, all wars – both 'old' and 'new' – carry military *and* (disproportionately) civilian casualties. For example, and as an advancement from the socioeconomic impacts observed by Hagan, et al (2012) (discussed in Chapter Three), in reviewing the health consequences of the 2003 Iraq War Levy and Sidel (2013) point out that civilians suffered widespread indirect consequences to their health as a result of the damage caused by war to Iraq's health infrastructure (see also McGarry and Walklate, 2015b). Akin to issues raised within chapters four and six, several million Iraqi civilians are also said to have been displaced by the war (Levy and Sidel, 2013). Furthermore, attendant to matters related to the 'soldier as victim' (discussed in Chapter Six), Levy and Sidel (2013) go on observe that tens of thousands of US military personnel also suffered psychological harm, and physical and traumatic injuries to their bodies as a consequence of participating in this war. Such interconnections of the consequences of war violence were therefore not lost on the 'Founding Fathers' of victimology or their predecessors, whether in the kind of comments promulgated by Mendelsohn (1982) vis-à-vis the 'monstrosity' of genocide, or that centred by Fassin and Rechtman (2009) vis-à-vis wartime trauma. Viewed in this way, they each offer an alternative appreciation of the 'dialectic' relationship between soldiers and civilians at war (discussed in Chapter Six).

Victimology and the Cold War era

However, as the post-Second World War era unfolded it is interesting to note that the interconnections pointed to above became an understated and much less prominent concern within victimological work as more widely understood. These gave way instead to a preference for rather more unidimensional and uni-factoral appreciations of criminal victimisation and its consequences. These appreciations reflected a tendency to focus on individual pathology rather than collective responsibility in their search for causal explanations of 'crime', with the matter of war violence becoming a more peripheral (but not obsolete) concern (as discussed in Chapter Two). Of course, the influential presence of this individualistic and individualised focus was in many ways inevitably political. Morrison (2015) suggests this emergent and subsequently dominant focus found within criminology (and indeed victimology) needs to be situated against the backcloth of the Cold War and the rise of North American intellectual, liberal imperialism. Here Morrison (2015) is alluding to the powerful ways in which wars, particularly post the Second World War, served as conduits for the imperial ambitions of North American liberal democratic values. These values traversed the globe in a different though not dissimilar way to that of the colonialism of the 19th century, and became epitomised in the European context via faith in the recourse to liberal law through initiatives like the International Criminal Court (ICC), for example, to tame the excesses of war (see also Chapter Four and our concluding Chapter Eight).

These observations certainly register with the telling question raised by Butler (2004) (discussed in Chapter Six) who asks: when is a life grievable? The rise of the 'superpowers' (that is, the US on the one hand and the Soviet Union on the other), set the context in which some lives were grievable and others were not. Such thinking, initially expressed as either being committed to liberal democracy and capitalism or being committed to communism, informed the McCarthy Era in the US during the 1950s and certainly fuelled foreign policy responses in the Northern hemisphere throughout the 1960s (as discussed in

Chapter Five). Against such a political backcloth some lives did indeed become grievable and others not. During the Cold War era much of the work developed under the lexicon of victimology lost sight of the war-time origins of the discipline and applied its early concepts (that is, victim proneness, victim culpability and victim precipitation) to what were considered to be much more ordinary and everyday criminal experiences, such as burglary, murder, and rape (although such foci were received somewhat contentiously in relation to the latter issue by the feminist movement during the 1970s; see for example Davies, 2018). During this time victimology, as an emergent discipline, did much to emulate criminology. It embraced familiar criminological pre-occupations of differentiation, determinism and pathology (Roshier, 1989) and with the development of the criminal victimisation survey in 1967 became characterised and latterly dominated by positivism (see for example Rock, 2018).

Whither victimology and war: a peace-time 'rendezvous science'?

In a similar way to criminology, victimology also became a meeting place for academics, policy-makers and practitioners all claiming to speak for the 'victim of crime'. Indeed, as Rock (1994: xvi) proclaimed, victimology became a 'rendezvous science defined by its attention to all things associated with victims, rather than a science unified by a common theory, practice, profession or institution'. From the late 1960s onwards the defining feature of victimhood came to be that typified by criminal victimisation; a perception of harm entrenched in individuality, ordinariness and mundanity. A normative view of 'crime' and thus victimisation became so embedded in theory and policy some commentators observed that the point had been reached whereby citizenship had become elided with and defined by victimhood (see Furedi, 1997; Young A., 1996). In this way the original foci of this area of investigation, that of genocide, war and their consequences, became lost in the peace-time drive to focus on the nature and extent of conventional crime. As a result, victims of war and genocide also became hidden from view within not only criminology but also victimology. That is until the ongoing Nuremberg Trials during the 1960s.

Karstedt (2010) traces the absent/present trajectory of victims' voices during this time. In reviewing this work, Shalhoub-Kevorkian and Braithwaite (2010: 1) state:

The profound contribution to victimology of Karstedt's work is the conclusion that the absence of any testimony from victims is one of the reasons the Nuremberg trials promoted a collective amnesia on the back of an interpretation that all this was the dirty work of just Hitler and his inner circle. Karstedt shows that it was not until a series of trials that started in the 1960s with the Eichmann trial in Israel that the German public were confronted with the voices of victims.

The silencing and then rediscovery of victims' voices alluded to in this analysis had consequences for the differential presence of war and its violence(s) in both criminology and victimology. One of which (discussed in Chapter Four) was the way the denial of genocide, and thus the denial of the collective violence(s) of the state, facilitated (albeit indirectly) the then emergent and subsequent contemporary ongoing criminological and criminal justice policy attention devoted to the 'deviant soldier' during 'old' and 'new' wars (discussed in Chapter Six). This attention has ranged from a concern with the 'spill-over effect' that preoccupied Bonger (1916, 1936), namely the problem of the returning soldier trained to kill but now expected to operate peaceably; to widely reported 'misdemeanours' of war, as contemporarily documented in the use of torture and other ceremonies of degradation during the war in Iraq (see for example, ICRC, 2004; Hamm, 2007; Lilly, 2007); to the more 'mundane' and 'ordinary' criminality committed in the course of soldiers 'doing their duty' (see Jeffreys, 2007, on sexual violence directed towards male and female colleagues, and Gartner and Kennedy, 2018, on the spill-over effects of violence more generally). Nevertheless, as earlier chapters have demonstrated, the criminological voices concerned with a wider appreciation of war were never completely silenced. However, for victimology, it took a while longer for its voice on understanding war and its violence(s) to reappear on the victimological agenda and be heard (see inter alia, Letschert et al, 2011; McGarry and Walklate, 2011; Rafter and Walklate, 2012). Indeed, as we shall come to learn, the presence of the victimological gaze on such questions still has much to offer.

Victimology, war and gender: identifying connections and making departures

To summarise, the silencing of victim voices post-Second World War combined with the ongoing focal attention paid to the deviant soldier need to be appreciated against the backcloth of the Cold War. During this time, the intellectual imperialism of North American liberal criminology (and here also read victimology) came to dominate how both disciplines took shape. These processes shaped what were considered to be legitimate and illegitimate substantive areas of investigation for each of these disciplines but they were not uniform in effect. As is documented elsewhere in this book, there were other voices pointing to and critically examining, the inclusionary and exclusionary processes involved in this agenda setting. However, the consequence of this (presumed) democratic liberal agenda afforded space for positivism to reign in both victimology and criminology. The resultant effect was that both became pre-occupied with a focus on the individual as a cause for and conduit of violent behaviour. Furthermore, both presumed that such behaviour was bounded by the different contexts in which violence occurred: war-time, peace-time or post-conflict situations. The cumulative impact of this has been a failure to see the continuities between each of these different contexts; one of which lies in an appreciation of the gendered relationships which underpin the patterns of gender-based violence, particularly sexual violence, found during times of war and 'peace' (see for example Cockburn, 2014).

While the notion of 'othering' has featured in earlier chapters in this book (the othering of states and communities post-9/11 discussed in Chapter Three for example), gender is historically and contemporarily also a key feature of 'othering' practices in which men constitute the measuring rod against which women are both valued and evaluated in both criminology and victimology. Indeed, as Carol Smart (1977: 178) astutely pointed out many years ago within *Women, Crime and Criminology: a Feminist Critique*:

> It is no surprise that our language and choice of words reflect the social 'invisibility' of women because in our culture, man is the centre of the universe and woman features only in her relation to him. Consequently within criminology we have studies of male criminal and male juvenile delinquents. Where are the women?

This is nowhere more the case than when considering the patterning of sexual violence(s) in both domestic contexts and the settings of war and genocide. As noted in chapter two, in her later essay/manifesto Jamieson (1998) pointed to understanding the gendered nature of warfare as a crucial component for establishing a 'criminology of war' in the ways Smart (1977) had advocated. In looking across the continuities between war, peace and post-conflict situations, and in making sense of the gendered interconnections across these contexts, it is possible to discern some of the analysis that both Smart (1977) and Jamieson (1998) had anticipated for the (now apparent) interconnected domains of war, crime and victimisation within criminology. However, before moving on to explore this further through our example of genocide, it is first worth offering a brief account on feminist thinking about war and its violence(s). Although a seemingly 'new horizon' for criminological studies of war, it is certainly not a novel undertaking for sociology.

Gendered perspectives on war

It almost goes without saying that war is predominantly perpetrated by men and that victims of war, in traditional conceptualisations of war (see Chapters One and Two), are predominantly – though not exclusively – also men. Of course, it is also the case that women fight in wars both as activists (see Oriola, 2012) and contemporarily as formally recruited members of the armed forces. Importantly women and children also constitute a major component of those who are victimised by all kinds of wars and their consequences; certainly, children are frequently victimised in war through their indoctrination and deployment as child soldiers. Historically and contemporarily however, war is considered to be 'men's work'. Indeed, feminist scholars have drawn attention to the way in which ideas about masculinity have been central to soldiering across different cultures (see for example Enloe, 1983) and it is this cross-cultural consistency that informs the gendered ways in which soldiers are trained to perceive 'success' as a valorised commodity, and 'failure' as an articulation of femininity (see also Zarkov, 2014). As Buss (2014: 5) notes, asking questions about the relative invisibility of women in accounts of war 'functions as a shorthand for a complex analytical process that seeks to unravel the multiple levels at which gender structures the practices and representations of war'. She goes on to observe that 'Women's lived reality of conflict also helps to challenge dominant conceptions of the very definitions of "war" and "armed conflict", the start and end of conflict and violence, the experiences of conflict-related violence, and the harms caused by conflict' (Buss, 2014: 6).

Indeed, the failure to appreciate the multi-layered presence of gender as a feature of war and war-making is tellingly revealed in Mann's (2014) analysis of 'sovereign masculinity' in the 'war on terrorism'. She states:

> If we want to understand the United States' vision of empire, we have to understand its culture and practices of gender, and if we want to understand gender as it is lived in the United States today, we need to understand sovereignty as it is imagined and practiced by the nation. The notion of 'sovereign masculinity' reminds us of this relation. (Mann, 2014: 4)

As per Buss' (2014) comments above, here Mann (2014) reminds us that gender permeates all levels and all aspects of social relations. The strike on the Twin Towers on 9/11 was a strike on the North American nation and its sovereignty, but it was also a strike that needs to be understood through the perspective of gender. It was a strike at the heart of North American neoliberal masculinity: intended to provoke a nation (of men) to respond. Moreover, despite women's groups and feminists protesting violent retaliation for 9/11 as a masculinist revalorisation of 'nationhood' (see Cockburn, 2007), the response came in classical, frontiersman style, overlaid with 'the construction of the West as the white male hero – as the civilised, advanced, rational, benevolent saviour – which disguises the reality of global international and economic relations' (Duncanson, 2013: 35).

This is a view which very quickly became constituted as defending the exploited, oppressed and racialised woman.

It is important to note that, broadly speaking, international relations is equally guilty of assuming their subject matter to be ungendered, which in making sense of war is additionally problematic (see, for example, Robinson, 2011). It is also evident that some feminist informed work in international relations has embraced the importance of gender in making sense of state, nation, security and terrorism (see, for example, Robinson, 2011; Wibben, 2016; and in relation to criminology see Walklate et al, 2019), with True (2012) exploring the gendered consequences of such relations. Other work, especially emanating from history, provides a good deal of insight into the different roles taken on by women during war as workers of all kinds, the impact of these roles on relationships with men, and the consequences these changes had (see also Carden-Coyne, 2012; Ericsson, 2015; Peniston-Bird and Vickers, 2017). However, less work has developed within criminology and victimology taking a gendered perspective on the multi-layered ways in which war and its consequences infiltrate women's (and some men's) everyday lives. For example, see Rueda (2018) on war and violence as work. Yet there is clearly a feminist informed agenda available to these areas of investigation which facilitates such a gendered analysis.

Women's experiences of gendered war violence

Since the publication of Susan Brownmiller's (1975) seminal work, *Against Our Will*, which put rape in war alongside other contexts in which rape occurs, feminists, particularly radical feminists, have been keen to encourage a recognition of the ways in which women's experiences of sexual violence(s) transcend the perceived boundaries between war-time, peace-time and post-conflict situations (Barberet, 2014). There are two conceptual devices which enable radical feminists (in particular) to situate these assumed different spheres of violence in the same frame of reference: the concept of 'patriarchy' and the concept of a 'continuum'. Indeed, the ongoing presence and importance of these as conceptual devices remains telling, as Connell (2016: 15) observes, the presence of,

> Not just a power-oriented masculinity but also a cultivated callousness is involved in organizing abductions of girls, suicide bombings, femicide, beheadings, and mass addiction. It seems close to the callousness involved in drone strikes, mass sackings, structural adjustment programmes, nuclear armaments, and the relentless destruction of our common environment.

The concept of a 'continuum' facilitates the connections Connell (2016) is making here. This concept has been deployed by different writers in different ways. In the context of criminology, L. Kelly (1988) introduced the concept of a 'continuum of sexual violence' developed from listening to women's voices and their experiences of sexual violence and its impact. This centred the sense-making of those experiences in ways not previously acknowledged by the discipline. Kelly's (1988) concept placed women's experiences from 'flashing' to murder, from those occurring in public to those occurring in private, from single offences to multiple offences, from single offenders to multiple offenders, all within the same conceptual space. This was violence as experienced by women over and through time.

In a parallel vein, Cockburn (2012, 2013, 2014) takes this idea further; rather than a single continuum she suggests thinking of 'continua' of violence(s) as experienced by individuals or as part of social structure, perpetrated at many levels and within different localities and across time, and enacted using various instruments of violence. As she points out:

For instance, a continuum of *scale of force*: so many pounds per square inch when a fist hits a jaw; so many more when a bomb hits a military target. A continuum on a *social scale*: violence in a couple, in a street riot, violence between nations. And *place*: a bedroom, a street, a police cell, a continent. *Time*: during a long peace, pre-war, in armed conflict, in periods we call 'postconflict'. And then *type of weapon*: hand, boot, machete, gun, missile. (Cockburn, 2013, online, emphasis added)

Taken together these interventions comprise a continuum of violence (Bourke, 2015), in which gender becomes the salient variable; not always and not everywhere, but a necessary conceptual device for making sense of ongoing patterns of violence. Indeed Cockburn (2007, 2014) argues gender needs to be placed along with, and of equal importance to, all variables put to the fore by other disciplinary perspectives when making sense of the violence(s) of war, peace and conflict. Of course, once gender is centred in this way the boundaries formally drawn between each of these different contexts become very blurred indeed.

Behind the intellectual story outlined above there is of course another one: that of feminist activism. Trivialised in many ways as the 'war between the sexes', campaigns emanating from the feminist movement have proved challenging in a wide range of contexts in both the Northern and the Southern hemispheres. Echoing the use of 'war' as a metaphor discussed above (and differently within Chapter Three), as Cockburn (2007) documents very well, these campaigns posed fundamental questions for not only whose knowledge counts but also to challenge the validity of war as a 'legitimate' response (Clausewitz, [1832] 1997) in and of itself to international conflicts both 'old' and 'new' (Kaldor, 2014). Feminist activism has also proved to be challenging to the consequences of war in divergent locations across the globe, such as Argentina (see Fisher, 1999), Srebrenica (noted in Chapter Six) (Simic and Daly, 2011), or indeed the long-lasting campaign against the presence of North American weapons at the RAF base in Greenham Common in the UK during the 1980s (see for example Young A., 1990; Roseneil, 1995). In concluding her 2007 book, *From Where We Stand: War, Women's Activism & Feminist Analysis,* Cockburn points out that there is not much you can teach a woman war slave about the nature of war, its violence(s), otherings and oppressions. Her experiences transcend all of these specificities and in many ways stand in support of Connell's (2002) assertion that in order to make a difference to these specificities, it is masculinity itself that must change. While that may well be the case, the question remains concerning what the shared perspective of victimology and the critical study of gender might bring to the scholarship of war within criminology.

Exploring the continuities of war's violence(s)

In a way it could be argued that the provocation to blur the boundaries between war, peace and post-conflict situations is not so profound. Feminist researchers and campaigners have long used the language of war to capture the nature of women's everyday lives. For example, Power-Cobbe (1878) talked of 'wife torture in England', Morgan (1989) talked of women's fears as everyday terrorism, and more recently Pain (2012) has analysed her findings on violence against women in a similar vein. If this body of knowledge is placed alongside other work documenting the experience of war as gendered – such as the extent of sexual violence within war and genocide documented by scholars such as Christopher Mullins (see, for example, Mullins 2009a, 2009b; Mullins and Visagaratnam, 2015; see also Davies and True, 2015), the disruption caused by war and conflict associated with sexual trafficking and labour exploitation (True, 2012), to the gendered nature of migration prompted by fleeing from conflicts (Hudson, 2016) – it is easy to see that all of these violence(s) are an everyday occurrence for those affected by them. Taken together they constitute powerful evidence to which feminism provides a conceptual framework to situate these experiences either on a continuum (Kelly, L., 1988) or between continua (Cockburn, 2012, 2013, 2014) within sociological, criminological and victimological work addressing war. Indeed, the work of Kelly (1988) and Cockburn (2012, 2013, 2014) challenges the idea that the experiences of such violence are separate and separable, particularly when viewed from the perspective of the harm generated by them (see Cockburn, 2007). This kind of conceptual standpoint however constitutes a profound challenge for the dominant individualistic orientation of mainstream criminology and/or victimology as outlined above. This point is well illustrated when revisiting our previous discussion of genocide earlier in this book (see Chapter Four).

Revisiting and rethinking genocide as a gendered experience

As discussed in Chapter Four, Rafter (2008) addressed the presence of Lombrosian thinking at the time of The Holocaust as criminology's 'darkest hour', and went on to state in her detailed analysis of genocide that 'Gender colours the conduct of genocide from start to finish' (Rafter, 2016: 180). And, while Alvarez (2010) has indicated that different genocides arise in different ways and are differently motivated, what they have in common is a planned and organised rationale in which people are exterminated for who they are assumed to be, or what they are constructed to represent (Jamieson, 1999; Short, 2010). In other words, as a gendered act genocide targets men and women differently, a conceptual problem captured by Jones (2000) in his notion of 'gendercide'.

Therefore, while conjuring mass state endorsed violence(s), genocide also conjures sex-selectivity in terms of victims, perpetrators, and behaviours. For example, in some genocides young men were singled out to be 'disappeared' (as in Kosovo or East Timor). While during others, women were singled out for rape, whereby sexual violence was used as a weapon of war to assault, dominate and debase women's bodies, and as a weapon of cultural degradation against a particular ethnic group (as in Serbia). In one of the most thorough and far reaching analyses of genocide written from a criminological perspective, Rafter (2016: 170) concludes: 'Genocide, my data shows, is always a gendered activity. Symbolically rape feminizes the victim group (including men who are raped or otherwise sexually violated), demonstrating its powerlessness, while at the same time it masculinizes the victors.'

The behaviours contributing to these processes are also sexual. They involve a wide variety of sexual acts and include violating those parts of the body associated with sexual identity or humiliation in committing such acts (often in public), or demanding the nakedness of those so targeted. As reported by Gettlemen (2017) and documented by Médecins Sans Frontières (2018), such harrowing sexual acts are evident in recent genocidal violence experienced by the Rohingya perpetrated by Myanmar authorities (noted in Chapter Four). Kaiser and Hagan (2015) have also discussed the impact of such experiences in Darfur.

These kinds of violence(s) can also be perpetrated and evidenced in more 'conventional' war contexts in which mass killings and atrocities can take on a gendered and sexualised character (see, for example, Bringedal-Houge, 2015). Who is, and who is not 'othered' as these processes unfold often depends on who is seen to be the victor ('victor's justice', as characterised by Zolo, 2010; also discussed in our concluding Chapter Eight). Indeed, in contradiction to more popular images of events associated with this period, Gebhardt (2016) evidences the nature and extent of sexual violence against German women at the end of the Second World War by *all* Armed Forces in Germany, not just the Red Army. Such specificities notwithstanding, all wars both 'old' and 'new' involve atrocities on all sides (Ruggiero, 2018) in which 'good men' do 'bad things'. Indeed, under some circumstances throughout history, as Ruggiero (2015: 29) observes, the gendered nature of masculine war violence has often been bestowed with such normalcy, how its perpetration is perceived has become warped so that 'torture becomes a patriotic act while rape may become an act of heroism'. In view of Cockburn's (2012) notion of such violence existing across 'continua', it is also important to remember from the victim/survivor's perspective that all of these acts are also sometimes perpetrated in the safe haven of the home during times defined as 'peaceful' (see also Carrington, 2015).

Of course, there is another component which emanates from a detailed appreciation of the disparities, as well as the similarities, between different genocides and/or atrocity crimes; some of which is alluded to above and has been mentioned in chapter four. For example, Rafter and Walklate (2012), on a close reading of the Armenian genocide (still denied in Turkey) developed the earlier work of Mendelsohn (noted above) and introduced the concept of 'victimality' to help make sense of some of the specific features of this relational process. This concept builds on Shaw's observation that it is important,

> we move away from the subjective meaning of genocidal action (for the perpetrator) to understanding the *typical social relations of genocide* (not only among perpetrators but crucially between them and the victims and indeed among victims) and therefore the structure of social relations that these set up. (Shaw, 2007: 82, emphasis added)

Rafter and Walklate reworked the traditional victimological concepts of 'victim proneness' and 'victim precipitation' into a separate concept of 'victimality', which

> refers to the potential of an individual for victimization, not fault. On the broader scale of national and international group conflicts, we can speak of a group's *victimality* or

> potential for victimization by another group (or by a state). This level can fluctuate, and it does not necessarily lead to genocide, although sometimes it does. (Rafter and Walklate, 2012: 517, emphasis added)

This echoes discussion by Smeulers (2011: 85) of the three case studies in her work, drawn from examples of involvement in extreme atrocities, who adds '[W]e sometimes have to take a more nuanced view towards perpetrators and victims alike and accept that victims and perpetrators are not always two mutually exclusive groups. Strange as it may seem sometimes people are victims and perpetrators at the same time'.

At first glance such an observation seems obvious. Yet on deeper reflection the challenge it poses for victimology (and criminology) vis-à-vis understanding war and genocide is indeed profound, in particular since it poses serious questions about what might be termed disciplinary 'either/orisms': here you are *either* a victim *or* an offender. Moreover, the continuities between war and genocide, recognised by Shaw (2003) are also lost in this aphorism (indeed the same overlap between offending and victimisation is also apparent with crime more associated with mainstream criminological work, like for example street crime).

These observations make the case, by implication, that understandings of genocide (and war's violence(s), whether characterised by features of genocide or not) are incomplete without an appreciation of gender and the processes associated with victimality (Rafter and Walklate, 2012). It is also evident that violence of this kind is perpetrated mostly on women and sometimes on other men, with these practices frequently endorsed by states peopled and governed by men (Connell, 2016). In recognising the kind of complexity underpinning the gendered nature of war violence, as typified by its sexual nature, it is possible to appreciate how such violence becomes 'folded into everyday life', an 'intertwining of the descent into the ordinary' in which 'ordinary people become scarred' (Das, 2007: 14). Indeed, the ordinariness of violence of this kind is captured in the United Nations (1993) *Declaration on Eliminating Violence Against Women* (quoted at length by Barberet, 2014) which brings to the fore taken for granted cultural practices (for example, female genital mutilation, forced sterilisation, and female infanticide) as well as the important role that state sponsored violence(s) play in harming women (and children). This is the 'ordinary' violence of peace, conflict and post-conflict contexts. This is an ordinariness that also includes men, not solely as perpetrators but also as victims of sexual and other war violence(s).

Criminology's fourth war?

Despite the apparent simplicity associated with bringing the continuities in the violence(s) of peace, conflict and post-conflict situations to the fore, the problems generated for mainstream criminology and victimology (and indeed sociology) are almost palpable. Rendering these interconnections visible makes the gendered violence(s) of war neither an aberration nor a pathological condition, nor solely related to Clausewitzean notions of 'war' as enacted between states, or as features of 'new' wars (which Kaldor, 2014, and others seem to have overlooked). Instead, grasping war as an inherently gendered set of activities renders its violence(s) profoundly normal, routine, and consequently a habitual concern for these disciplines, particularly when understood as being perpetrated and experienced on a 'continuum' (Kelly, L., 1988) or across 'continua' (Cockburn, 2012; 2013, 2014). Jock Young (2011) offers a compelling argument that if criminology is to make sense of issues prescient across the globe, such as war violence, it needs to loosen the conceptual and methodological hold that, what he calls the 'bogus of positivism', has over the discipline. The hold of positivism projects North American (liberal) values – particularly those centring individualism – on criminology across the globe. This projection of values is developed in Morrison's (2015) elucidation of criminology's 'nomos' and the imperialistic processes inherent in this. This liberal vision of knowledge and the knowledge production process makes liberal analyses of othering, demonisation, and denial much easier. All of which are prescient in treating violence(s) against women and the violence(s) of war as separate and separable, as discussed here.

One way out of this conundrum is for the discipline of criminology to begin to think differently about the gendered interconnections with which this chapter has been concerned. Here we have foregrounded genocide as an example through which the gendered nature of war can be rethought and reconsidered. Perhaps another way in which to do this is to think of these issues as a further feature of the 'dialectics of war' as articulated by Shaw (1988a) and discussed in chapter six. If considered in this vein, the 'dialectic of war' presented here centres gender in the practices of war in all its forms and at every level (individual, institutional, state, global). At each of these levels patriarchal social relations and dominant forms of masculinity are produced and reproduced. This is evidenced in the practices of sexual violence towards civilians, combatants and others both male and female (not only by military personnel but by others in the field of war). In the reproduction of the male (Western) hero, sent to save the downtrodden racialised woman as directed within northern foreign policy, and in the intellectual (male dominated) denial/minimisation of the interconnections between, for example, the recourse to 'lone wolf' terrorism and violence against women (Hamm and Spaaji, 2017). This dialectical relationship between gender, war and peace is hidden but is nonetheless real in its consequences. It has been evidenced in the pages of this book in the absence of gendered thinking around genocide, 'new wars', 'old wars', the Cold War, and the 'war on terrorism'. To parody LaFree's (2009) assertion of the relative attention paid to wars waged against various nouns within criminology (that is, crime, drugs and terrorism), centring gender is arguably criminology's (and victimology's) 'fourth war' since mainstream criminology and victimology have been complicit in hiding this dialectic as a result of their own entrenched imperialistic intellectual ambitions.

Conclusion

What we have chosen to foreground within this chapter are the perspectives of victimology, feminism and the study of gender, and the interconnections that can be made between the critical issues each of these raises for the wider study of war within criminology and sociology. We have, of course, provided insights into victims, victimisation and victimhood throughout previous chapters of this book as a means by which to shift the conceptual focus of studying war to the disproportionate harms experienced by civilians. Within this chapter however we have made this connection more explicit by linking the emergence and development of the sub discipline victimology to the Second World War, and more specifically the Holocaust. By centring the 'monstrosity' of genocide (Mendelsohn, 1982) as a heuristic device and exposing it to a reinterpretation based on gendered ways of understanding its violence(s), it becomes clear that acts of war and genocide are almost exclusively sanctioned, legitimised and perpetrated under the gendered mantle of hegemonic masculinity (Connell, 2005). When viewed and understood as a gendered enterprise rather than a rational act of statism (Clausewitz, [1832] 1997) it is possible to begin appreciating that the violence(s) of war (including genocide) are experienced differently for men and women; both as perpetrators and receivers of such harm, issues which the international crime of genocide further complicates.

We consider such ways of thinking about war in victimological and gendered terms, as presented throughout this chapter, to offer a useful conceptual prism (rather than a monocular or binocular 'lens') through which to look back on, and critically reconsider, arguments we have made throughout this book. Following Enloe (1993), pertinent interventions could, for example, be made regarding our discussion of the Cold War in chapter five and the absence of gender informing some of that literature. The absence of a gendered appreciation of the terms listed by Buss (2014) (noted above) within articulations of 'old war', 'new war', and the 'war on terrorism' discussed in earlier chapters of this book would also be worthy of reflection and critique. Indeed, the notion of 'militarism' has been evident since the inception of criminological studies of war (Bonger, 1916) and underpins the relational 'dialectics of war' as discussed in chapter six, and as well represented in fig 6.1 and the cover image of this book. This is a concept that has, for some considerable time, been a core focal point of critique for feminist scholars addressing war and critically analysing the ways in which 'militarism' impacts and governs women's lives across the globe (see inter alia Enloe, 2000, 2016). We of course welcome, encourage and support others to make further specific critiques of the work we have presented throughout this book vis-à-vis the gendered nature of war for criminology.

In conclusion, we wish to make a final conceptual observation on the connection gendering war and its violence(s) makes between sociology and criminology. The crux of the gendered problem inherent in a significant amount of literature covered in all previous chapters (One to Six) is usefully captured by Wibben (2016: 3) who points out that, 'Much writing on war and violence (without explicitly stating this) is on man and the state.' For example, as interpreted via the work of Malešević (2010a) (discussed in Chapter Two), the scholarship of the 'Founding Fathers' of Metropolitan 'classical' sociology (that is, Marx, Weber and Durkheim) paid scarce attention to gender vis-à-vis war; nor for that matter did early criminologists engaged in the study of war, such as Bonger, Mannheim, Sutherland, Glueck, Radzinowicz and (as noted above) Mendelsohn. As Cockburn (2007) notes, research on war taking gender seriously has been generally absent from the origins of the formation of the 'sociology of war' as now contemporarily understood (see Creighton and Shaw, 1987); although the recent intervention by Malešević (2010a) has offered a minor corrective to this problem. As our earlier discussions in this chapter make clear, gender is a maligned concept within these disciplines. This, of course, is not a unique observation. However, it is the marginal role assigned to matters relating to gender from central concerns within the 'sociology of war' past and present which clearly connects with the discipline of criminology. Returning to the earlier words of Carol Smart (1977: 178), she further instructs:

> Criminology and the sociology of deviance must become more than the study of men and crime if it is to play any significant part in the development of our understanding of crime, law and the criminal process and play any role in the transformation of existing social practices.

We hope these sage words remain ringing in the ears of scholars who wish to undertake criminological and sociological studies of war in the years following the publication of this book. Only by doing so will the historical neglect of gender vis-à-vis the study of war, crime *and* victimisation become an uncomfortable (but not forgotten) artefact of the discipline.

EIGHT

Conclusion: Beyond a 'New' Wars Paradigm: Bringing the Periphery into View

Introduction

In this book we have endeavoured to connect extant sociological and criminological literature to the contested subject of 'war'. By foregrounding what for some might be regarded as 'subjugated knowledge' (Foucault, 2004), we have attempted to demonstrate in preliminary ways how criminological literature addressing war might be revisited and developed from additional sociological insights. In Chapters Two to Seven we demonstrated that there have been some meaningful criminological contributions on 'old' and 'new' wars (Kaldor, 2014), including the First and Second World Wars and the Holocaust, the Cold War era, further genocides throughout the 20th and 21st centuries, the Balkans wars, the conflict in Northern Ireland and most recently wars perpetrated under the lexicon of the 'war on terrorism' post-9/11. What we hope to have made clear is that the study of war is not new to criminology (or sociology). We also hope to have illuminated some of the 'negative evidence' (Lewis and Lewis, 1980) inherent in the literature we have presented. In so doing it becomes apparent that not all wars, armed conflicts and genocides have caught the attention of the discipline. For example, the Falklands War stands out for its near complete absence. Moreover, with few notable exceptions, other wars and conflicts – including the 1991 Gulf War (see White, R., 2008) and Israel's 'colonial-territorial project' of occupied East Jerusalem in the West Bank of historic Palestine against Palestinian land (Shalhoub-Kevorkian, 2017: 1280) – have been significantly underrepresented within criminological scholarship on war. Furthermore, with the exception of recent substantive work documenting genocidal violence across some African nations, and parts of South and Southeast Asia (noted in Chapter Four), so the (in) visibility of war and conflict occurring in other parts of the Global South (and North for that matter) become noticeable by their lack of coverage in much of the conventional literature. By implication these absences are suggestive of both the normative disciplinary interests of (mainstream) criminology and the orientation of its metropolitan knowledge base, a point to which we shall return.

In this extended conclusion we wish to underscore that there is more work to do to ensure criminological scholarship has something relevant and critical to contribute to the interdisciplinary study of war. To help explore this assertion further, and before we turn to address the overarching question we posed in our Introduction (that is, can there be a 'criminology of war'?), there is a farther-reaching message we wish to convey. Within this final chapter, as a way of providing some overall assessment for the arguments we have constructed throughout this book, we offer a critique of the conceptual framework of the 'new wars' paradigm framing our discussion. Indeed, our own view, that the study of war is not necessarily a 'new horizon' for the discipline of criminology, is a critique similarly reflected in the supposed newness of contemporary forms of war.

Revisiting the conceptual framework of the (not so) 'new' wars paradigm

Used as a general framework to capture much of the literature covered throughout this book, Kaldor's (2014) notions of 'old' and 'new' wars have helped conceptualise the changing nature of war across a variety of hitherto unconnected criminological and sociological literatures. However, notwithstanding the convenience afforded by these ideas, what has come to be known as the 'new wars paradigm' is not without its own critics. For Malešević (2010a: 319), the efficacy of a new wars paradigm is put in doubt due to 'shaky foundations', particularly its broad empirical and theoretical claims. For example, Malešević (2010a) suggests that inter- and intra-state wars are not easily separable acts of war making historically. Intra-state wars (that is, civil wars) are often the catalysts for inter-state wars between nations, and conversely civil wars have been funded and supported by external sovereign nations with global economic power (Malešević, 2010a). The asymmetrical tactics of war fighting as found with guerrilla war are also not unique to new wars and have been used throughout the centuries by smaller socio-cultural and political groups and organisations to combat larger invading and occupying powers (Malešević, 2010a).

In more targeted criticisms, Malešević (2010a: 320) suggests connecting new wars so tightly to the economic forces of globalisation participates in a 'structuralist economic reductionism'. This has several permutations: war making cannot be merely devolved to economic motivations; structural economic changes do not have a democratic impact on all locales in the same way; and wars past and present have always been fought for a variety of ideological and geopolitical reasons not just those which relate to economics and globalisation (Malešević, 2010a). So too warlords, criminals and privatised forms of violence have been present within war making historically (see Tilly, 1985), and proposing the capture of geopolitical territory as *not* a significant motivation for the contemporary enactment of war is an untenable suggestion (Malešević, 2010a). Nation-states have demonstrably grown and developed from competing economic (Mann, 1988), political (Giddens, 1985), and military developments (Tilly, 1975; on the military in particular see Finer, 1975, and Malešević, 2010a). As Malešević (2010a) continues, military force also remains the most certain guarantee of economic development and nation-states have found ways to monopolise militarised violence via different means of negotiation, surveillance (Giddens, 1985), policing (Tilly, 1975; in particular Bayley, 1975, on the police) and privatised security (noted later). However, nation-states still require forms of nationalism to further support and afford 'legitimacy' for their war making (see Weber, discussed in Chapter Two), even when national public backing for war is to be gained from a benign base of support rather than overt and enduring jingoism (as discussed in Chapter Six; see also Malešević, 2010a). The 'new' wars argument also stipulates it is less the advancements in technology that define them than it is the macro socioeconomic changes of globalisation (Kaldor, 2014). However, for Malešević (2010a) the advent of the revolution in military affairs has made military powers reliant on advanced weapons technologies of war to fight 'uncooperative' governments in smaller more incisive armed conflicts. As such, technologies are far from a moot issue in contemporary war making. Indeed, they are a central feature of the capacity of nation-states and their militaries to perpetrate violence in what we have discussed as 'risk-transfer wars' (Shaw, 2005, discussed in Chapter Six), or what Castells (2010: 484–91) has differently described as 'instant wars'. As he suggests, 'we must be strongly reminded that instant, surgical, secluded, technology-driven wars are the privilege of technologically dominant nations', without forgetting that 'slow-motion' wars (for example civil wars, or indeed as the 2001 and 2003 wars in Afghanistan and Iraq turned out to be) 'are still, and will be for the foreseeable future, the hideous sign of our destructive capacity' (Castells, 2010: 489).

Building an instrument of critique for this book

Put simply then, the crux of many criticisms regarding the 'new wars paradigm' is that its main tenets are far from unique. However, by using this approach as a way of generally framing the literature for our discussions, the emphasis placed on the characteristics of new wars has subsequently informed omissions within our own argument. A telling instance of this is the absence of issues relating to the gendered masculine nature of war whether deemed 'old' or 'new'. As discussed in Chapter Seven, this conceptual problem was largely absent from the analysis offered in previous chapters (One to Six) and helps signify the more general inattention to issues of gender within much of the sociological and criminological literature addressing war (and indeed crime). Once apparent, the analysis of war as presented throughout this book begins to look precarious, not only for its general inattention to matters related to gender but for a deeper lack of acknowledgement about the intersectional issues (vis-à-vis gender, 'race', ethnicity, class, sexuality and so on) that a gendered analysis brings to the fore when studying war as a form of 'masculinity by other means' (Horne, 2004, cited in Cockburn, 2007: 249). Indeed, as Cockburn (2007: 257) concludes, '[t]he gender drama is never absent: the male as subject, the female as alien, aliens as effeminate. This is why a theory of war is flawed if it lacks a gender analysis.'

Following Horne (2004, cited in Cockburn, 2007: 249) noted above, we will offer a further reinterpretation of Clausewitz's ([1832] 1997) adage of war in due course. For now, two further dimensions not addressed in detail within this book are technologies and a preoccupation with state-centric wars. For example, even when war is understood not to have prioritised the capturing of geographical terrain (as per 'new' wars), the spatiality of war making (Holmqvist, 2014) has been assumed as perpetrated within and upon the physical and topographical environment. Yet it is abundantly clear in contemporary times that 'instant wars, and their technologically induced temporality, are an attribute of informational societies' (Castells, 2010: 491). Indeed, for Aas (2013), digital landscapes are an intellectual frontier of significant importance to the study of criminology vis-à-vis globalisation, security and surveillance (that is, cybercrime and cybersecurity) when understood through the lens of temporality to which Castells (2010) refers. Therefore, taken in view of the concerns here, an engagement with *cyberwars* as an extension of growing criminological interests in technologies could add meaningfully to future studies concerned with 'war'. However, ten years on from the launch of the *International*

Journal of Cyber Criminology, when outlining a future research agenda for the following decade, no mention was made of 'war' (see Ngo and Jaishankar, 2017). Nevertheless, scholars such as Yar (2013) have included 'cyberterrorism' in critical criminological accounts of cybercrime, while others such as Karatzogianni (2006, 2009, 2013) have long since been developing sociological insights related to war and conflict in virtual realms. Recent developments have also occurred from across these supposed disciplinary divides. Contributions from Kirton (2016) and Mair et al (2016) offer innovative demonstrations of how the role and use of technologies such as digitally recorded footage of warfare, when presented through internet and social media platforms, can add to and further advance our critical understanding of how war violence is captured, (re)presented, problematised and used.

Returning to the work of Kaldor (2014), in opposition to her argument, for Drake (2007: 640) the 'midrange explanatory account' of war in this work as derived 'upwards from the evidence of case studies' is its main flaw. Drake states Kaldor's (2014) argument is 'inadequate' as it derives from an analysis of state-centric wars that have been perpetrated by formal military powers. It therefore overlooks 'the 'other side' of new wars – the power of invention' (Drake, 2007: 645) from states in the Global North and South where insurgent, para- or private military actors are influential in the perpetration of war violence. Our own discussions herein have also fallen into this conceptual state-centric trap. By way of explanation rather than excuse, this is in part because our arguments have been guided by an intention to present subjugated knowledge (Foucault, 2004). In doing so it becomes apparent that criminological studies of war have largely focused on wars perpetrated by nation-states with formalised military structures. However, more recently authors such as Adam White have excavated matters relating to war and military issues with regards to private military contractors, including their political economy (see for example, White, 2010, 2012) and statuses as criminals and victims (White, 2016), in the aftermath of war as 'private military veterans' (White, 2018a), or indeed as relevant criminological subject matter (White, 2018b).

Thus the shortcomings of the new wars paradigm become evident and provide space for further critique. For the remainder of this chapter this critique will be the instrument through which we build a further assessment of the work presented in this book.

Some central critiques of the 'new wars paradigm'

A key critique raised of Kaldor's (2014) 'new' wars thesis is the way in which the deviant nature of war was to be addressed with 'cosmopolitan' responses. For Kaldor (2014), 'new' wars require a democratic (metropolitan) project to counter the violence and 'politics of exclusivism' which they perpetrate. She suggests:

> What is needed is an alliance between local defenders of civility and transnational institutions which would guide a strategy aimed at controlling violence. Such a strategy would include political, military and academic components. It would operate within a framework of international law that comprises both the 'laws of war' and human rights law, which could perhaps be termed cosmopolitan law, and it would put an emphasis on various forms of transitional justice. (Kaldor, 2014: 12)

However, as advocated in chapter two and reflected in subsequent chapters, when viewed critically there is very little to suggest the processes and functions of international, criminal and transitional justice (as promoted by Kaldor, 2014) are not corrupt or corrupting. Predesignating war as a form of criminality, advocating for its regulation within the universalism of the laws of war, and promoting 'cosmopolitan' solutions to tackle war as a means of pacification are notions requiring further elicitation and reinterpretation. Indeed, we need to consider 'war is the motor behind institutions and order ... we have to interpret the war that is going on beneath peace; peace itself is a coded war' (Foucault, 2004: 50–1). Here we offer some preliminary 'decoding' of Kaldor's (2014) 'cosmopolitan' solutions to 'new' wars through the concepts of crime, policing, justice and power. Working through these concepts brings other peripheral, but important, issues of globalisation, colonialism and the proclivities of metropolitan criminological knowledge to the fore.

Decoding war as 'crime', 'policing' and 'justice'

In chapters three, four and five in particular we have reflected on the general problem of law and crime as socially constructed normative systems of order. In brief, and as Kaldor (2014) has observed, the laws of war de facto afford legitimacy to war-making as a rational state act (in accordance with Clausewitzean thought), an approach generally incompatible with understanding the social phenomenon of 'war' from critical vantage points (discussed in Chapter Two). Certainly, when addressing matters of crime and law, given that for some political power exists as a facilitator of war-making and that social and judicial structures are borne out of the violence of warfare, acts of war and the laws that govern them must not be simply considered rational tools of pacification (Foucault, 2004). When translated in terms of 'conflict' vis-à-vis social relations, the notion of war exists in many enclaves of power within society (Foucault, 2004), including crime and the law. As discussed in chapter three, this is evident in the metaphorical uses of waging 'wars' against crime, drugs and terrorism throughout 'criminology's three wars' (LaFree, 2009). Equally, social institutions such as the law, police and judiciary do not operate peacefully, particularly when constituted to regulate international kinds of social (dis)order. When framed as a corrective to this problem, war in its more literal forms can therefore be operationalised as a modality of juridical pacification.

With regards to criminality and 'new' war, Drake (2007) accuses Kaldor's (2014) analysis of a 'downward gaze' on crime, a criticism often levelled at mainstream criminology. He suggests that the financing of 'new' wars are overlooked by Kaldor as 'predatory economic globalisation' (Drake, 2007: 643). This he argues is overgeneralised by Kaldor (2014) as facilitated by 'diasporic communities' consisting of migrant workers 'who provide an ideologically manipulable source of expatriate finance and a reservoir of socially disembedded recruits for the new wars' (Drake, 2007: 643). Instead, Drake (2007) suggests that 'diasporic communities' who are affected by war and conflict should be understood sensitively as those frequently exposed to exploitation, disempowerment and essentialism (as discussed in Chapter Four). In rudimentary terms, for Drake (2007) the non-state actors perceived to be helping facilitate state-perpetrated 'new' wars in Kaldor's (2014) analysis are perhaps akin to 'folk devils' (Cohen, [1972] 2011). Whether 'new' wars constitute a 'moral panic' is more of a moot question, but the 'war on terrorism' has long since been known to engender essentialism and fear of the 'other' in the way Drake (2007) implies (see Young, J., 2007; Walklate and Mythen, 2014). The same is also true of 'war' when understood as colonial violence, a point which we will return to shortly.

The general tenor of the 'cosmopolitan' solutions to war proposed by Kaldor (2014) to tackle such 'deviance' can also been understood as constructing wars as criminal acts requiring global 'policing' responses. As Kaldor (2014: 12) acknowledges '[s]ince the new wars are, in a sense, a mixture of war, crime and human rights violations, so the agents of cosmopolitan law-enforcement have to be a mix of soldiers and police'.

Noted as one of the three key themes of a 'criminology of war' in chapter two (Carrabine, 2018), transnational policing at war has indeed been addressed at length within criminological literature (see for example, Degenhardt, 2016b; Delaforce, 2016; McCulloch, 2016). For Holmqvist (2014), addressing wars in terms of global policing refutes Clausewitzean thought on war as a forcible act (noted in our Introduction). War instead has been transformed into a normative exploit of (Western) global order maintenance and a form of coercion and control. Indeed, as Holmqvist (2014: 16) points out, 'In the narrative of policing war, the eventually coercive nature of war is obscured. War by liberal states is rationalised not as war proper but as a necessary corrective to disorder – a fantasy that has proved extraordinarily lasting in the liberal imagination.'

In her account of war as 'policing', Holmqvist (2014) provides several perspectives on how war has been conceptualised as illegitimate: either in reductionist terms as a collapse of normative perceptions of (dis)order within 'failed states' (almost exclusively residing in the Global South); or as a 'clash of civilisations' whereby war is deemed an inevitable and deterministic outcome of cultural, religious and social constructions of certain identities. War is also conceptualised in terms of 'banal' criminality or 'dramatic' acts of terrorism (Holmqvist, 2014). War as a form of criminality has been the preoccupation of each of our previous chapters in one form or another, but for Holmqvist (2014) the presentation of war in such ways frequently strips it of historical, social and theoretical complexity and reduces it to a banal problem of disorder. The latter issue of terrorism (discussed in Chapter Three) is frequently understood as a 'phenomenon distinct from war' reducing the motivations for violence to individualised acts of pathology or irrationality (Holmqvist, 2014: 29). Terrorism and counterterrorism thereby become 'an essential part of the metaphor of policing' and abstracted from any form of political legitimacy and historical struggle (Holmqvist, 2014: 29). For Holmqvist (2014), these 'narratives of disorder' emerging from (Western) perceptions of 'failed states', culturally deterministic (internal) conflicts, criminality and terrorism (see also Drake, 2007, commenting on Kaldor) have become conjoined with the notion of international (policing) responses serving the restoration of global order. Indeed, Kaldor's (2014) argument for 'cosmopolitan' solutions to 'new' war appears enmeshed in such normativity.

A further conceptual hurdle bound up in Kaldor's (2014) appeal to 'cosmopolitan' solutions is an understanding of war as a crime perpetrated by nation-states and its actors. Thus, this is a form of criminality requiring a different juridical response vis-à-vis international instruments of 'justice'. Adopting an approach more closely aligned with that charted in chapter two and demonstrated throughout subsequent chapters, another way of viewing elements of Kaldor's (2014) 'cosmopolitan' approach is through an 'upward gaze' on criminality. However, within much of the criminological literature presented earlier in this book (particularly Chapters Two to Six) the corrective to war as a form of 'state crime' has frequently been the recourse to international mechanisms of justice. Despite being mentioned on several occasions throughout this book, we are acutely aware that we have not addressed in detail the workings of the UN Charter and the UN Security Council, Geneva Conventions, or the Rome Statute and International Criminal Court, or other apparatuses of international criminal justice such as the ad hoc tribunals of the UN International Criminal Tribunal for the former Yugoslavia (ICTY) or the UN International Criminal Tribunal for Rwanda (mentioned in Chapter Four). Other criminological scholars have addressed these matters in considerable detail. A high-profile example is, of course, Sheldon Glueck (discussed in Chapters Two and Four) who was influential in establishing international standards of justice for aggressive war, genocide and crimes against humanity at the Nuremberg trials (see Hagan and Greer, 2002). Others have been directly involved in observing specific cases such as the Balkans (Hagan, 2003) and 2003 Iraq war (Kramer and Michalowski, 2005; Rothe and Mullins, 2006, chapter six; Hagan et al, 2015), some have appeals to criminological analysis more generally (Savelsberg, 2010, chapter 6), and others have developed historical practices that question the involvement of victims in the process of 'justice' (Karstedt, 2010; Rothe, 2014). However, Kaldor's (2014) support for a 'cosmopolitan' form of justice through these sorts of instruments is unsettled if reconsidered via the notion of 'victor's justice' (Zolo, 2010).

For Zolo (2010) the conceptual problem of law as related to war is grounded in the criminalisation of war making itself. This does not mean that war should not be deemed criminal and harmful. The key premise from Zolo (2010: 30) is that the trials established in Nuremberg and Tokyo to prosecute Nazi and Japanese atrocities during the Second World War, rather than pursuing justice impartially and equitably in the name of the law and for global benefit, instead established a 'dual standard system of international justice' formulated by the victorious nations (that is, the US, UK and Soviet Union) to serve their future geopolitical interests. Key to this dual system of justice, as noted in Chapters Five and Six, is that atrocities committed by Allied Forces during the Second World War, including the nuclear bombings of Hiroshima and Nagasaki, and terror bombings of civilians within German cities were not considered for prosecution, thereby legitimising their perpetration (Zolo, 2010). Considered in this way, and notwithstanding the criminal prosecutions brought to Nazi and Japanese war criminals, Zolo (2010: 30) argues that the construction of these trials set a precedent for a 'dual standard system of international justice' since replicated at the ICTY (organised by the UN) and Iraq Special Tribunal; the latter was constituted by Iraqi magistrates to try Saddam Hussein for previous crimes against humanity, but was unlawfully implemented and governed by the US as an occupying force under the Geneva Conventions (Zolo, 2010). The 'quality' of justice dispensed in such trials, Zolo suggests, is therefore of little integrity, due to the impunity with which global powers (such as the US, NATO and the UN) operate without accountability for their own war crimes. Their 'exemplarity', which is said to pander to global (read metropolitan) punitive populism, often prioritises degradation over due process and hides the presumed retribution 'paradigm' within which they operate. Therefore, challenging Kaldor's (2014) 'cosmopolitan' solutions to 'new' wars from such a position illuminates ways of problematising established international legal organs and mechanisms of 'justice'. Zolo (2010) maintains the moral position that war-making in all its manifestations constitutes inhumane and merciless acts of brutality, demanding accountability for *all* who perpetrate the gendered violence(s) of war.

Reinterpreting the baseline definition of ('old') Clausewitzean war as 'power'

A final point of departure from Kaldor's (2014) 'cosmopolitan solutions' is the misconception within the 'new wars paradigm' (Malešević, 2010a) that war making is mainly motivated by identity politics (as discussed in Chapter Six). For our purposes this can be understood in two oppositional ways, leading us to the problem transcending Kaldor's (2014) emphasis on global economic relations: the issue of 'power'.

Further to the assertion that war can be understood as a form of 'masculinity by other means' (Horne, 2004, cited by Cockburn, 2007: 249), another well-known reinterpretation of Clausewitz's ([1832] 1997) adage vis-à-vis power is presented by Michel Foucault. In a series of public lectures during 1976, later published in *Society Must be Defended*, Foucault (2004) proposed a consideration of 'war' that challenged its legitimacy as a rational act of state sovereignty, and urged for a critical appreciation of war to surpass its meaning as a manifestation of economic relations and statism (discussed in Chapter Two). In questioning the 'exercise of power' as a 'relationship of force' rather than that which is 'primarily the perpetuation and renewal of economic relations' (Foucault, 2004: 15), Foucault suggests that the notion of power should be questioned as operating *merely* as a form of economic repression. If power is considered as the 'implementation and deployment of a relationship of force', rather than war being understood as a modality of 'politics by other means' (Clausewitz, [1832] 1997), Foucault suggested instead that 'Power is war, the continuation of war by other means ... we can invert Clausewitz's proposition and say that *politics is the continuation of war by other means*' (Foucault, (2004: 15, emphasis added).

For Foucault (2004) this inversion of Clausewitzean thought implies that social relations as contemporarily arranged were at one time initially established by acts of violent war-making. Moreover, although often being considered an instrument of ending war and instituting peace, for Foucault political power operating in this way does so 'perpetually to use a sort of silent war to reinscribe that relationship of force, and to reinscribe it in institutions, economic inequalities, language, and even bodies of individuals [that is, biopolitics]' (Foucault, (2004: 16, our insert).

Proposed within a broader discussion of 'subjugated knowledges', for Foucault Clausewitz's ([1832] 1997) adage was the inversion of how the origins of power had been historically arranged. Rather than war being initially understood as 'politics by other means' (Clausewitz, [1832] 1997), for Foucault it was more historically and conceptually accurate to suggest politics vis-à-vis power relations should first be conceptualised as the 'continuation of war by other means'. Indeed, as he further states, 'we are always writing the history of the same war, even when we are writing the history of peace and its institutions' (Foucault, 2004: 16).

Thus, when power relations are understood as acts of war they can be perceived as forms of identity politics and biopolitics (and indeed necropolitics, as discussed in Chapter Six), as much as they can be rationalised in terms of motivations for economic and geopolitical gain. For Drake (2007) however, the rationale of 'new' wars being fought for ideological reasons or via the exercise of biopower, justifies Kaldor (2014) advocating *for* cosmopolitan forms of justice in her argument as a response to contemporary war making. What this sacrifices however, is the opportunity to open up the conceptual space to critique cosmopolitan forms of justice as contemporary displays of imperialism (Drake, 2007). In opposition to Kaldor's (2014) argument, then, it is not 'the unimportance of space but the illegitimacy of territorial conquest' that is at stake in contemporary wars (Malešević, 2010a: 323). From this perspective, both Drake (2007) and Malešević (2010a) argue the motivations of new wars have not changed. Identity politics inform political and ideological motivations for war making and have long been inseparable matters. For Malešević (2010a: 329), what is more likely to have changed is that it is no longer perceived as 'legitimate' to invade, occupy and treat a nation and its citizens 'as a culturally and racially inferior species'. Powerful (Western) nation-states have instead adopted a 'softer' geopolitics of coercion and bargaining when waging war; however, what is being fought for remains historically and contemporarily consistent, namely economic, territorial, geopolitical and ideological gain (Malešević, 2010a).

In a defence of her thesis however, Kaldor (2014) notes that the terms 'old' and 'new' were not intended to render pre-Second World War violence obsolete, but instead were introduced to help inform policy makers to think differently about how war making had developed since 1945 and required different responses. Yet, although Malešević (2010a) suggests that introducing such 'new' paradigmatic thinking can help present unique and competing ways of conceptualising the social phenomenon of war, we suggest it is also equally useful to reorient this framework to facilitate alternative ways of understanding the globalised and historical contexts of war. Bluntly put, 'when it comes to interstate wars, Western powers have clearly done most of the fighting, and the global South is where most of it has occurred' (Wimmer, 2014: 174).

'Out of the North parts …': bringing the periphery into view

Following Drake (2007), we acknowledge Kaldor's (2014) concept of 'new' wars had taken little account of a longer view of war making historically (indeed Holmqvist, 2014, suggested this view to be ahistorical), and her analysis is displaced from perceptions of nation building. Revising this thinking brings into view some further glaring absences of the 'new' wars paradigm. This puts to the fore important yet often peripheral issues for the study of war, and allows us to finish with a critical reflection on the discipline of criminology and the perceived 'origin stories' of a 'criminology of war'.

To help bring into view issues overlooked in both the new wars paradigm and criminological studies of war more generally, Drake

(2007) directs us to the work of Tarak Barkawi. In *Globalization & War*, Barkawi (2006) provides an alternative appreciation of war from that offered by Kaldor (2014). Pointing to the work of Martin Shaw (1988a) (discussed in Chapter Six), Barkawi (2006: 28) suggests a Western-centric 'war and society' approach (as generally mobilised throughout this book) has dominated both the historicising and intellectualising of war within the social sciences past and present. Conceptualised in broadly Clausewitzean terms, and conducted outwardly from Westphalian positions (that is, between sovereign nation-states) and metropolitan experiences (that is, of Europe and the US), these perspectives have shaped how war is understood in global terms within mainstream social science (Barkawi, 2006). Akin to our discussions of classical sociology in Chapter Two, the liberal assumptions that globalisation is a facilitator of pacification and stands in opposition to war has influenced scholarship in ways that make it 'particularly bad at addressing how such a [Westphalian] world came about' (Barkawi, 2006: 34). To think of a 'war and society' approach in terms of the historical and dialectic relationship between metropolitan war making and those most affected by it outwith the Global North, Barkawi (2006) encourages us to consider how the arrangement of military force has not merely been organised through the 'monopoly' of violence from sovereign armies emerging 'out of the North parts' (in the manner of the image on the cover of this book and as noted in Figure 6.1), but instead as a means of 'globalising' a 'war and society' approach. Thus, by fully and critically appreciating the role of imperialism and colonialism as central (rather than peripheral) concerns for sociological studies of war, Barkawi (2006) encourages us to understand the organisation of military force as more fragmented and widespread across nations colonised by metropolitan powers as acts of Empire and empire building. Barkawi (2006), for example, foregrounds the British Indian Army as an historical exemplar of the centrality of colonialism within metropolitan war-making.

In addition to the co-option of Indigenous peoples into colonial armies to fight on behalf of the sovereign interests imposed on them, as Cunneen and Tauri (2016: 45) make clear, '[e]very part of Indigenous society was attacked during the colonial process. Early contact often involved open warfare, to be replaced later by government controls.' Within the context of criminology, Mark Brown (2014) has similarly foregrounded the British penal code in colonised and postcolonial India (see Brown, 2017a) as a way of critically accounting for criminal justice and penal mechanisms as key impositions of the governmental 'civilising' control of Indigenous peoples. As Brown (2017b: from personal conference notes—*RMc*) later pointed out, extrapolating the nuances between 'settler' and 'extractive' colonialism offers further specificity on what is meant by the 'colonial state' and the 'depth and penetration' that this has had on the lives of Indigenous peoples (Barkawi, 2006). Indeed, Brown (2017b) notes the term 'colonial rule' is a more effective means of critically analysing the processes of colonialism. In this regard, addressing the colonisation of Indigenous peoples in Australia and Aotearoa New Zealand, as Cunneen and Tauri (2016) observe, the first step in the imposition of 'colonial rule' (Brown, 2017a) was invasion, brutality and violence. Facilitated by the racialisation of Indigenous peoples as 'inferior', threatening and requiring control (that is, 'civilising'), colonialists of all nationalities are widely evidenced to have subjected the populaces of nations throughout history to domination, subjugation and eradication (Cunneen and Tauri, 2016). Indeed, as Cunneen and Tauri (2016: 49) continue, 'It is clear that imperial justifications for colonisation, even by way of discovery and settlement, allowed for the conduct of war against resisting Indigenous peoples … In some cases, wars against Indigenous peoples can be seen as genocide.'

Of course, one of the central features of the new wars paradigm, held as a core tenet of this book, is the disproportionate targeting of civilians as victims of war violence. However, in view of the reorientation in thinking urged by Barkawi (2006) (for sociology) and Cunneen and Tauri (2016) (for criminology), a further key limitation of the new wars paradigm is its neglect of the historical massacres and genocides by colonial powers in accounts of overall civilian deaths. Moreover, as one of the foremost engagements within criminological studies of war has been the crime of genocide (as discussed in Chapters Four and Seven), it is imperative that such violence is not further overlooked as acts of colonialism which have shaped historical and contemporary geopolitics vis-à-vis war (see for example, Short, 2010, 2016).

As demonstrated in Chapter Seven, the inclusion of the study of gender encouraged a re-evaluation of the work covered throughout this book. Taking genocide as a key focal and gendered subject, a critical reanalysis of the work presented in Chapter Four would point to elements of our discussion as a 'first generation' perspective (Woolford, 2013). Woolford (2013) notes that unlike Friedrich's (2000) take on the 'crime of the century' (noted in Chapter Four), critical genocide scholars are less inclined to defer to the applied legal definition of genocide often found in critical criminological work. Indeed, with few exceptions (including Jamieson, 1998, 1999; Morrison, 2006; Mullins and Rothe, 2008), for Woolford (2013: 169) it is often via concerns with 'canonical case studies' imbued with themes of perpetration, prevention and 'clothed in criminological theory' that criminologists studying genocide enter the field for the first time as 'first generation' genocide scholars. This is not to undermine the influential work done in these areas, but instead acknowledges the imposition of historical moments, theoretical concepts and the limited cultural and geographical reach of northern scholarship on the study of genocide within criminology (see Woolford, 2006). Importantly, for Buss (2014) a questionable feature of later work on atrocity crimes points to the dangers inherent in assuming genocide and crimes against humanity as a 'third world' or 'African problem'. Here the spectre of Orientalism emerges, melding with the intellectual imperialism of northern theorising (Connell, 2007, discussed later). Addressing the colonisation of Indigenous peoples in Canada, Woolford's (2013) suggestion is for a 'second generation' approach to genocide within criminology (and sociology) to be more fully recognised to understand the perpetration of genocide as a historical set of processes akin to the ways advocated above by Barkawi (2006) and Cunneen and Tauri (2016).

Barkawi's (2006) account of war in these altered globalised terms forces us to reassess our historical awareness and points of departure for how we – as social scientists – have formed our own appreciations of studying war and its origins. In closing, we follow Connell's (2007; 2017: from personal conference notes—RMc) suggestion to take account of colonialism as a 'low intensity war over one hundred years'. This approach further recognises the postcolonial era as continuing to demonstrate the 'coloniality of power' through globalised violence such as the 'war on terror' (Connell, 2017: from personal conference notes—RMc), or ongoing colonising territoriality such as that perpetrated by Israel in Gaza and the West Bank of historic Palestine for example (Short, 2016; Shalhoub-Kevorkian, 2017). Thus, we can also begin to better appreciate the ways in which such global processes have profoundly shaped the colonisation of knowledge within the social sciences. To this end, we wish to offer some disruption to the 'origin stories' of criminology and war as presented within this book.

Disrupting the origin stories of a 'criminology of war'

As we have argued in Chapter Three, Jamieson's (1998) proposition for a 'criminology of war' quickly became synonymous with the 'war on terrorism'. Taken as a problem of the selective view of the 'criminological imagination' (Young, J., 2011) this has yet to adopt a more complete interdisciplinary embrace of the study of war. Following

Brad Evans (2013) we further suggest that within the confines of such metropolitan knowledge (politically, publicly and academically) we are frequently encouraged to only reach back in history to selective moments, such as 9/11, to understand the past and to think critically about the present. This, Evans (2013) suggests, is the narrow conceptual and historical framework through which the present is often viewed, and through which we suggest contemporary criminological studies of war (ours included) have often taken as their points of engagement and departure. Notwithstanding his previous extensive work on the Balkans war, Iraq war, and Darfur genocide (discussed in Chapters Six, Three and Four, respectively), Hagan's (2015: 4, emphasis added) more recent assertion of '*American* criminology', also being caught 'sleeping' with regards to analysing the 2003 Iraq War as a war of aggression stands as an exemplar of this problem. Barkawi's (2006) critique of sociological studies of war (noted earlier) can be extended to implicate these criminological approaches. Of course, writing prior to 9/11 Jamieson (1998) was well aware of the need for a longer view of war in relation to history which extended beyond the Second World War. Observing Bonger (1916), Jamieson suggested we should appreciate 'the relationship between war and crime to be inextricably linked to social structures and imperatives. In his 1916 text, Bonger forcibly argued that militarism was closely linked to colonialism (the external struggle for the expansion of markets) and internal pacification' (Jamieson, 1998: 485)

Thus, a reading of Jamieson's (1998) call for intellectual moves 'towards a criminology of war in *Europe*' to be merely tethered to the geography and knowledges of the Global North (Barkawi, 2006; Connell, 2007) would be inaccurate. In reconnecting with the work of Bonger (1916) as the earliest substantive contribution within criminology to the study of war (noted in Chapter Two), Jamieson (1998) brings some of the concerns tabled by Barkawi (2006), M. Brown (2014, 2017a), and Cunneen and Tauri (2016) into view which had been hitherto peripheral concerns for criminology.

Some of the most recent substantive intellectual movements within criminology have begun to offer a sustained corrective to the problems noted here. Taking influence from the work of Raewyn Connell's (2007) *Southern Theory*, 'southern criminology' (see for example, Carrington et al, 2018, 2019) encourages us to take a historical and more globally oriented (rather than 'international') view of crime, violence and victimisation that transcends the metropolitan hegemonic knowledge base of criminology. Considered as a means with which to challenge the 'origin stories' of what we read, teach and study, as Hogg and colleagues outline:

> It is important to stress that it is *not an oppositional or rejectionist project* ... all societies are marked by centre/periphery relationships and hierarchies, reminding us that North/South should be regarded not simply or primarily as a geographical divide so much as a metaphor for power relations that are pervasive. At the same time, dominant northern and hegemonic theories and accounts are often limited by their own restricted 'northern' gaze, failing to fully appreciate, if they acknowledge it at all, the effects of imperial context and entwined histories on their own societies and institutions. (Hogg et al, 2017: 5, emphasis added)

In view of the observations from Barkawi (2006), Cunneen and Tauri (2016) and Connell (2007) we suggest that the central argument of this book – that study of war is not a new endeavour for the discipline of criminology – is brought into different relief when recognised as being underpinned by, prioritising, and perpetuating metropolitan knowledge in unreflexive ways (Connell, 2007).

Furthermore, as Carrington and colleagues note, the critical position of a 'southern criminology' is:

> As an *essentially peace-time endeavour*, much criminological research has concentrated on justice as 'a domestic (national) project, confined to local or national interests' (Barbaret [sic] 2014: 16), overlooking major historical and contemporary forms and trends in criminal justice practice outside the metropolitan centres of the northern hemisphere. (Carrington et al, 2016: 3, emphasis added)

However, while we concur with the premise and direction of this agenda, we also recognise that it is not without existing critique (see for example, Moosavi, 2019; Travers, 2019) or open to further examination. By way of the latter, we care to point out that when reflecting on the subject matter covered throughout this book observations of criminology being 'essentially a peace-time endeavour' (Carrington et al, 2016) begin to appear questionable. Although the study of criminology and the knowledge base it produces has indeed been confined to domestic projects of pacification through national criminal justice interests, conversely – as we have evidenced – scholarship during times of war (that is, not 'peace-time') has also been a persistent feature of criminology for those frequently working at the margins of the discipline's interests.

However, the study of war within criminology past and present has established its hegemonic gaze on the subject of war so that only certain types of Clausewitzean 'old' or 'new' wars (Kaldor, 2014) are afforded some attention. As we have discussed, this attention is frequently arranged around certain normative criminological assumptions related to crime, law, (dis)order and victimisation transposed onto international issues of inter- or intra-state violence often described in macro terms of state-centric war and state crime. Importantly, the predominant criminological literature addressing war has a limited history originating from the First World War. Following Barkawi's (2006) insights noted above vis-à-vis globalisation, war and colonialism, so too is there an urgent requirement for criminology to have a longer view of history that is not tied to normative matters of pacification. As Carrington et al (2016: 3) continue:

> Much research in criminology takes for granted a high level of internal peace within what is assumed to be a stable nation state system. This has led to the obfuscation of the historical role of state violence in nation-building, the expansion of colonialism across the global South and the neglect of contemporary violent phenomena, like armed conflict, drug wars and ethnic cleansing, that are more common in the Global South.

This observation notwithstanding however, despite the advocacy of scholars such as Barkawi (2006), the newly emerged southern criminology agenda has perhaps inadvertently displaced war and genocide from its central attentions. Nevertheless, as a corrective to the hegemonic criminological views of war presented herein, future studies of wars, armed conflict, state violence and genocides must take these concerns seriously. In doing so, and as a concluding note, we may wish to not only question – for one final time – how 'war' is being defined here, but additionally ponder whose worldview is being depicted in what we have been studying.

Concluding thoughts: can there be a 'criminology of war'?

Throughout this book we have been necessarily selective with the material we have chosen to engage with, and we therefore realise that there are – of course – limitations to what we present. For example, we have not been able to excavate all possible avenues within historical or classical sociology, the 'sociology of war' and 'military sociology', nor looked to connect the subject of war to all corners of criminology. This was not however the purpose nor intention of this book. We are also fully aware that the study of war is vast, and what we have attempted to present here is indeed an ambitious undertaking which strains against the confines of one book. Indeed, what has perhaps been risked in what we have presented in these chapters is a roaming discussion of some breadth and limited depth, or a series of targeted discussions with some depth but limited reach. Worse still we may have achieved neither of these things. We therefore appreciate our arguments include omissions we are well aware of, and others that may come to light in the years after its publication.

The general unease with which the 'new wars paradigm' has been received within disciplines such as sociology and security studies as, among other things, offering an ahistorical view of war making and presiding over issues that are far from 'new', is a conceptual problem similarly reflected in the underpinning argument of this book. In foregrounding and arranging the literature presented throughout chapters two to seven, it is our contention that the study of war is not necessarily a 'new horizon' of criminology any more than a 'new' wars paradigm offers any particular newness to the study of war more generally. Nevertheless, we consider what has been presented here is a useful way of arranging previously disconnected criminological work, situated within and further developed by relevant sociological literature.

Returning to the problematique posed in the comments of Martin Shaw (1984) from the Introduction, we now revisit the overarching question, and indeed the title, of this book: can there be a 'criminology of war'? The answer to this question is open to interpretation. For some the response may be 'yes', particularly given the efforts we have gone to throughout this book to foreground extant criminological work that has been concerned to address the topic of war. For others the answer may be 'no', perhaps due to war being a social phenomenon like any other and, in view of the further work we have presented here, might demonstrate the sociological relevance of this position. Indeed, conversely some may not care for this question at all or consider it an irrelevance. Whichever way one responds to this question however, when all is said and done readers of this book would do well to keep in mind that the study of war is not intended to be captured or conceptualised (nor colonised) as a criminological 'specialism'. We are, of course, not the first to make this point. This has been made clear previously by Ruth Jamieson (2012) in an article within *Studi Sulla Questione Criminale,* and the introduction to the long-awaited edited reader *The Criminology of War* (Jamieson, 2014). As Jamieson (2012) suggested, the study of war within criminology – as one of many disciplines within the social sciences – remains as important as it has ever been, but fundamentally, 'what it comes down to is not so much a question of what people call it ... Rather *it is a question of how the study of war is imagined and achieved*' (Jamieson, 2012, emphasis added). We concur.

References

Aas, K.F. (2013) *Globalization & Crime* (2nd edn). London: Sage.

Agamben, G. (1995) *Homo Sacer: Sovereign Power and Bare Life*. Stanford, CA: Stanford University Press.

Agamben, G. (2005) *State of Exception*. Chicago, IL: The University of Chicago Press.

Agnew, R. (2010) A general strain theory of terrorism. *Theoretical Criminology* 14(2): 131–54.

Albertson, K., Irving, J. and Best, D. (2016) A social capital approach to assisting veterans through recovery and desistance transitions in civilian life. *The Howard Journal of Criminal Justice*, 54: 384–96.

Albertson, K., Best, D., Pinkney, A., Murphy, T., Irving, J. and Stevenson, J. (2017) *"It's Not Just About Recovery": The Right Turn Veteran-Specific Recovery Service Evaluation. Final Report*. www.fim-trust. org/wp-content/uploads/2017/06/Albertson-et-al-Right-Turn-evaluation-final-report-June-2017-p.pdf

Al Hussein, Z.R. (2017) Human Rights Council 36th session Opening Statement by Zeid Ra'ad Al Hussein, United Nations High Commissioner for Human Rights, 11 September. www.ohchr.org/EN/NewsEvents/Pages/DisplayNews.aspx?NewsID=22041&LangID=E

Alvarez, A. (1997) Adjusting to genocide: the techniques of neutralization and the Holocaust. *Social Science History*, 21(2): 139–78.

Alvarez, A. (2010) *Genocidal Crimes*. Oxon: Routledge.

Alvarez, A. (2016) Borderlands, climate change, and the genocidal impulse. *Genocide Studies International*, 10(1): 27–36.

Alvarez, A. (2017) *Unstable Ground: Climate Change, Conflict and Genocide*. Lanham, MD: Rowman & Littlefield.

Amoore, L. (2014) Security and the incalculable. *Security Dialogue*, 45(5): 423–39.

Ashworth, A. and Zedner, L. (2014) *Preventive Justice*. Oxford: Oxford University Press.

Banks, J. and Albertson, K. (2018) Veterans and violence: an exploration of pre-enlistment, military and post-service life. *European Journal of Criminology*, 16(6): 730–47.

Barak, G. (2009) Christopher W. Mullins, Dawn L. Rothe: Blood, Power, and Bedlam: Violations of International Criminal Law in Post-Colonial Africa. *Theoretical Criminology*, 17: 75–7.

Barberet, R. (2014) *Women, Crime, and Criminal Justice*. London: Routledge.

Barkawi, T. (2006) *Globalization and War.* Oxford: Rowman & Littlefield.

Barnouw, E. (1970) *Hiroshima Nagasaki.* A CMC Production: Centre for Mass Communication. New York City: Columbia University Press. [video project]

Bartrop, P.R. (2015) *Genocide: The Basics.* Oxon: Routledge.

Bauman, Z. (1989) *Modernity and the Holocaust.* Cambridge: Polity.

Bayley, D.H. (1975) The police and political development in Europe. In Tilly, C. (ed) *The Formation of National States in Europe.* Princeton, NJ: Princeton University Press.

Beck, U. (2009) *World at Risk.* London: Sage.

Blaustein, J. (2015) *Speaking Truths to Power: Police Ethnography and Police Reform in Bosnia and Herzegovina.* Oxford: Oxford University Press.

Bonger, W.A. (1916) *Criminality and Economic Conditions.* Boston, MA: Little, Brown and Company.

Bonger, W.A. (1936) *An Introduction to Criminology.* London: Methuen.

Bourke, J. (2015) *Deep Violence.* University of California, Berk: Counterpoint Press.

Braithwaite, J. (2010) Loose talk of just war. *Pakistan Journal of Criminology,* 2(1): iii–vii.

Braithwaite, J. and D'Costa, B. (2018) *Cascades of Violence: War, Crime and Peacebuilding Across South Asia.* Acton: Australia National University Press. https://press.anu.edu.au/node/4135/download

Braithwaite, J. and Rashed, T. (2014) Nonviolence and reconciliation among the violence in Libya. *Restorative Justice: an International Journal,* 2(2): 185–204.

Braithwaite, J. and Wardak, A. (2013) Crime and war in Afghanistan: Part I: The Hobbesian solution. *The British Journal of Criminology,* 53: 179–96.

Brennan, A.-M. (2017) Ratko Mladić convicted – but justice hasn't entirely been served in the Hague. *The Conversation,* 24 November. http://theconversation.com/ratko-mladic-convicted-but-justice-hasnt-entirely-been-served-in-the-hague-88094

Bringedal-Houge, A. (2015) Conflict related sexual violence. In Ericsson, K. (ed) *Women in War: Examples from Norway and Beyond.* Fareham: Ashgate Publishing.

Bromberg, W. (1943) The effects of war on crime. *American Sociological Review,* 8(6): 685–91.

Brown, M. (2014) *Penal Power and Colonial Rule.* Oxon: Routledge.

Brown, M. (2017a) Postcolonial penality: liberty and repression in the shadow of independence, India c. 1947. *Theoretical Criminology,* 21(2): 186–208.

Brown, M. (2017b) As criminology looks back: State crime and the colonial turn. *Crime and Justice in Asia and the Global South Conference*, co-hosted by the Crime and Justice Research Centre, QUT, and the Asian Criminological Society, Cairns: Australia, 11 July.

Brown, W.B. (2008) Another emerging storm: Iraq and Afghanistan Veterans with PTSD in the criminal justice system. *Justice Policy Journal,* 5(2). www.cjcj.org/news/5574

Brown, W.B. (2010) War, Veterans, and crime. In Herzog-Evans, M. (ed) *Transnational Criminology*. The Netherlands: Wolf Legal Publishers.

Brown, W.B. (2011) From war zones to jail: veteran reintegration problems. *Justice Policy Journal,* 8(1). www.cjcj.org/news/5579

Brown, W.B. (2015) Veteran coming-home obstacles: short and long-term consequences of the Iraq and Afghanistan wars. In Walklate, S. and McGarry, R. (eds) *Criminology and War: Transgressing the Borders.* Oxon: Routledge.

Brownmiller, S. (1975) *Against Our Will*. New York: Bantam Books.

Burns, K. and Novick, L. (2017) *The Vietnam War.* Arlington, VA: Public Broadcasting Service.

Buss, D. (2014) Seeing sexual violence in conflict and post-conflict societies: the limits of visibility. In Buss, D., Lebert, J., Rutherford, B. and Sharkey, D. (eds) *Sexual Violence in Conflict and Post-Conflict Societies.* London: Routledge.

Butler, J. (2004) *Precarious Life: The Powers of Mourning and Violence.* London: Verso.

Caforio, G. (2006) (ed) *Handbook of the Sociology of the Military.* New York: Springer.

Caldwell, R.A. and Mestrovic, S.G. (2011) The war on terror in the early twenty-first century: applying lessons from sociological classics and sites of abuse. In Carlton-Ford, S. and Ender, M.G. (eds) *The Routledge Handbook of War and Society: Iraq and Afghanistan.* Oxon: Routledge.

Camilleri, R. (2012) *Impact of Counter-Terrorism on Communities: France Background Report.* London: Institute for Strategic Dialogue.

Carden-Coyne, A. (2012) *Gender and Conflict since 1914.* London: MacMillan-Palgrave.

Carrabine, E. (2016) Book review: The Crime of all Crimes: Towards A Criminology of Genocide, by Nicole Rafter. *The British Journal of Criminology,* 56(6): 1310–12.

Carrabine, E. (2018) Traces of violence: representing the atrocities of war. *Criminology & Criminal Justice,* 18(5): 631–46.

Carrington, K. (2015) *Feminism and Global Justice: New Directions in Critical Criminology*. Oxon: Routledge.

Carrington, K., Hogg, R. and Sozzo, M. (2016) Southern criminology. *The British Journal of Criminology*, 56(1): 1–20.

Carrington, K., Hogg, R. and Sozzo, M. (2018) (eds) *The Palgrave Handbook of Criminology and the Global South*. Basingstoke: Palgrave Macmillan.

Carrington, K., Hogg, R., Scott, J., Sozzo, M. and Walters, R. (2019) *Southern Criminology*. Oxon: Routledge.

Carruthers, S.L. (2014) 'Casualty aversion': media, society and public opinion. In Scheipers, S. (ed) *Heroism and the Changing Character of War*. Basingstoke: Palgrave Macmillan.

Castells, M. (2010) *The Rise of the Network Society: Volume 1* (2nd edn). West Sussex: Blackwell Publishing.

Center for Political Ecology (2014) Environment, health, and other human rights concerns associated with nuclear weapons testing, fallout, involuntary displacement, human subject experimentation, and the failure to achieve durable solutions that protect the environment and safeguard the rights of the people of the Marshall Islands. *Submission to the United Nations Universal Periodic Review of the Republic of the Marshall Islands. Second Cycle–Twenty Second Session of the UPR Human Rights Council April–May 2015.* www.culturalsurvival.org/sites/default/files/media/upr_statement_by_cpe_-_rmi_nuclear_issues-1.pdf

Chinkin, C. (2012) Rethinking legality/legitimacy after the Iraq war. In Falk, R., Juergensmeyer, M. and Popovski, V. (eds) *Legality and Legitimacy in Global Affairs*. Oxford: Oxford University Press.

Clausewitz, C.V. ([1832] 1997) *On War* (trans. J. Graham). Ware, Herts: Wordsworth Editions.

Clinard, M.B. (1946) Criminological theories of violations of wartime regulations. *American Sociological Review*, 11(3): 258–70.

Coates, C.H. and Pelligrin, R.J. (1965) *Military Sociology: A Study of the American Military Institution and Military Life*. Maryland: Social Science Press.

Cockburn, C. (2007) *From Where We Stand: War, Women's Activism and Feminist Analysis*. London: Zed Books.

Cockburn, C. (2012) *Anti-militarism: Political and Gender Dynamics of Peace Movements*. Basingstoke: Palgrave Macmillan.

Cockburn, C. (2013) Towards a Different Common Sense: from Battlefield to Household – Reducing Violence, Transforming Gender Relations. https://www.cynthiacockburn.org/BlogCommonsenseNorwich.pdf

Cockburn, C. (2014) A continuum of violence: gender, war and peace. In Jamieson, R. (ed) *The Criminology of War*. London: Ashgate.

Cohen, S. ([1972] 2011) *Folk Devils and Moral Panics. Routledge Classic.* Oxon: Routledge.

Cohen, S. (1993) Human rights and crimes of the state: the culture of denial. *Australian and New Zealand Journal of Criminology,* 26(2): 97–115.

Cohen, S. (2001) *States of Denial: Knowing About Atrocities and Suffering.* Cambridge: Polity.

Collins, R. (2008) *Violence: A Micro-Sociological Theory*. Princeton, NJ: Princeton University Press.

Connell, R. (2002) *Gender.* Cambridge: Polity.

Connell, R.W. (2005) *Masculinities* (2nd edn). Cambridge: Polity.

Connell, R. (2007) *Southern Theory: The Global Dynamics of Knowledge in Social Science.* Cambridge: Polity.

Connell, R. (2016) 100 Million kalashnikovs: gendered power on a world scale debate. *Feminista,* 51: 3–17.

Connell, R. (2017) Keynote presentation: Decolonizing knowledge for criminology, Crime and Justice in Asia and the Global South Conference, co-hosted by the Crime and Justice Research Centre, QUT, and the Asian Criminological Society, Cairns: Australia, 11 July.

Cottee, S. (2011) Jihadism as a subcultural response to social strain: extending Marc Sageman's 'bunch of guys' thesis. *Terrorism and Political Violence,* 23: 730–51.

Cottee, S. (2014) We need to talk about Mohammad: criminology, theistic violence and the murder of Theo Van Gogh. *The British Journal of Criminology,* 54(6): 981–1001.

Crawford, A. (2014) Thinking about sustainable security: metaphors, paradoxes and ironies. In Schuilenburg, M., van Steden, R. and Oude Breuil, B. (eds) *Positive Criminology: Reflections on Care, Belonging and Security.* The Hague: Eleven International Publishing.

Creighton, C. and Shaw, M. (1987) (eds) *The Sociology of War and Peace.* Explorations in Sociology 24: British Sociological Association. Basingstoke: Macmillan Press Ltd.

Cunneen, C. and Tauri, J. (2016) *Indigenous Criminology.* Bristol: Policy Press.

Dalgaard-Nielsen, A. (2010) Violent radicalization in Europe: what we know and what we do not know. *Studies in Conflict & Terrorism,* 33(9): 797–814.

Danilova, N. (2015a) *The Politics of War Commemoration in the UK and Russia.* Basingstoke: Palgrave MacMillan.

Danilova, N. (2015b) The politics of mourning: the virtual memorialisation of British fatalities in Iraq and Afghanistan. *Memory Studies,* 8(3): 267–81.

Das, V. (2007) *Life and Words.* Berkeley, C: University of California Press.

Davies, P. (2018) Feminist voices, gender and victimisation. In Walklate, S. (ed) *Handbook of Victims and Victimology* (2nd edn). Oxon: Routledge.

Davies, S.E. and True, J. (2015) Reframing conflict-related sexual and gender-based violence: bringing gender analysis back in. *Security Dialogue,* 46(6): 495–512.

Dawson, G., Dover, J. and Hopkins, S. (2016) (eds) *The Northern Ireland Troubles in Britain: Impacts, Engagements, Legacies and Memories.* Manchester: Manchester University Press.

Degenhardt, T. (2010) Representing war as punishment in the war on terror. *International Journal of Criminology and Social Theory,* 3: 343–58.

Degenhardt, T. (2015a) Crime, justice and the legitimacy of military power in the international sphere. *Punishment & Society,* 17(2): 139–62.

Degenhardt, T. (2015b) The overlap between war and crime: unpacking Foucault and Agamben's studies within the context of the war on terror. *Journal of Theoretical and Philosophical Criminology,* 5(2): 29–58.

Degenhardt, T. (2016a) Criminology and War: Transgressing the Borders. *Criminal Law and Criminal Justice Book Reviews,* March. http://clcjbooks.rutgers.edu/books/criminology-and-war-transgressing-the-borders/

Degenhardt, T. (2016b) An analysis of the war-policing assemblage: the case of Iraq (2003–2015). In McGarry, R. and Walklate, S. (eds) *The Palgrave Handbook of Criminology and War.* Basingstoke: Palgrave Macmillan.

Delaforce, R. (2016) Police, pluralisation and private security. In McGarry, R. and Walklate, S. (eds) *The Palgrave Handbook of Criminology and War.* Basingstoke: Palgrave Macmillan.

de Lint, W. and Virta, S. (2004) Security and ambiguity: towards a radical security politics. *Theoretical Criminology,* 8: 465–89.

Detter, I. (2013) *The Laws of War.* Oxon: Routledge.

DiPietro, S.M. (2016) Criminology and war: where are we going and where have we been? *Sociology Compass,* 10: 839–48.

DiPietro, S.M. (2019) Roads diverged: An examination of violent and nonviolent pathways in the aftermath of the Bosnian war. *Criminology,* 57(1): 74–104.

Drake, M.S. (2007) Sociology and new wars in the era of globalisation. *Sociology Compass,* 1(2): 637–50.

Duncanson, C. (2013) *Forces for Good? Military Masculinities and Peacebuilding in Afghanistan and Iraq*. London: Palgrave Macmillan.

Durkheim, E. (2013) *The Rules of Sociological Method and Selected Texts on Sociology and its Method* (2nd edn), S. Lukes (ed). Basingstoke: Palgrave MacMillan.

Edkins, J. (2003) *Trauma and the Memory of Politics*. Cambridge: Cambridge University Press.

Elias, N. (1994) *The Civilizing Process*. Oxford: Blackwell.

Ellis-Petersen, H. (2018a) Myanmar army rejects UK MPs' 'one-sided accusations' about Rohingya, *The Guardian*, 7 March. www.theguardian.com/world/2018/mar/07/myanmar-army-rejects-uk-mps-one-sided-accusations-about-rohingya

Ellis-Petersen, H. (2018b) Rohingya crisis: 132 MPs across region call for Myanmar to be referred to ICC, *The Guardian*, 24 August. www.theguardian.com/world/2018/aug/24/rohingya-crisis-132-mps-across-region-call-for-myanmar-to-be-referred-to-icc

Enloe, C. (1983) *Does Khaki Become You? The Militarisation of Women's Lives*. Boston, MA: South End Press.

Enloe, C. (1993) *The Morning After: Sexual Politics at the End of the Cold War*. Berkley and Los Angeles: University of California Press.

Enloe, C. (2000) *Manoeuvres: The International Politics of Militarizing Women's Lives*. Berkley and Los Angeles: University of California Press.

Enloe, C. (2016) *Globalization and Feminism: Feminists Make the Link*. Lanham, MD: Rowman & Littlefield.

Ericsson, K. (2015) *Women in War: Examples from Norway and Beyond*. Farnham: Ashgate.

Eulriet, I. (2010) Durkheim and Approaches to the Study of War. *Durkheim Studies*, 16: 59–76.

Evans, B. (2013) *Liberal Terror*. Cambridge: Polity.

Evans, K. (2017) War and peace: is militarisation the new norm? In Amatrudo, A. (ed) *Social Censure and Critical Criminology: After Sumner*. Basingstoke: Palgrave Macmillan.

Falk, R., Juergensmeyer, M. and Popovski, V. (2012) (eds) *Legality and Legitimacy in Global Affairs*. Oxford: Oxford University Press.

Fassin, D. (2011) The trace: violence, truth and the politics of the body. *Social Research*, 78(2): 281–98.

Fassin, D. and Rechtman, R. (2009) *The Empire of Trauma: An Inquiry into the Condition of Victimhood*. Princeton, NJ: Princeton University Press.

Fein, H. (1990) Genocide: a sociological concept. *Current Sociology: The Journal of the International Association*, 38(1): 8–25.

Finer, S.E. (1975) State and nation-building in Europe: the role of the military. In Tilly, C. (ed) *The Formation of National States in Europe*. Princeton, NJ: Princeton University Press.

Finnane, M. (2013) Terrorism and government: between history and criminology. *Australian and New Zealand Journal of Criminology*, 46(2): 159–77.

Fisher, J. (1999) *Mothers of the Disappeared*. London: Zed Books.

Ford, M., Mills, H., Grimshaw, R. and Allison, C. (2016) *Profile of Supervision for Armed Forces Veterans Under Probation Supervision*. Forces in Mind Trust. www.fim-trust.org/wp-content/uploads/2017/02/Veterans-Probation-Report.pdf

Fossey, M., Cooper, L., Godier, L. and Cooper, A. (2017) *A Pilot Study to Support Veterans in the Criminal Justice System. Project Report.* Forces in Mind Trust. http://arro.anglia.ac.uk/701663/1/RFEA_Nova_Document.pdf

Foucault, M. (2004) *Society Must be Defended: Lectures at the Collège de France, 1975–76* (trans. David Macey). London: Penguin Books Ltd.

Friedrichs, D.O. (1985) The nuclear arms issue and the field of criminal justice. *Justice Professional,* 1: 5–9.

Friedrichs, D.O. (2000) The crime of the century? The case for the Holocaust. *Crime, Law & Social Change,* 34: 21–41.

Friedrichs, D.O. (2010) *Trusted Criminals: White Collar Crime in Contemporary Society* (4th edn). Belmont, CA: Wadsworth Cengage Learning.

Freilich, J.D. and LaFree, G. (2014) Criminology theory and terrorism: introduction to the special issue. *Terrorism and Political Violence: Special Issue on Criminological Theory and Terrorism,* 27(1): 1–8.

Furedi, F. (1997) *Culture of Fear*. London: Cassell Continuum.

Futter, A. (2015) *The Politics of Nuclear Weapons.* London: Sage.

Gartner, R. and Kennedy, L. (2018) War and postwar violence. *Crime and Justice* 47(1): 1–67.

Gault, R.H. (1918) Delinquency in war time. *Journal of the American Institute of Criminal Law and Criminology,* 8(5): 651–2.

Gebhardt, M. (2016) *Crimes Unspoken: The Rape of German Women at the End of the Second World War.* Cambridge: Polity.

Gettlemen, J. (2017) Rohingya recount atrocities: 'they threw my baby into a fire'. *The New York Times*, 11 October. www.nytimes.com/2017/10/11/world/asia/rohingya-myanmar-atrocities.html

Giddens, A. (1985) *The Nation-State and Violence*. Cambridge: Polity.

Glueck, S. (1944) *War Criminals: Their Prosecution and Punishment.* New York: Knopf.

Glueck, S. (1946) *The Nuremberg Trial and Aggressive War.* New York: Knopf.

Green, P. and Ward, T. (2004) *State Crime: Governments, Violence and Corruption.* London: Pluto Press.

Green, P. and Ward, T. (2009) The transformation of violence in Iraq. *The British Journal of Criminology,* 49(5): 609–27.

Green, P., MacManus, T. and de la Cour Venning, A. (2015) *Countdown to Annihilation: Genocide in Myanmar.* London: Queen Mary University of London, International State Crime Initiative. http://statecrime. org/data/2015/10/ISCI-Rohingya-Report-PUBLISHED-VERSION.pdf

Green, P., MacManus, T. and de la Cour Venning, A. (2018) *Genocide Achieved, Genocide Continues: Myanmar's Annihilation of the Rohingya.* London: Queen Mary University of London, International State Crime Initiative. http://statecrime.org/data/2018/04/ISCI-Rohingya-Report-II-PUBLISHED-VERSION-revised-compressed.pdf

Greer, S. (2010) Anti-terrorist laws and the United Kingdom's 'suspect Muslim community': a reply to Pantazis and Pemberton. *The British Journal of Criminology,* 50: 1171–90.

Hagan, J. (2003) *Justice in the Balkans: Prosecuting War Crimes in The Hague Tribunal.* Chicago: Chicago University Press.

Hagan, J. (2015) While criminology slept: a criminal war of aggression in Iraq. *The Criminologist: The Official Newsletter of the American Society of Criminology,* 40(6): 2–4.

Hagan, J. and Greer, S. (2002) Making war criminal. *Criminology,* 40(2): 231–64.

Hagan, J. and Rymond-Richmond, W. (2009) *Darfur and the Crime of Genocide.* Cambridge: Cambridge University Press.

Hagan, J. and Kaiser, J. (2011) The displaced and dispossessed of Darfur: explaining the sources of a continuing state-led genocide. *The British Journal of Sociology,* 62(1): 1–25.

Hagan, J., Kaiser, J., Rothenberg, D., Hanson, A. and Parker, P. (2012) Atrocity victimization and the costs of economic conflict crimes in the battle for Baghdad and Iraq. *European Journal of Criminology,* 9(5): 481–98.

Hagan, J., Kaiser, J. and Hanson, A. (2015) *Iraq and the Crimes of Aggressive War: The Legal Cynicism of Criminal Militarism.* Cambridge: Cambridge University Press.

Hall, M. (2017) Exploring the cultural dimensions of environmental victimisation. *Palgrave Communications,* 3(17076), DOI:10.1057/palcomms.2017.76

Ham, P. (2013) *Hiroshima Nagasaki*. London: Doubleday.

Hamm, M.S. (2007) 'High crimes and misdemeanors': George W. Bush and the sins of Abu Ghraib. *Crime Media Culture*, 3(3): 259–84.

Hamm, M. and Spaaij, R. (2017) *The Age of Lone Wolf Terrorism*. New York: Columbia University Press.

Hamourtziadou, L. (2016) Lest we forget. www.iraqbodycount.org/analysis/beyond/lest-we-forget/

Harding, R. (1983) Nuclear energy and the destiny of mankind – some criminological perspectives. *Australian & New Zealand Journal of Criminology,* June, 16: 81–92.

Hayward, K. and Morrison, W. (2002) Locating 'Ground Zero': caught between the narratives of crime and war. In Strawson, J. (ed) *Law After Ground Zero*. London: Glasshouse Press.

Hediger, R. (2017) Animals in war. In Maher, J., Pierpoint, H. and Beirne, P. (eds) *The Palgrave International Handbook of Animal Abuse Studies*. Basingstoke: Palgrave Macmillan.

Heinecken, L. (2015) The military, war and society: the need for a critical sociological engagement. *Scientia Militaria, South African Journal of Military Studies,* 43(1): 1–16.

Hickman, M., Thomas, L., Silvestri, L.and Nickels, H. (2011) Suspect communities? Counter-terrorism policy, the press and impact on Muslim and Irish communities. London: London Metropolitan University. http://openaccess.city.ac.uk/8735/1/suspect-communities-report-july2011.pdf

Hillyard, P. (1993) *Suspect Community: People's Experiences of the Prevention of Terrorism Acts in Britain*. London: Pluto Press.

Hoffman, H (1992) What did Mendelsohn really say? In David, S.B. and Kirkhoff, G.F. (eds) *International Faces of Victimology*. Mönchengladbach: WSV Publishing.

Hogg, R., Scott, J. and Sozzo, M. (2017) Special edition: Southern criminology. Guest editor's introduction. *International Journal for Crime, Justice and Social Democracy*, 6(1): 1–7.

Holmes, O. (2017a) Massacre at Tula Toli: Rohingya recall horror of Myanmar army attack, *The Guardian*, 7 September. www.theguardian.com/world/2017/sep/07/massacre-at-tula-toli-rohingya-villagers-recall-horror-of-myanmar-army-attack

Holmes, O. (2017b) Fact check: Aung San Suu Kyi's speech on the Rohingya crisis, *The Guardian*, 7 September. www.theguardian.com/world/2017/sep/20/fact-check-aung-san-suu-kyi-rohingya-crisis-speech-myanmar

Holmqvist, C. (2012) War/space: shifting spatialities and the absence of politics in contemporary accounts of war. *Global Crime,* 13(4): 219–34.

Holmqvist, C. (2014) *Policing Wars: On Military Intervention in the Twenty-First Century.* Basingstoke: Palgrave Macmillan.

Hood, R. (2004) Hermann Mannheim and Max Grünht: criminological pioneers in London and Oxford. *British Journal of Criminology,* 44: 469–95.

Howard League for Penal Reform (2011) *Report of the Inquiry into Former Armed Service Personnel in Prison.* London: Howard League for Penal Reform.

Howie. L. (2012) *Witnesses to Terror.* London: Palgrave Macmillan.

Hudson, B. (2009) Justice in a time of terror. *British Journal of Criminology,* 49: 702–17.

Hudson, B. and Walters, R. (2009) (eds) Introduction. Special issue: criminology and the war on terror. *The British Journal of Criminology,* 49(5): 603–8

Hudson, B. and Ugelvik, S. (2012) Introduction: new landscapes of security and justice. In Hudson, B. and Ugelvik, S. (eds) *Justice and Security in the 21st Century.* London: Routledge.

Hudson, V. (2016) Europe's man problem. *Politico,* 11 January. www. politico.eu/article/europes-man-problem/

ICAN (International Committee to Abolish Nuclear Weapons) (2018) Signature/ratification status of the Treaty on the Prohibition of Nuclear Weapons. www.icanw.org/status-of-the-treaty-on-the-prohibition-of-nuclear-weapons/

ICAN (n.d.) About ICAN. http://uk.icanw.org/campaign/

ICRC (International Committee of the Red Cross) (2004) Report of the International Committee of the Red Cross (ICRC) on the Treatment by the Coalition Forces of Prisoners of War and Other Protected Persons by the Geneva Conventions in Iraq During Arrest, Internment and Interrogation. www.globalsecurity.org/military/library/report/2004/icrc_report_iraq_feb2004.pdf

Iraq Body Count (2018) Iraq Body Count. www.iraqbodycount.org

Jamieson, R. (1998) Towards a criminology of war in Europe. In Ruggiero, V., South, N. and Taylor, I. (eds) *The New European Criminology: Crime and Social Order in Europe.* London: Routledge.

Jamieson, R. (1999) Genocide and the social production of immorality. *Theoretical Criminology,* 3(2): 131–46.

Jamieson, R. (2003) Introduction. Special Issue: War, crime and human rights. *Theoretical Criminology,* 7(3): 259–63.

Jamieson, R. (2012) On war as an object of analysis for criminologists. *Studi Sulla Questione Criminale*, 3/2012: 97–114.

Jamieson, R. (2014) (ed) *The Criminology of War*. Surrey: Ashgate.

Jaworski, G.D. (1993) Pitirim A. Sorokin's sociological anarchism. *History of the Human Sciences*, 6(3): 61–77.

Jeffreys, S. (2007) Double jeopardy: women, the US military and the war in Iraq. *Women's Studies International Forum*, 30(1): 16–25.

Jessop, B. (1986) A. Giddens: The Nation State and Violence. Reviewed by Bob Jessop. *Capitalism & Class*, 10(2): 216–20.

Joas, H. (2003) *War and Modernity*. Cambridge: Polity.

Jones, A. (2000) Gendercide and genocide. *Journal of Genocide Research*, 2(2): 185–211.

Kaiser, J. and Hagan, J, (2015) Gendered genocide: the socially destructive process of genocidal rape, killing and displacement in Darfur. *Law and Society Review* 49 (1): 69–107.

Kaldor, M. (2014) *New and Old Wars: Organized Violence in a Global Era* (4th edn). Stanford: Stanford University Press.

Karatzogianni, A. (2006) *The Politics of Cyber Conflict*. Oxon: Routledge.

Karatzogianni, A. (2009) (ed) *Cyber-Conflict and Global Politics*. Oxon: Routledge.

Karatzogianni, A. (2013) (ed) *Violence and War in Culture and the Media: Five Disciplinary Lenses*. Oxon: Routledge.

Karstedt, S. (2010) From absence to presence, from silence to voice: victims in international and transitional justice since the Nuremberg trials. *International Review of Victimology*, 17: 9–30.

Kauzlarich, D. (1994) Nuclear threats by the United States in the Korean and Vietnam wars: towards a grounded theory of international governmental crime. Unpublished PhD thesis. Kalamazoo, Michigan: Western Michigan University.

Kauzlarich, D. (1995) A criminology of the nuclear state. *Humanity & Society*, 19(3): 37–57.

Kauzlarich, D. (1997) Nuclear weapons on trial: the battle at the International Court of Justice. *Social Pathology*, Fall (3): 157–64.

Kauzlarich, D. and Kramer, R.C. (1995) The nuclear terrorist state. *Peace Review*, 7(3/4): 333–7.

Kauzlarich, D. and Kramer, R.C. (1998) *Crimes of the American Nuclear State: At Home and Abroad*. Boston: Northeastern University Press.

Kauzlarich, D. and Kramer, R.C. (2006) Nuclear weapons production. In Michalowski, R.J. and Kramer, R.C. (eds) *State-Corporate Crime: Wrongdoing at the Intersection of Business and Government*. New Brunswick, NJ: Rutgers University Press.

Kauzlarich, D. and Matthews. R.A. (2006) Taking stock of theory and research. In Michalowski, R.J. and Kramer, R.C. (eds) *State-Corporate Crime: Wrongdoing at the Intersection of Business and Government*. New Brunswick, NJ: Rutgers University Press.

Kauzlarich, D., Kramer, R.C. and Smith, B. (1992) Towards the study of governmental crime: nuclear weapons, foreign intervention, and international law. *Humanity & Society*, 16(4): 543–63.

Kauzlarich, D., Matthews, R.A. and Miller, W.J. (2001) Toward a victimology of state crime. *Critical Criminology*, 10: 173–94.

Kelly, J. (2014) The needs of ex-service personnel in the criminal justice system: evidence from two surveys. Analytical summary. London: Ministry of Justice. www.gov.uk/government/uploads/system/uploads/attachment_ data/file/389856/the-needs-of-ex-service-personnel-in-the-cjs-analytical-summary.pdf

Kelly, L. (1988) *Surviving Sexual Violence*. Oxford: Polity.

Kennison, P. and Loumansky, A. (2007) Shoot to kill – understanding police use of force in combating terrorism. *Crime, Law & Social Change,* 47: 151–68.

Killean, R. (2018) Constructing victimhood at the Khmer Rouge Tribunal: visibility, selectivity and participation. *International Review of Victimology*, 24(3): 273–96.

King, A. (2010) The Afghan War and 'postmodern memory': commemoration and the dead of Helmand. *The British Journal of Sociology,* 61(1): 1–25.

Kirton, A. (2016) Online engagements: war and social media. In McGarry, R. and Walklate, S. (eds) *The Palgrave Handbook of Criminology and War*. Basingstoke: Palgrave Macmillan.

Kramer, R.C. (2010a) From Guernica to Hiroshima to Baghdad: the normalization of the terror bombing of civilians. In Chambliss, W.J., Michalowski, R. and Kramer, R.C. (eds) *State Crime in the Global Age*. Devon: Willan.

Kramer, R.C. (2010b) Resisting the bombing of civilians: challenges from a public criminology of state crime. *Social Justice,* 36(3): 78–97.

Kramer, R.C. and Kauzlarich, D. (2010) Nuclear weapons, international law, and the normalization of state crime. In Rothe, D. and Mullins, C. (eds) *State Crime: Current Perspectives*. New Jersey, NJ: Rutgers University Press.

Kramer, R.C. and Marullo, S. (1985) Towards a sociology of nuclear weapons. *The Sociological Quarterly: Special Feature: The Sociology of Nuclear Threat*, 26(3): 277–92.

Kramer, R.C. and Michalowski, R.J. (2005) War, aggression and state crime: a criminological analysis of the invasion and occupation of Iraq. *British Journal of Criminology,* 45(4): 446–69.

Kramer, R.C. and Michalowski, R.J. (2006) The invasion of Iraq. In Michalowski, R.J. and Kramer, R.C. (eds) *State-Corporate Crime: Wrongdoing at the Intersection of Business and Government.* New Brunswick, NJ: Rutgers University Press.

Kramer, R.C. and Smith, A.M. (2014) 'Death flies down': the bombing of civilians and the paradox of international law. In Rothe, D.L. and Kauzlarich, D. (eds) *Towards a Victimology of State Crime.* Oxon: Routledge.

Kraska, P.B. (2007) Militarization and policing – its relevance to 21st century police. *Policing,* 1(4): 501–13.

Kreuger, A. and Maleckova, J. (2003) Education, poverty and terrorism: is there a causal connection? *The Journal of Economic Perspectives,* 17(4): 119–44.

LaFree, G. (2009) Criminology's third war. *Criminology & Public Policy: Special Issue on Terrorism and Responses to Terrorism,* 8(3): 431–44.

LaFree, G. and Dugan, L. (2015) How has criminology contributed to the study of terrorism. In Deflem, M. (ed) *Terrorism and Counterterrorism Today. Sociology of Crime and Deviance,* vol. 20. Bingley: Emerald Group Publishing Limited.

LaFree, G. and Freilich, J.D. (2016) Introduction: bringing criminology into the study of terrorism. In LaFree, G. and Freilich, J.D. (eds) *The Handbook of the Criminology of Terrorism.* West Sussex: Wiley Blackwell.

Laufer, W.S. (1999) The forgotten criminology of genocide. In Laufer, W.S. and Adler, F. (eds) *The Criminology of Law.* New Brunswick: Transaction Publishers.

Lea, J. (2015) Postscript: From the criminalisation of war to the militarisation of crime control. In Walklate, S. and McGarry, R. (eds) *Criminology and War: Transgressing the Borders.* Oxon: Routledge.

Lea, J. (2016) War, criminal justice and the rebirth of privatisation. In McGarry, R. and Walklate, S. (eds) *The Palgrave Handbook of Criminology and War.* Basingstoke: Palgrave Macmillan.

Lee, Y. (2018) Report of the Special Rapporteur on the situation of human rights in Myanmar. www.ohchr.org/EN/HRBodies/HRC/RegularSessions/Session37/Documents/A-HRC-37-70.docx

Lemkin, R. (1944) *Axis Rule in Occupied Europe: Laws of Occupation, Analysis of Government, Proposals for Redress.* Washington, D.C: Carnegie Endowment for International Peace, Division of International Law.

Lemkin, R. (1945) Raphael Lemkin, 'Genocide: a modern crime'. In Totten, S. and Bartrop, P.R. (2009) (eds) *The Genocide Studies Reader.* Oxon: Routledge.

Letschert, R., Haveman, R., de Brouwer A-M. and Pemberton, A. (2011) (eds) *Victimological Approaches to International Crimes: Africa.* Cambridge: Intersentia.

Levy, B.S. and Sidel, V.W. (2013) Adverse health consequences of the Iraq War. *The Lancet*, 381: 949–58.

Lewis, G.H. and Lewis, J.F. (1980) The dog in the night-time: negative evidence in social research. *British Journal of Sociology*, 31(4): 544–58.

Lilly, R.J. (2007) COUNTERBLAST: Soldiers and rape: the other band of brothers. *The Howard Journal*, 46(1): 72–5.

Loader, I. and Percy, S. (2012) Bringing the 'outside' in and the 'inside' out: crossing the criminology/IR divide. *Global Crime,* 13(4): 213–18.

Logan, M.W. and Pare, P.-P. (2017) Are inmates with military backgrounds 'army strong'. *Criminal Justice Policy Review*, 28(8): 814–41.

Lowe, D. and Joel, T. (2013) *Remembering the Cold War: Global Contest and National Stories.* Oxon: Routledge.

Lunden, W.A. (1952) Military service and criminality. *Criminal Law, Criminology & Police Science*, 42: 766–73.

MacLeish, K. (2015) The ethnography of good machines. *Critical Military Studies,* 1(1): 11–22.

MacManus, D., Fossey, M., Watson, S.E. and Wessely, S. (2015) Former armed forces personnel in the criminal justice system. *The Lancet*, 2: 121–2.

MacManus, D., Dean, K., Bakir, Al., Iversen, A.C., Hull, L., Fahy, S., Wessely, S. and Fear, N.T. (2012) Violent behaviour in UK military personnel returning home after deployment. *Psychological Medicine,* 42: 1663–73.

MacManus, D., Dean, D., Jones, M., Rona, R.J., Greenberg, N., Hull, L., Fahy, T., Wessley, S. and Fear, T.N. (2013) Violent offending by UK military personnel deployed to Iraq and Afghanistan: a data linkage cohort study. *The Lancet*, 381: 907–17.

Maier-Katkin, D., Mears, D.P. and Bernard, T.J. (2009) Towards a criminology of crimes against humanity. *Theoretical Criminology,* 13(2): 227–55.

Mair, M., Elsey, C., Smith, P.V. and Watson, P.G. (2016) The violence you were/n't meant to see: representations of death in an age of digital reproduction. In McGarry, R. and Walklate, S. (eds) *The Palgrave Handbook of Criminology and War.* Basingstoke: Palgrave Macmillan.

Maira, S. (2009) *Missing.* Durham NC: Duke University Press.

Malešević, S. (2010a) *The Sociology of War and Violence*. Cambridge: Cambridge University Press.

Malešević, S. (2010b) How pacifist were the founding fathers? War and violence in classical sociology. *European Journal of Social Theory*, 13(2): 193–212.

Mann, B. (2014) *Sovereign Masculinity Gender Lessons from the War on Terror*. Oxford: Oxford University Press.

Mann, M. (1984) Capitalism and militarism. In Shaw, M. (ed) *War, State and Society*. London: Palgrave Macmillan.

Mann, M. (1988) *State, War and Capitalism*. Oxford: Basil Blackwell Ltd.

Mannheim, H. (1941) *War and Crime*. London: Watts & Co.

Mannheim, H. (1965) *Comparative Criminology: A Text Book, Volume Two*. London: Routledge & Kegan Paul.

Maras, H. (2013) *Counterterrorism*. London: Jones and Burlington.

Marsavelski, A., Sheremeti, F. and Braithwaite, J. (2017) Did nonviolent resistance fail in Kosovo? *The British Journal of Criminology*, 58(1): 218–36.

Martinsen, K.D. (2013) *Soldier Repatriation: Popular and Political Responses*. Surrey: Ashgate.

May, D.C., Stives, K.L., Wells, M.J. and Wood, P.B. (2017) Does military service make the experience of prison less painful? Voices from incarcerated veterans. *Criminal Justice Policy Review*, 28(8): 770–89.

Mbembe, A. (2003) Necropolitics. *Public Culture*, 15(1): 11–40.

McCartney, H.B. (2011) Hero, victim or villain? The public image of the British soldier and its implications for defense policy. *Defense & Security Analysis*, 27(1): 43–54.

McClanahan, B. and Brisman, A. (2015) Climate change and peacemaking criminology: ecophilosophy, peace and security in the 'war on climate change'. *Critical Criminology: An International Journal*, 23: 417–31.

McCulloch, J. (2004) Blue armies, khaki police and the cavalry on the new American frontier: critical criminology for the 21st century. *Critical Criminology: An International Journal*, 12: 309–26.

McCulloch, J. (2016) Violence, policing and war. In McGarry, R. and Walklate, S. (eds) *The Palgrave Handbook of Criminology and War*. Basingstoke: Palgrave Macmillan.

McCulloch, J. and Sentas, V. (2006) The killing of Jean Charles de Menezes: hyper-militarism in the neoliberal economic free-fire zone. *Social Justice*, 33(4): 92–106.

McCulloch, J. and Wilson, D. (2016) *Pre-crime: Pre-emption, Precaution and the Future.* Oxon: Routledge.

McDonnell, M.A. and Moses, D. (2005) Raphael Lemkin as historian of genocide in the Americas. *Journal of Genocide Research,* 7(4): 501–29.

McEvoy, K. and Mika, H. (2002) Restorative justice and the critique of informalism in Northern Ireland. *The British Journal of Criminology,* 42: 534–62.

McGarry, R. (2015) War, crime and military victimhood. *Critical Criminology: An International Journal,* 23(3): 255–75.

McGarry, R. (2016) Hierarchical victims of terrorism and war. In Spencer, D. and Walklate, S. (eds) *Critical Victimology: Reconceptualizations, Interventions and Possibilities.* Lexington Books: Maryland.

McGarry, R. and Walklate, S. (2011) The soldier as victim: peering through the looking glass. *The British Journal of Criminology,* 51(6): 900–17.

McGarry, R. and Walklate, S. (2015a) Introduction: placing war within criminology. In Walklate, S. and McGarry, R. (eds) *Criminology and War: Transgressing the Borders.* Abingdon: Routledge.

McGarry, R. and Walklate, S. (2015b) *Victims: Trauma, Testimony and Justice.* Abingdon: Routledge.

McGarry, R. and Walklate, S. (2016) The criminology of war, what is it good for? In McGarry, R. and Walklate, S. (eds) *The Palgrave Handbook of Criminology and War.* Hampshire: Palgrave.

McGarry, R. and Walklate, S. (2018) Criminology, war, and the violence(s) of militarism. In DeKeseredy, W. and Dragiewicz, M. (eds) *The Routledge Handbook of Critical Criminology* (2nd edn). Oxon: Routledge.

McGarry, R., Mythen, G. and Walklate, S. (2012) The soldier, human rights and the military covenant: a permissible state of exception? *International Journal of Human Rights. Special Issue: New Directions in the Sociology of Human Rights,* 16(8): 1183–95.

Mendelsohn, B. (1976) Victimology and contemporary society's trends. *Victimology: An International Journal,* 1(1): 8–28.

Mendelsohn, B. (1982) Socio-analytic introduction to research in a general victimological and criminological perspective. In Schneider, H.J. (ed) *The Victim in International Perspective.* Berlin: Walter de Gruyter.

Michalowski, R. and Dubisch, J. (2001) *Run for the Wall: Remembering Vietnam on a Motorcycle Pilgrimage.* New Brunswick: Rutgers University Press.

Michalowski, R.J. and Kramer, R.C. (2006) The critique of power. In Michalowski, R.J. and Kramer, R.C. *State-Corporate Crime: Wrongdoing at the Intersection of Business and Government*. New Brunswick: Rutgers University Press.

Mills, C.W. ([1956] 2000) *The Power Elite*. Oxford: Oxford University Press.

Mills, C.W. (1959) *The Causes of World War Three*. London: Martin Secker & Warburg Ltd.

Ministry of Defence (2015) Operations in Afghanistan: British fatalities in Afghanistan. www.gov.uk/government/fields-of-operation/afghanistan

Moosavi, L. (2019) A friendly critique of 'Asian criminology' and 'Southern criminology'. *The British Journal of Criminology*, 59(2): 257–75.

Morgan, R. (1989) *The Demon Lover*. London: Mandarin.

Morrison, W. (2006) *Criminology, Civilisation and the New World Order*. Oxon: Routledge.

Morrison, W. (2015) War and normative visibility: interactions in the nomos. In Francis, P., Wyatt, T. and Davies, P. (eds) *Invisible Crimes and Social Harms*. London: Palgrave Macmillan.

Moshman, D. (2001) Conceptual constraints on thinking about genocide. *Journal of Genocide Research*, 3(3): 431–50.

MSF (Médecins Sans Frontières) (2018) 'No one was left': death and violence against the Rohingya in Rakhine State, Myanmar. http://cdn.msf.org/sites/msf.org/files/msf_death_and_violence_report-2018.pdf

Mullins, C.W. (2009a) 'We are going to rape you and taste Tutsi women': rape during the 1994 Rwandan genocide. *The British Journal of Criminology*, 49(6): 719–35.

Mullins, C.W. (2009b) 'He would kill me with his penis': rape during the Rwandan genocide as a state crime. *Critical Criminology: An International Journal*, 17(1): 15–33.

Mullins, C.W. (2011) War crimes in the 2008 Georgia–Russia conflict. *The British Journal of Criminology*, 51(6): 918–36.

Mullins, C.W. and Rothe, D.L. (2007) The forgotten ones: the Darfuri genocide. *Critical Criminology: An International Journal*, 15: 135–58.

Mullins, C.W. and Rothe, D.L. (2008) *Blood and Bedlham: Violations of International Criminal Law in Post-Colonial Africa*. New York: Peter Lang.

Mullins, C. and Visagaratnam, N. (2015) Sexual and sexualised violence in armed conflict. In Walklate, S. and McGarry, R. (eds) *Criminology and War: Transgressing the Borders*. Oxon: Routledge.

Mullins, C. and Young, J. (2012) Cultures of violence and terrorism: a test of the legitimating-habituation model. *Crime and Delinquency*, 58(1): 28–56.

Murphy, T. and Whitty, N. (2013) Making history: academic criminology and human rights. *The British Journal of Criminology*, 53(4): 568–87.

Murray, E. (2015). Criminology and war: can violent veterans see blurred lines clearly? In Walklate, S. and McGarry, R. (eds) *Criminology and War: Transgressing the Borders*. Oxon: Routledge.

Murray, E. (2016) The 'veteran offender': a governmental project in England and Wales. In McGarry, R. and Walklate, S. (eds) *The Palgrave Handbook of Criminology and War*. Hampshire: Palgrave Macmillan.

Mythen, G., Walklate, S. and Khan, F. (2009) 'I'm a Muslim, but I'm not a terrorist': risk, victimization and the negotiation of risky identities. *The British Journal of Criminology*, 49(6): 736–54.

Mythen, G., Walklate, S. and Khan, F. (2013) 'Why should we have to prove we're alright?' Counter-terrorism, risk and partial securities. *Sociology*, 47(2): 383–98.

Ngo, F. and Jaishankar, K. (2017) Commemorating a decade in existence of the International Journal of Cyber Criminology: a research agenda to advance the scholarship on cyber crime. *International Journal of Cyber Criminology*, 11(1): 1–9.

Nikolic-Ristanovic, V. (1998) War and crime in the former Yugoslavia. In Ruggiero, V., South, N. and Taylor, I. (eds) *The New European Criminology: Crime and Social Order in Europe*. London: Routledge.

Nikolic-Ristanovic, V. (1999) Living without democracy and peace: violence against women in the former Yugoslavia. *Violence Against Women*, 5(1): 63–80.

O'Brien-Mòr, A. (1994) Churchill and the Tonypandy riots. *Welsh Historical Review*, 17(1): 67–99.

OHCHR (Office of the United Nations High Commissioner for Human Rights) (2017) Report of OHCHR mission to Bangladesh: Interviews with Rohingyas fleeing from Myanmar since 9 October 2016. Flash Report, 3 February. www.ohchr.org/Documents/Countries/MM/FlashReport3Feb2017.pdf

Okafo, N. (2009) Book review: Mullins, C.W., & Rothe, D.L. (2008) Blood, Power, and Bedlam: Violations of International Criminal Law in Post-Colonial Africa. *International Criminal Justice Review*, 19(3): 357–59.

Oriola, T. (2012) The delta creeks, women's engagement and Nigeria's oil insurgency. *The British Journal of Criminology*, 52(3): 534–55.

O'Sullivan, C. and Walters, R. (2016) Criminology, war and environmental despoliation. In McGarry, R. and Walklate, S. (eds) *The Palgrave Handbook of Criminology and War*. Hampshire: Palgrave Macmillan.

Packer, H.L. (1964) Two models of the criminal process. *University of Pennsylvania Law Review*, 113(1): 1–68.

Pain, R. (2012) Everyday terrorism: how fear works in domestic abuse. Durham: Centre for Social Justice and Community Action, Durham University and Scottish Women's Aid. http://womensaid. scot/wp-content/uploads/2017/07/EverydayTerrorismReport.pdf

Pantazis, C. and Pemberton, S. (2009) From the 'old' to the 'new' suspect community: explaining the impacts of recent UK counter-terrorism legislation. *The British Journal of Criminology*, 49: 464–66.

Pantazis, C. and Pemberton, S. (2011) Restating the case for a 'suspect community': a reply to Greer. *The British Journal of Criminology*, 51: 1054–62.

Parmantier, S. and Weitekamp, E.G.M. (2014) Victimisation during and after war: empirical findings from Bosnia. In Rothe, D.L. and Kauzlarich, D. (eds) *Towards a Victimology of State Crime*. Oxon: Routledge.

Peniston-Bird, P. and Vickers, E. (2017) (eds) *Gender and the Second World War*. London: Palgrave Macmillan.

Phillips, S. (2014) Former members of the armed forces and the criminal justice system: a review on behalf of the Secretary of State for Justice. www.gov.uk/government/uploads/system/uploads/ attachment_data/file/389964/former-mem bers-of-the-armed-forces-and-the-criminal-justice-system.pdf

Picart, K. (2017) *American Self-Radicalizing Terrorists and the Allure of 'Jihadi Cool/Chic'*. Cambridge: Cambridge Scholar Publishing.

Pollard, R.S.W. (1941) Liberty and war time: new criminal law. *The Howard Journal*, 6(1): 59–64.

Post, J.M. (2007) *The Mind of the Terrorist*. New York: Palgrave Macmillan.

Powell, C. (2007) What do genocides kill? A relational concept of genocide. *Journal of Genocide Research*, 9(4): 527–47.

Power-Cobbe, F. (1878) Wife-torture in England. *The Contemporary Review*, 32: 55–87.

Radzinowicz, L. (1999) *Adventures in Criminology*. London: Routledge.

Rafter, N. (2008) Criminology's darkest hour: biocriminology in Nazi Germany. *The Australian and New Zealand Journal of Criminology*, 41(2): 287–306.

Rafter, N. (2009) Darfur and the Crime of Genocide by John Hagan and Wenona Rymond-Richmond: a symposium. *Theoretical Criminology,* 13(4): 475–11.

Rafter, N. (2016) *The Crime of all Crimes: Towards a Criminology of Genocide.* New York: New York University Press.

Rafter, N. and Walklate, S. (2012) Genocide and the dynamics of victimization: some observations on Armenia. *European Journal of Criminology,* 9(5): 514–526.

Riga, L. (2011) Book review: Sinisa Malešević, The Sociology of War and Violence. *Canadian Journal of Sociology,* 36(2): 239–41.

Robinson, F. (2011) *Ethics of Care: A Feminist Approach to Human Security.* Philadelphia, PA: Temple University Press.

Rock, P. (1994) Introduction. In Rock, P. (ed) *Victimology.* Aldershot: Dartmouth Publishing.

Rock, P. (2018) Theoretical perspectives on victimisation. In Walklate, S. (ed) *Handbook of Victims and Victimology* (2nd edn). Oxon: Routledge.

Roseneil, S. (1995) *Disarming Patriarchy: Feminism and Political Action at Greenham.* Milton Keynes: Open University Press.

Roshier, B. (1989) *Controlling Crime.* London: Lyceum Books.

Rothe, D.L. (2006) Iraq and Haliburton. In Michalowski, R.J. and Kramer, R.C. (eds) *State-Corporate Crime: Wrongdoing at the Intersection of Business and Government.* New Brunswick: Rutgers University Press.

Rothe, D.L. (2014) Can an international justice system address victims' needs? In Rothe, D.L. and Kauzlarich, D. (eds) *Towards a Victimology of State Crime.* Oxon: Routledge.

Rothe, D.L. and Kauzlarich, D. (2014) (eds) *Towards a Victimology of State Crime.* Oxon: Routledge.

Rothe, D.L. and Mullins, C.W. (2006) *Symbolic Gestures and the Generation of Global Social Control: The International Criminal Court.* Plymouth: Lexington Books.

Rothe, D.L. and Mullins, C.W. (2010) Beyond the juristic orientation of international criminal justice: the relevance of criminological insight to international criminal law and its control. A commentary. *International Criminal Law Review,* 10: 97–110.

Rueda, G.M. (2018) Working in violence: moral narratives of paramilitaries in Colombia. *Theoretical Criminology,* OnlineFirst: https://doi.org/10.1177/1362480618792747

Ruggiero, V. (2005) Criminalizing war: criminology as ceasefire. *Social & Legal Studies,* 14(2): 239–57.

Ruggiero, V. (2006) *Understanding Political Violence: A Criminological Analysis.* Maidenhead: Open University Press.

Ruggiero, V. (2015) War and the death of Achilles. In Walklate, S. and McGarry, R. (eds) *Criminology and War: Transgressing the Borders.* Oxon: Routledge.

Ruggiero, V. (2018) Fiction, war and criminology. *Criminology & Criminal Justice,* 18(5): 604–16.

Sagan, C. (1983) Nuclear war and climate catastrophe: some policy implications. *Foreign Affairs,* 62(2): 257–92.

Sampson, R.J. and Laub, J.H. (1993) *Crime in the Making: Pathways and Turning Points through Life.* Cambridge: Harvard University Press.

Sampson, R.J. and Laub, J.H. (1996) Socioeconomic achievement in the military life course of disadvantaged men: military service as a turning point, circa 1940–1965. *American Sociological Review,* 61(June): 347–67.

Savelsberg, J.J. (2010) *Crime and Human Rights.* London: Sage.

Schabas, W.A. (n.d.) United Nations Convention for the Prevention and Punishment of the Crime of Genocide. *United Nations: Audiovisual Library of International Law.* http://legal.un.org/avl/pdf/ha/cppcg/cppcg_e.pdf

Schabas, W.A. (2005) Crimes against humanity. In Totten, S. and Bartrop, P.R. (2009) (eds) *The Genocide Studies Reader.* Oxon: Routledge.

Schell, J. (1982) *The Fate of the Earth.* New York: Konpf.

Schneider, H.J. (1982a) Acknowledgments of the editor. In Schneider, H.J. (ed) *The Victim in International Perspective.* Berlin: Walter de Gruyter.

Schneider, H.J. (1982b) Victims of genocide. In Schneider, H.J. (ed) *The Victim in International Perspective.* Berlin: Walter de Gruyter.

Schwendinger, H. and Schwendinger, J. (1970) Defenders of order or guardians of human rights? *Issues in Criminology,* 5(2), Summer: 123–57.

Scraton, P. (2002) (ed) *Beyond September 11: An Anthology of Dissent.* London: Pluto Books.

Scraton, P. (2007) *Power, Conflict and Criminalisation.* Oxon: Routledge.

Scruton, R. (1987) Notes on the sociology of war. *The British Journal of Sociology,* 38(3): 259–309.

Scruton, R. (1988) Reply to Martin Shaw. *The British Journal of Sociology,* 39(4): 619–23.

Shalhoub-Kevorkian, N. (2017) The occupation of the senses: the prosthetic and aesthetic of state terror. *The British Journal of Criminology,* 57(6): 1279–300.

Shalhoub-Kevorkian, N. and Braithwaite, J. (2010) Victimology between the local and the global. *International Review of Victimology*, 17: 1–8.

Shaw, M. (1984) Introduction: war and social theory. In Shaw, M. (ed) *War, State and Society*. London: Palgrave Macmillan.

Shaw, M. (1988a) *Dialectics of War: An Essay in the Social Theory of Total War and Peace*. London: Pluto Press.

Shaw, M. (1988b) The real sociology of war: a reply to Roger Scruton. *The British Journal of Sociology*, 39(4): 615–18.

Shaw, M. (1991) *Post Military Society: Militarism, Demilitarization and War at the End of the Twentieth Century*, Cambridge: Polity.

Shaw, M. (2003) *War & Genocide: Organized Killing in Modern Society*. Cambridge: Polity.

Shaw, M. (2005) *The New Western Way of War*. Cambridge: Polity.

Shaw, M. (2007) *What is Genocide?* Cambridge: Polity.

Shaw, M. (2010) Book reviews: Hagan, J. and Rymond-Richmond, W., Darfur and the Crime of Genocide. *The British Journal of Sociology*, 61(2): 388–90.

Short, D. (2010) Cultural genocide and indigenous peoples: a sociological approach. *The International Journal of Human Rights*, 14(6): 833–48.

Short, D. (2016) *Redefining Genocide: Settler Colonialism, Social Death and Ecocide*. London: Zed Books.

Siebold, G.L. (2001) Core issues and theory in military sociology. *Journal of Political & Military Sociology*, 29(1): 140–59.

Simic, O. and Daly, K. (2011) 'One pair of shoes, one life': steps toward accountability for genocide in Srebrenica. *International Journal of Transitional Justice*, 5(3): 477–91.

Skocpol, T. (1987) Review: The Nation-State and Violence: Volume Two of a Contemporary Critique of Historical Materialism. *Social Forces*, 66(1): 294–6.

Smart, C. (1977) *Women, Crime and Criminology: A Feminist Critique*. Routledge Revivals. Oxon: Routledge.

Smeulers, A. (2011) Eroding the myth of pure evil. In Letschert, R. and Pemberton, A. (eds) *Victimological Approaches to International Crimes: Africa*. (Series Supranational Criminal Law: Capita selecta, Vol. 13). Cambridge: Intersentia.

Smeulers, A. and Haveman, R. (2008) (eds) *Supranational Criminology: Towards a Criminology of International Crimes*. Antwerp: Intersentia.

Soeters, J. (2018) *Sociology and Military Studies: Classical and Current Foundations*. Oxon: Routledge.

Sorokin, P.A. ([1937] 1962) *Social and Cultural Dynamics, Volume Three: Fluctuations of Social Relationships, War, and Revolution.* New York: The Bedminster Press.

Sorokin, P.A. (1944) The conditions and prospects for a world without war. *American Journal of Sociology,* 49(5): 441–9.

South, N. (1998) A green field for criminology? *Theoretical Criminology,* 2(2): 211–33.

Steinert, H. (2003) The indispensable metaphor of war: on populist politics and the contradictions of the state's monopoly of force. *Theoretical Criminology,* 7(3): 265–91.

Sutherland, E.H. (1942) Review: War and Crime by Hermann Mannheim. *American Journal of Criminology,* 47(4): 638–9.

Sutherland, E.H. (1949) *White Collar Crime.* New York: Holt, Rinehart and Winston.

Sykes, G.M. and Matza, D. (1957) Techniques of neutralization: a theory of delinquency. *American Sociological Review,* 22(6): 664–70.

Tham, H.K. (1990) Crime in Scandinavia during World War II. *Journal of Peace Studies,* 27(4): 415–28.

Tilly, C. (1975) (ed) *The Formation of National States in Europe.* Princeton, NJ: Princeton University Press.

Tilly, C. (1985) War making and state making as organized crime. In Whyte, D. (2008) (ed) *Crimes of the Powerful: A Reader.* Maidenhead: Open University Press.

Tombs, S. and Whyte, D. (2003) Scrutinizing the powerful: crime, contemporary political economy and critical social research. In Tombs, S. and Whyte, D. (eds) *Unmasking Crimes of the Powerful.* New York: Peter Lang Publishing, Inc.

Totten, S. and Bartrop, P.R. (2009) (eds) *The Genocide Studies Reader.* Oxon: Routledge.

Travers, M. (2019) The idea of a southern criminology. *International Journal of Comparative and Applied Criminal Justice.* 43(1): 1–12.

Treadwell, J. (2016) The forces in the firing line? Social policy and the 'acceptable face' of violent criminality. In McGarry, R. and Walklate, S. (eds) *The Palgrave Handbook of Criminology and War.* Hampshire: Palgrave.

True, J. (2012) *The Political Economy of Violence Against Women.* New York: Oxford University Press.

UN (United Nations) (1948) General Assembly resolution 260 (III) of 9 December 1948 (Prevention and Punishment of the Crime of Genocide). www.un.org/ga/search/view_doc.asp?symbol=a/res/260(III)

UN (2017) Treaty on the Prohibition of Nuclear Weapons. https://treaties.un.org/doc/Treaties/2017/07/20170707%2003-42%20PM/Ch_XXVI_9.pdf

UNAMA (United Nations Assistance Mission in Afghanistan) (2018a) Afghanistan: protection of civilians in armed conflict annual report 2017. https://unama.unmissions.org/sites/default/files/afghanistan_protection_of_civilians_annual_report_2017_final_6_march.pdf

UNAMA (2018b) Afghanistan: human rights and protection of civilians in armed conflict. Special report: Airstrikes in Dasht-e-Archi district, Kunduz province, 2 April. https://unama.unmissions.org/sites/default/files/unama_protection_of_civilians_special_report_2_april_aerial_operations_final.pdf

UNHCR (United Nations High Commissioner for Refugees) (2017) 100 days of horror and hope: a timeline of the Rohingya crisis, 1 December. www.unhcr.org/news/stories/2017/12/5a1c313a4/100-days-horror-hope-timeline-rohingya-crisis.html

UNHCR (United Nations High Commissioner for Refugees) (2018) Rohingya emergency, 7 January. www.unhcr.org/uk/rohingya-emergency.html

UNHRC (United Nations Human Rights Council) (2016) Situation of human rights of Rohingya Muslims and other minorities in Myanmar. Report of the United Nations High Commissioner for Human Rights. www.ohchr.org/EN/HRBodies/HRC/RegularSessions/Session32/Documents/A_HRC_32_18_AEV.docx

UNHRC (2018) Report of the Independent International Fact-Finding Mission on Myanmar Report of the United Nations High Commissioner for Human Rights. www.ohchr.org/Documents/HRBodies/HRCouncil/FFM-Myanmar/A_HRC_39_64.pdf

UNICTR (United Nations International Criminal Tribunal for Rwanda) (n.d.) Legacy website of the International Criminal Tribunal for Rwanda. http://unictr.unmict.org/en/tribunal

UNICTY (United Nations International Criminal Tribunal for the former Yugoslavia) (n.d.a) Legacy website of ICTY / TPIY / MKSJ. www.icty.org

UNICTY (n.d.b) Ratko Mladić case – Key information & timeline. www.icty.org/en/cases/ratko-mladic-case-key-information-timeline

UN News (2013) Guatemala: UN rights chief welcomes 'historic' genocide conviction of former military leader. 13 May. https://news.un.org/en/story/2013/05/439412-guatemala-un-rights-chief-welcomes-historic-genocide-conviction-former-military

UNODA (United Nations Office for Disarmament Affairs) (n.d.a) Treaty on the Non-Proliferation of Nuclear Weapons. www.un.org/disarmament/wmd/nuclear/npt/

UNODA (n.d.b) Treaty on the Non-Proliferation of Nuclear Weapons: Status of the Treaty. http://disarmament.un.org/treaties/t/npt

UNODA (1968) Treaty on the Non-Proliferation of Nuclear Weapons: Text of the Treaty.

UNODA (1996) Comprehensive Nuclear-Test-Ban Treaty (CTBT) www.un.org/disarmament/wmd/nuclear/ctbt/

UNODA (2017) Treaty on the Prohibition of Nuclear Weapons. www.un.org/disarmament/wmd/nuclear/tpnw/

UNODA (2018) Treaty on the Prohibition of Nuclear Weapons: Status of the Treaty. http://disarmament.un.org/treaties/t/tpnw; http://disarmament.un.org/treaties/t/npt/text

Wagley, P.V. (1943) Some criminogenic implications of the returning soldier. *Crime, Law & Criminology*, 43, 311–14.

Walklate, S. and McGarry, R. (2015) Competing for the 'trace': the legacies of war's violence(s) In Walklate, S. and McGarry, R. (eds) *Criminology and War: Transgressing the Borders.* Oxon: Routledge.

Walklate, S. and Mythen, G. (2014) *Contradictions of Terrorism: Security, Risk and Resilience.* Oxon: Routledge.

Walklate, S. and Mythen, G. (2016) Splintered lives, splintered knowledge? Making criminological sense of the Paris 2015 attacks. *Critical Criminology: An International Journal*, 24(3): 333–46.

Walklate, S., McCulloch, J. Fitz-Gibbon, K. and Maher, J.M. (2019) Criminology, gender and security in the Australian context: making women's lives matter. *Theoretical Criminology*, 23(1): 60–77.

Wall, T. and Monahan, T. (2011) Surveillance and violence from afar: the politics of drones and liminal security-scapes. *Theoretical Criminology*, 15(3): 239–54.

Wardak, A. and Braithwaite, J. (2013) Crime and war in Afghanistan: Part II: the Jeffersonian alternative. *The British Journal of Criminology*, 53: 197–214.

Ware, V. (2009) Why critical whiteness studies needs to think about warfare. *Sociologisk Forskning*, 46(3): 57–64.

Weber, M. (1919) Politics as a vocation. In Whyte, D. (2008) (ed) *Crimes of the Powerful: A Reader.* Maidenhead: Open University Press.

West, B. and Matthewman, S. (2016) Towards a strong program in the sociology of war, the military and civil society. *Journal of Sociology*, 52(3): 482–99.

White, A. (2010) *The Politics of Private Military Security: Regulation, Reform and Re-Legitimation.* Basingstoke: Palgrave Macmillan.

White, A. (2012) The new political economy of private security. *Theoretical Criminology*, 16(1): 85–101.

White, A. (2016) Private military contractors as criminals/victims. In McGarry, R. and Walklate, S. (eds) *The Palgrave Handbook of Criminology and War*. Basingstoke: Palgrave Macmillan.

White, A. (2018a) Beyond Iraq: the socioeconomic trajectories of private military veterans. *Armed Forces & Society*, 44(3): 387–407.

White, A. (2018b) Private military contractors: a criminological approach. In Wadham, B. and Goldsmith, A (eds) *Criminologies of the Military: Militarism, National Security and Justice*. Onati Book Series. Oxford: Hart Publishing.

White, R. (2008) Depleted uranium, state crime and the politics of knowing. *Theoretical Criminology*, 12(1): 31–54.

Whyte, D. (2007) Crimes of the neo-liberal state in occupied Iraq. *The British Journal of Criminology*, 47(2): 177–95.

Whyte, D. (2015) Civilizing the corporate war. In Walklate, S. and McGarry, R. (eds) *Criminology and War: Transgressing the Borders*. Oxon: Routledge.

Wibben, A.T.R. (2016) Introduction: feminists study war. In Wibben, A.T.R. (ed) *Researching War: Feminist Methods, Ethics and Politics*. Oxon: Routledge.

Willbach, H. (1948) Recent crimes and the veterans. *Journal of Criminal Law and Criminology*, 38(5): 501–8.

Wimmer, A. (2014) War. *The Annual Review of Sociology*, 40: 173–97.

Winter, J. (2014) *Sites of Memory, Sites of Mourning*. Cambridge: Cambridge University Press.

Woolford, A. (2006) Making genocide unthinkable: three guidelines for a critical criminology of genocide. *Critical Criminology: An International Journal*, 14: 87–106.

Woolford, A. (2013) The next generation: criminology, genocide studies and settler colonialism. *Revista Crítica Penal y Poder. Special Issue: Redefining the Criminal Matter: State Crime, Mass Atrocities and Social Harm*, September: 163–85.

Yacoubian, G.S. (2000) The (in)significance of genocidal behavior to the discipline of criminology. *Crime, Law & Social Change*, 34(1): 7–19.

Yar, M. (2013) *Cybercrime and Society*. London: Sage.

Young, A. (1990) *Femininity in Dissent*. London: Sage.

Young, A. (1996) *Imagining Crime*. London: Sage.

Young, J. (1999) *The Exclusive Society*. London: Sage.

Young, J. (2003) Merton with energy, Katz with structure: the sociology of vindictiveness and the criminology of transgression. *Theoretical Criminology*, 7(3): 389–414.

Young, J. (2007) *The Vertigo of Late Modernity.* London: Sage.

Young, J. (2011) *The Criminological Imagination.* Cambridge: Polity.

Young, J. ([1973] 2013) Introduction to 40th anniversary edition. In Taylor, I., Walton, P. and Young, J. (eds) *The New Criminology: For a Social Theory of Deviance.* Oxon: Routledge.

Zarkov, D. (2014) Warriors: cinematic ontologies of the Bosnian war. *European Journal of Women's Studies,* 2(3): 180–93.

Zedner, L. (2000) The pursuit of security. In Hope, T. and Sparks, R. (eds) *Crime, Risk and Insecurity.* London: Routledge.

Zedner, L. (2009) *Security.* Oxon: Routledge.

Zehfuss, M. (2009) Hierarchies of grief and the possibility of war: remembering UK fatalities in Iraq. *Millennium: Journal of International Studies,* 38(2): 419–40.

Zehfuss, M. (2012) Killing civilians: thinking the practice of war. *British Journal of Politics and International Relations,* 14: 423–40.

Zolo, D. (2010) *Victors' Justice: from Nuremberg to Baghdad.* London: Verso.

Index